THE COLLECTIONS OF THE DETROIT INSTITUTE OF ARTS

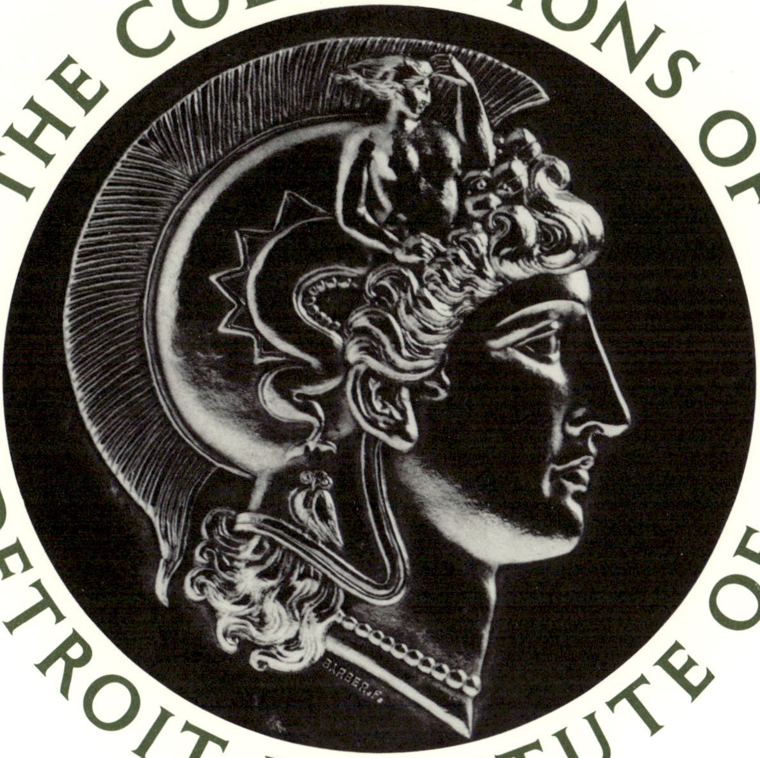

Flemish and German Paintings of the 17th Century

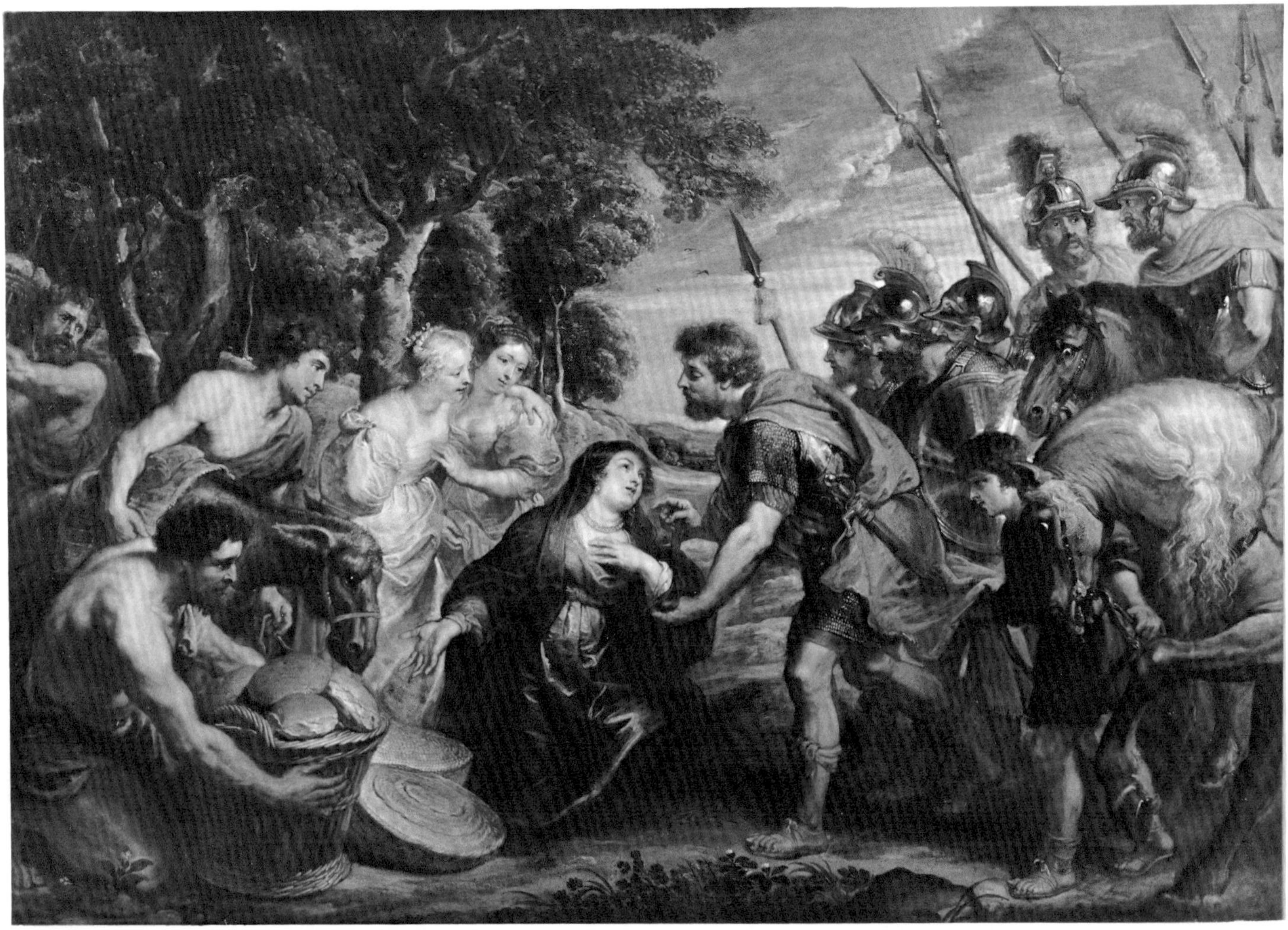

THE
COLLECTIONS
OF THE
DETROIT
INSTITUTE
OF ARTS

Flemish and German Paintings of the 17th Century

JULIUS S. HELD

THE DETROIT INSTITUTE OF ARTS

FRONTISPIECE:
Peter Paul Rubens, *The Meeting of David and Abigail.*

Library of Congress Cataloguing in Publication Data
Held, Julius Samuel, 1905-
Flemish and German paintings of the 17th century.
(The Collections of the Detroit Institute of Arts)
Bibliography: pp. 129-134
Includes indexes.
1. Painting, Flemish–Catalogs. 2. Painting, Modern–17th-18th centuries–Belgium–Flanders–Catalogs. 3. Painting, German–Catalogs. 4. Painting, Modern–17th-18th centuries–Germany–Catalogs. 5. Painting–Michigan–Detroit–Catalogs. 6. Detroit Institute of Arts–Catalogs. I. Detroit Institute of Arts. II. Title. III. Series.
ND625.H44 759.3'074'017434 82-5152
ISBN 0-89558-092-6 AACR2

PRINTED IN THE UNITED STATES OF AMERICA

TABLE OF CONTENTS

TABLE OF COLOR PLATES

INTRODUCTION

In 1985 the Detroit Institute of Arts will celebrate the 100th anniversary of its foundation. During its first century, the museum has benefited from the collective support of the Detroit community—including its generous donors—and from the individual efforts of directors, curators, and scholars whose knowledge and research have contributed to the building of one of America's finest collections of European paintings. As we approach our centennial year, it is entirely appropriate to pause and survey the results of these endeavors. The Art Institute is proud, therefore, to inaugurate a series of catalogues of the permanent collections at this time. The present volume dedicated to the Flemish and German schools of the 17th century, and prepared by Professor Julius S. Held, is the first in this series.

In 1889, four years after its establishment as the major cultural institution in the city, the Detroit Museum of Art, as it was then known, received the magnificent gift of the James E. Scripps Collection, which included paintings representing all the European schools. This donation formed the nucleus of the museum's holdings and brought Detroit immediately to the forefront of public collections in America. Many Flemish pictures were included in the Scripps gift, works that reflected the donor's refined taste as well as his interest in the works of lesser-known artists represented by examples of the highest artistic merit. In addition to masterpieces such as Rubens' *David and Abigail*—one of eight works by this artist or his studio now owned by the museum—paintings by Steenwijck and Van Kessel were also included, prefiguring the modern interest in these lesser-known painters. Scripps' determination to purchase works of quality, regardless of the artist's reputation, had its rewards: the *Portrait of a Married Couple*, acquired as a work by Cornelis de Vos, was later correctly identified by W. R. Valentiner, then the Art Institute's director, as an autograph double portrait by Van Dyck.

The Valentiner years (1921-45) were rich in additions to the already existing collection of 17th-century Flemish paintings. This is hardly surprising considering Dr. Valentiner's personal interest in Northern European painting, a passion he shared with his mentor, Wilhelm von Bode. In 1929 Dr. Valentiner organized a major exhibition at the Art Institute of works by Van Dyck. During his tenure at the Art Institute, works by Fyt, Joos de Momper, Abraham and Jan Brueghel, Sweerts, Teniers, and Rubens were purchased. Also important for the Flemish and German collections was Dr. Valentiner's role as adviser to Detroit collectors who eventually gave or bequeathed to the museum the masterpieces acquired with his assistance. Thus brought into the collection were such major paintings as *The Holy Family with Saint Anne* by Jordaens, donated by Mrs. Ralph Harman Booth a year after Dr. Valentiner's departure from Detroit, and Rubens' magnificent sketch *Briseis Given Back to Achilles*, bequeathed in 1953 by Mr. and Mrs. Edgar B. Whitcomb.

In more recent years the Northern European collections have not been neglected. Purchases have been made to complement the superb works already brought together: paintings by Snyders and Rubens acquired within the last five years, for instance, have added significantly to the diversity of the Art Institute's holdings. In the case of Rubens, these acquisitions illustrate the versatility and stylistic range of a master already well represented in the collection, and with Snyders' *Still Life with Fruit, Vegetables, and Dead Game*, a particularly splendid example of a characteristic type of Flemish painting has been brought to Detroit.

It is this collection to which Professor Held has devoted his enthusiastic attention for many years, preparing a catalogue that is both a model of scholarly research and a stimulating and enjoyable analysis. To read the entries is to look at each painting with a fresh eye. Professor Held has indeed fulfilled the hope—expressed by James E. Scripps in his introduction to his 1889 catalogue—that "some one will come forward and take up the work where I leave it, and pursue it with all the interest, devotion and confidence that I have been able to bring to its inception."

A number of individuals have contributed to the realization of this project. The catalogue's elegant design is the work of Klaus Gemming, New Haven. Several Art Institute staff members, past and present, participated in other aspects of its creation. In particular, I would like to thank J. Patrice Marandel, Curator of European Painting, and his predecessor, Dewey F. Mosby (Picker Art Gallery, Colgate University); Abraham Joel and Barbara Heller, Conservation Services Laboratory, and Teresa Hensick (Fogg Art Museum); Marianne DePalma and Patricia Miller, Development Office; and Dirk Bakker and Robert Hensleigh, Photography Department. Editing and production coordination were ably handled by Susan L. Caroselli and Andrea P. A. Belloli, who received conscientious assistance from Cynthia Jo Fogliatti, Publications Department. Gratitude is also due Susan F. Rossen (Art Institute of Chicago).

This catalogue could not have been developed without the generosity of the National Endowment for the Arts, which provided funds for research and preparation of the text, and the Ford Foundation, which generously subsidized the volume's production from its innovative matching-grant program to encourage the cataloguing of major American collections. We are deeply grateful to both of these foundations for their support.

FREDERICK J. CUMMINGS

Director, The Detroit Institute of Arts

EDITOR'S NOTE

Sequence

The catalogue entries are arranged alphabetically by the artist's surname (for example, Dyck rather than Van Dyck, Momper rather than De Momper) or by nationality when the artist is not known. If the collection includes two or more works by an artist, the entries are in chronological order.

Attribution

Paintings either signed or considered to be autograph are designated by the master's name. If a reasonable doubt exists concerning the authorship of a work, the term "attributed to" has been used. The following terms have also been used to clarify a master's contribution to works not believed to be autograph:

"Studio of": the painting is the work of an unidentified artist in the master's studio and based on his invention, with or without some degree of participation by the master himself.

"Circle of": the painting is the work of an unidentified artist who is stylistically related to the master, possibly trained or directly influenced by him, and proximate in time and place.

"Style of": the painting is similar stylistically to the work of the master, but direct influence may be lacking; this phrase implies a distance in time and/or place from the master.

"Copy after": the painting is a copy by an unidentified artist of a known or suspected original by the master but not produced in his studio; a copy may range in date from a work contemporary with the original to a modern version.

Medium and dimensions

Both the medium and support are identified. Dimensions are given in both centimeters and inches; height precedes width. Measurements were taken at the time each painting was examined by Art Institute conservators.

Conservation

Condition reports were prepared by Teresa Hensick, formerly of the Art Institute's Conservation Services Laboratory. The letters "CSL" after a conservator's name signify that he or she is (or was) a member of the Art Institute staff.

Provenance

The history of each painting has been traced as completely as possible. Dealers have been so designated to distinguish them from collectors (of course, in some cases the two categories overlap, but it is usually impossible to determine whether a work was in a dealer's private collection). In the case of sales, the owner's name, if known, precedes the place and date of the sale. The phrase "offered for sale" indicates that the painting was not sold at that time.

Exhibitions and References

All known exhibition and bibliographical information has been included, with the exception of references to illustrations that convey no information about a work (for example, annual reports and picture books published by the Art Institute). Also, no reference has been made to paintings catalogues of the Art Institute prior to the 1930 edition, all earlier versions being only checklists.

Within the entries, exhibition and bibliographical references are indicated by a short form consisting of the city and date of the exhibition in the former case, the author's name and date of publication in the latter. Complete citations can be found in the bibliography (pages 129-134).

CATALOGUE

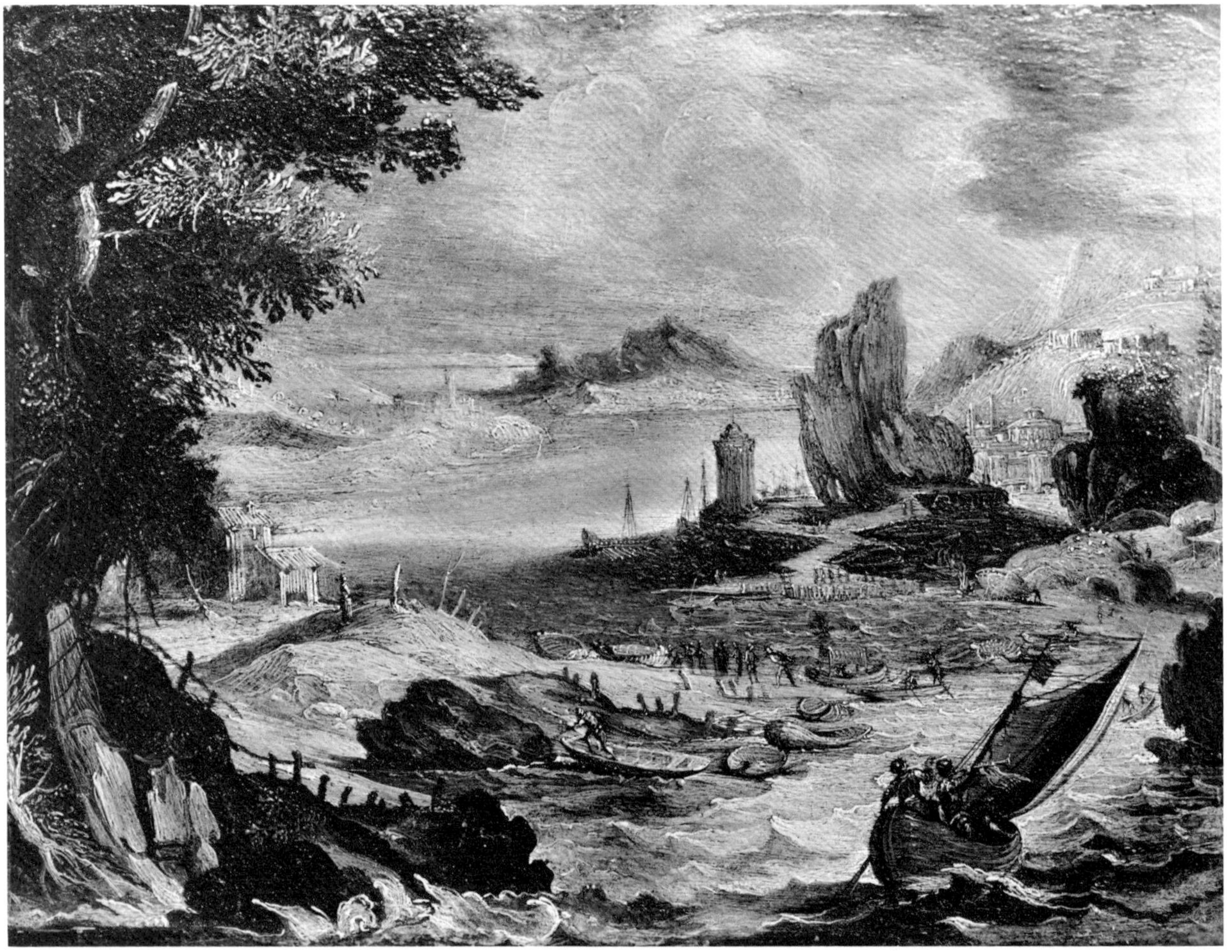

Attributed to Bril, *Landscape Fantasy*.

Paul Bril

1554 ANTWERP – ROME 1626

PAUL BRIL and his older brother, Mattheus the Younger, were the sons of Mattheus Bril the Elder, also a painter. In 1574 Paul left for France and is known to have been active in Lyon. In 1582 he was recorded in Rome, where his brother had preceded him (Mattheus the Younger died soon after, in 1583). Paul became one of the most successful landscape painters in Rome in the later 16th and early 17th centuries. At the beginning of his Roman stay, he was much in demand as a painter of murals; his wall decorations are still to be found in the Vatican and in various churches and palaces (the Palazzo Rospigliosi, for example) of Rome. Toward the end of his life, however, he concentrated more on the production of smaller easel paintings.

Bril's earlier works are characterized by picturesque arrangements of landscape elements and violent contrasts of light and dark. Under the influence of Annibale Carracci and, above all, Adam Elsheimer, however, he began executing calm, bucolic scenes in which the elements of nature are no longer broken up and rendered as if in turbulent motion, but are pulled together into solid shapes, firmly rooted in the ground. His late style, "governed by Latin clarity and at the same time of an entirely northern sensibility in rendering light and vegetation" (Charles Sterling in Paris 1936: 12), exercised a strong influence on later Flemish landscape painters and was crucial to the formation of Claude Lorrain's conception of classical landscape.

Attributed to Bril

Landscape Fantasy

☾ The attribution of this small but striking landscape (formerly called *Harbor Scene*) to Bril is not entirely certain; if by him, it must belong among his earliest works executed in Italy. Some analogies can indeed be found with Bril's early paintings, such as two landscapes in the Galleria Borghese, Rome (nos. 206 and 207), and some of his early drawings (Chatsworth Settlement, Courtauld Institute, London).

The compositional scheme, with its framing tree on one side and the zigzag design of the wave pattern used as a device to create depth, continues a Flemish tradition of the mid-16th century that can be seen in works by Pieter Bruegel the Elder. Yet the lively interplay of light and shade and the loose, almost sketchy brushwork give to this little painting a highly personal character. The highlights on the foliage at the left and on the crests of the waves have the sparkling vivacity of a fireworks display.

The human activity depicted in the composition corresponds to the agitated character of the scenery. It is not clear what the artist had in mind when he painted the many boats of all sizes and the tiny figures in them or on the shore; that they are engaged in some kind of military undertaking is suggested by the two men in armor in the small boat in the foreground, one of whom may be giving a signal by blowing a bugle. However, it seems perfectly possible that Bril did not intend to depict a definite historical event, but rather to enliven the landscape scene with these figures, a device to sustain the mood of excitement already created by the natural elements.

c. 1580/90

Oil on copper, 23 × 30 cm ($9\frac{1}{16} \times 11\frac{13}{16}$ in.)

Inscription: A "signature" in the form of a pair of spectacles (*bril*) once visible at lower right (Detroit 1944: 17-18, no. 443) can no longer be located.

Conservation: The copper plate is very slightly uneven, indented particularly along the top edge. The paint film is in very good condition with small, scattered losses and inpainting along the top edge, in the lower right corner, and in the central sky area. Blisters were secured and the painting was completely cleaned and restored in 1965 by Edward O. Korany.

Provenance: Sale, Müller, Amsterdam, 1927. Galerie Dr. Schäffer (dealer), Berlin, 1930. Acquired in 1930.

Exhibitions: Los Angeles 1955. Colorado Springs 1955.

References: Scheyer 1937: 51, fig. 22; 53. Detroit 1944: 17-18, no. 443.

Founders Society Purchase, Adelaide B. Haberkorn Bequest Fund (30. 389).

Abraham Brueghel

1631 ANTWERP – NAPLES 1697

THERE ARE few families in the history of art in which artistic talent persisted at a respectable level through four generations, as it did in the Brueghel (Bruegel, Breughel) family of Antwerp. The greatest talent was obviously Pieter the Elder (c. 1525-1569); both his sons, Jan the Elder and Pieter the Younger, were painters, as was Jan's son, Jan the Younger. Abraham Brueghel was the latter's son, and was probably trained by his father. He settled in Rome in 1659 and never, as far as we know, returned to the Netherlands. In 1670 he was elected a member of the Roman painters' guild, the Accademia di San Luca. He gained a devoted patron in Antonio Ruffo of Messina (there is some evidence that Brueghel had a low opinion of another artist patronized by Ruffo,

Abraham Brueghel, *Still Life of Fruit and Flowers.*

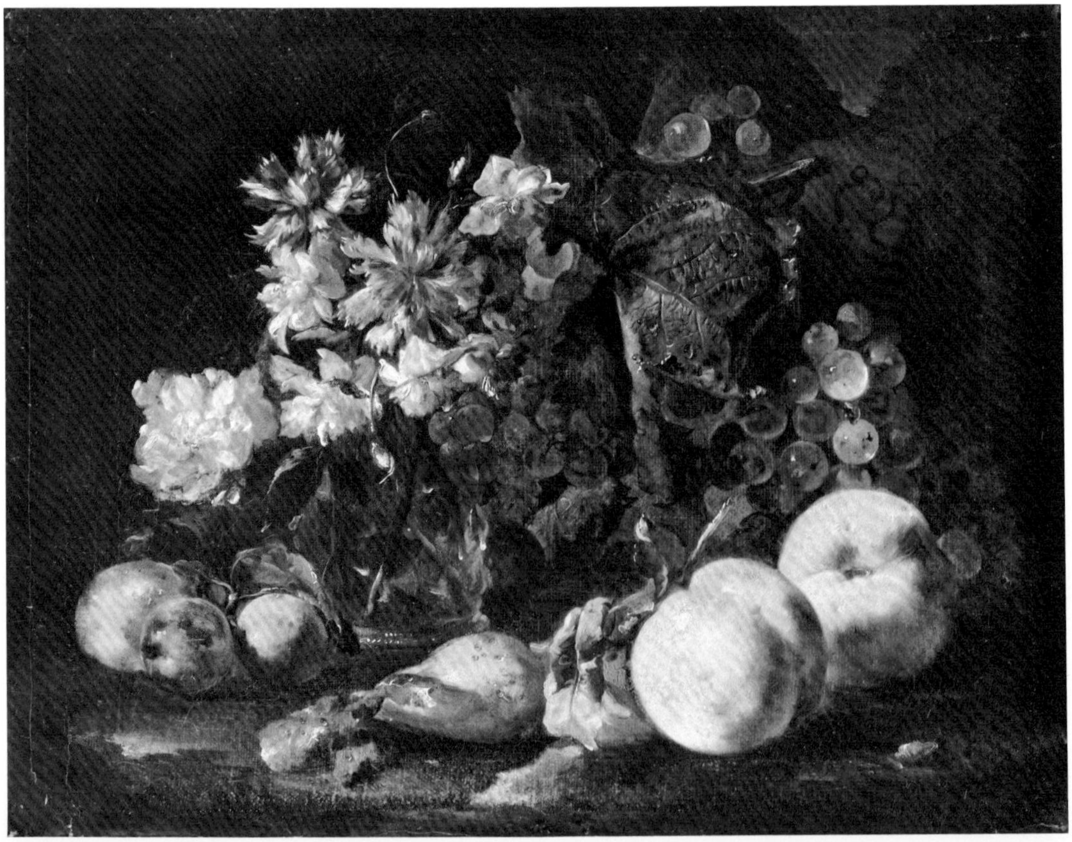

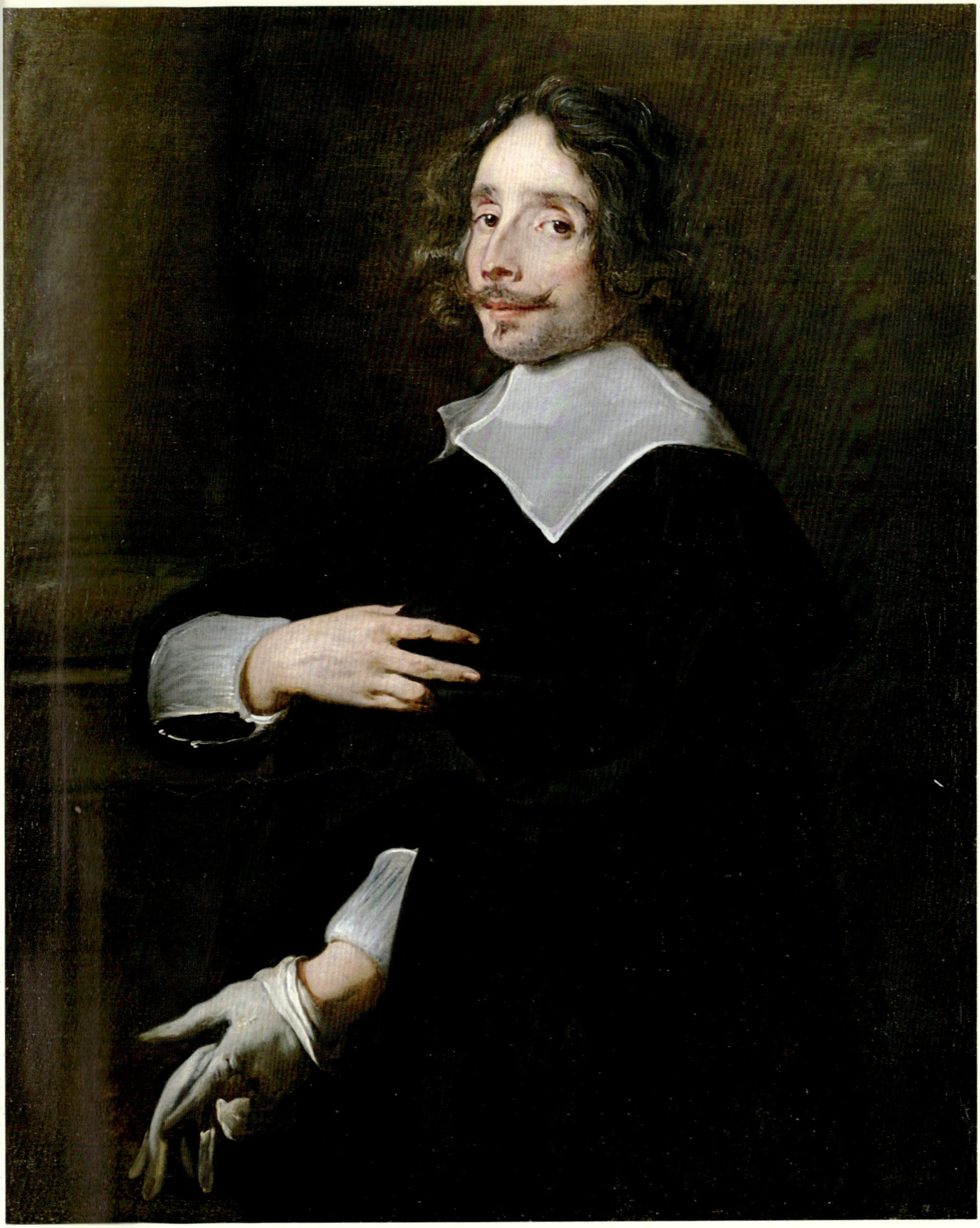

PLATE II. Cossiers, *Portrait of a Gentleman* (*Jan van Balen*?).

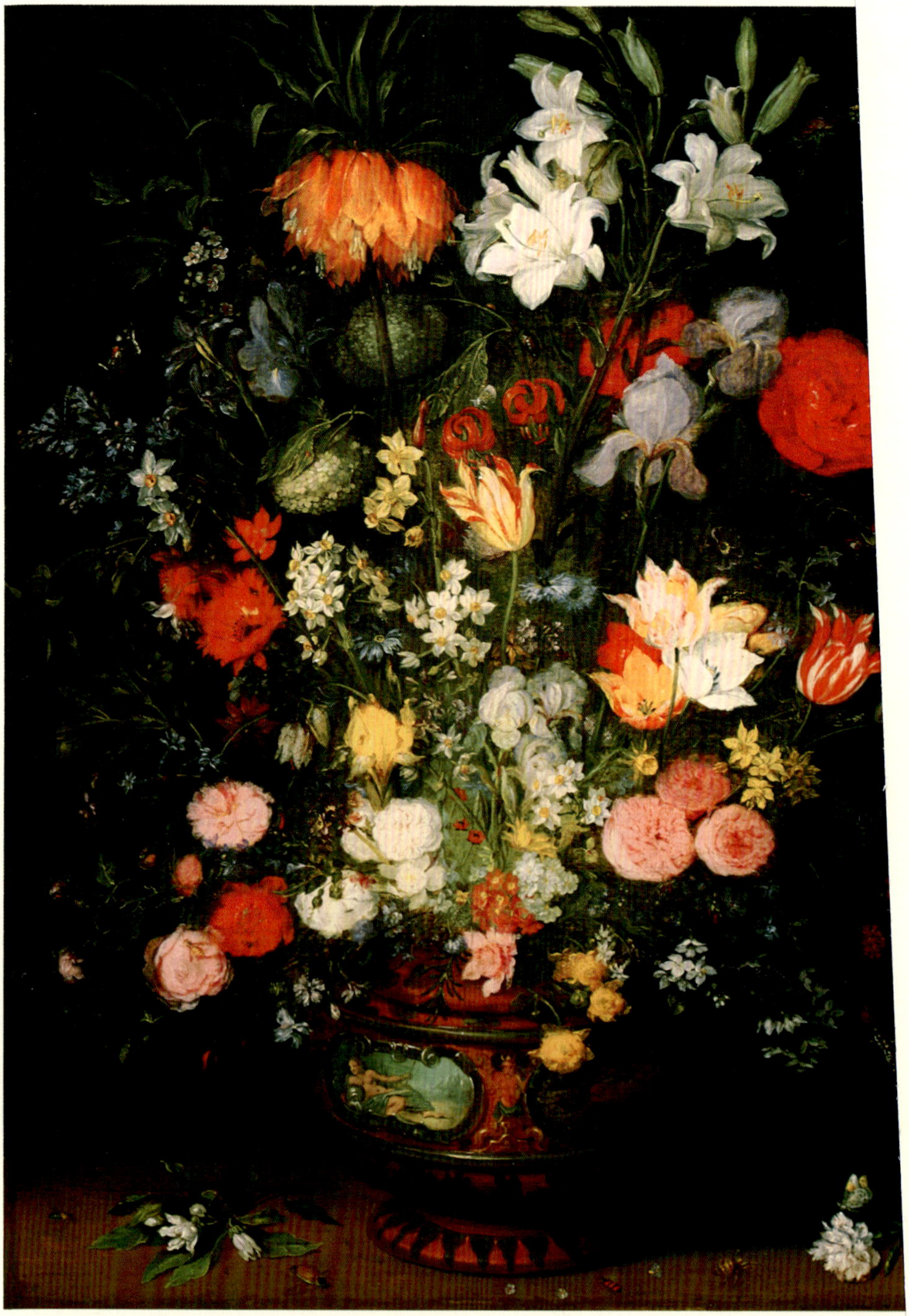

PLATE I. Jan Brueghel the Elder, *Still Life of Flowers.*

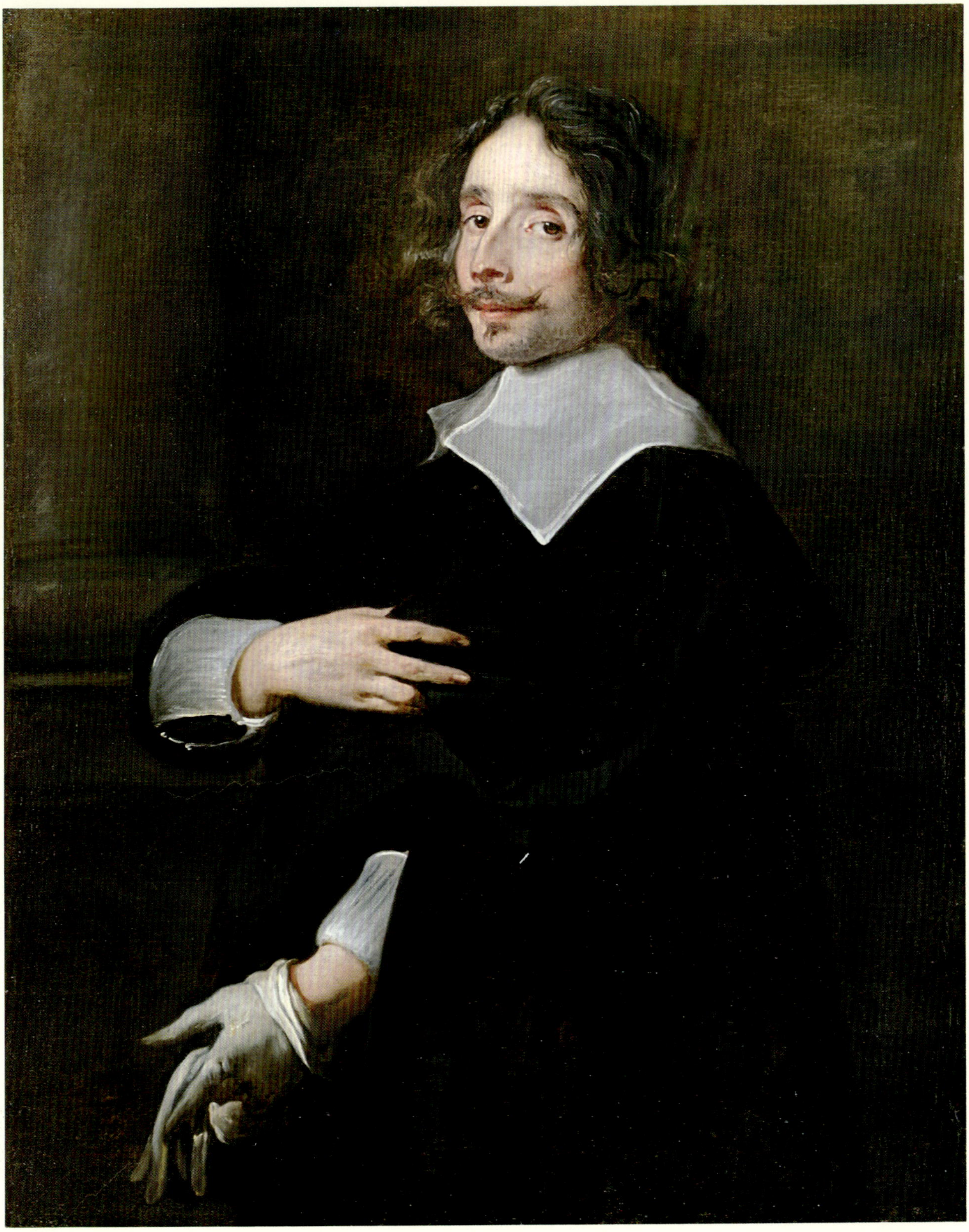

PLATE II. Cossiers, *Portrait of a Gentleman* (*Jan van Balen*?).

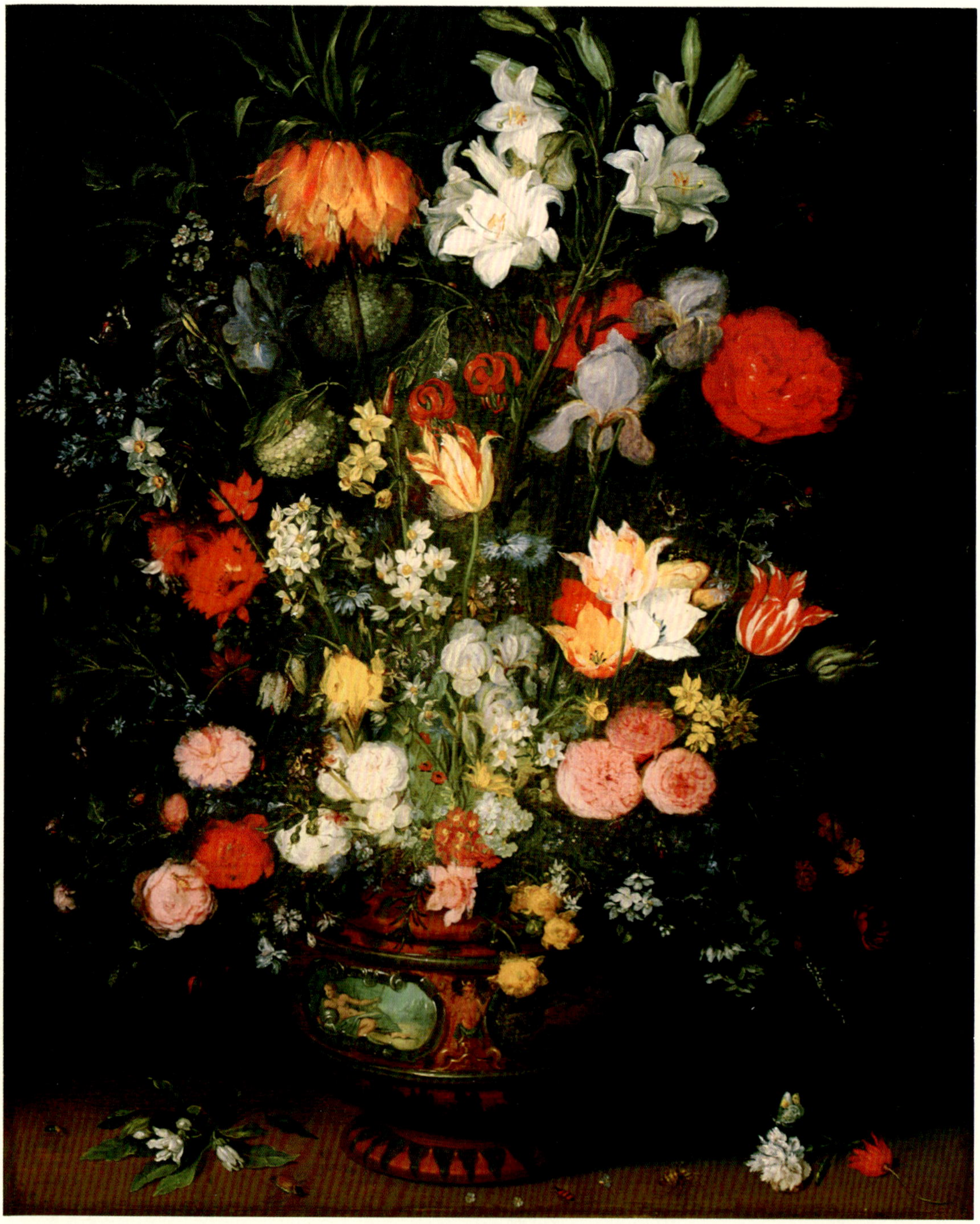

PLATE I. Jan Brueghel the Elder, *Still Life of Flowers*.

Rembrandt van Rijn). Between 1671 and 1674, Brueghel made two trips to Sicily, and from 1675 until his death he resided in Naples (a city his great-grandfather, Pieter the Elder, had visited about 125 years before). Abraham surely owed his technique to his training in the reliable tradition of Flemish still-life painting, yet, stylistically, his works are indebted to the Neapolitan school of still life, represented by such masters as Luca Forte and Paolo Porpora. The figures in Brueghel's works were occasionally painted by other artists, including Giacinto Brandi, Baciccio, and Carlo Maratti.

Still Life of Fruit and Flowers

Although this handsome still life of a variety of flowers placed in a glass, surrounded by an arrangement of peaches, plums, pears, and grapes, is not signed, its traditional attribution to Abraham Brueghel may well be correct; it has never been disputed. The striking chiaroscuro, muted colors, and strongly plastic forms place it squarely in the Italian still-life tradition of the middle and second half of the 17th century, but in its finely observed textures and cleverly rendered illusionistic effects (such as the translucent drops of water on the fruit and grape leaves) it reveals the sound technique the painter derived from his Northern upbringing and training.

c. 1670/80

Oil on canvas, 34.5 × 43 cm ($13\frac{9}{16}$ × $16\frac{15}{16}$ in.)

Conservation: The painting was wax-lined, cleaned, inpainted, and provided with a new stretcher by Edward O. Korany in 1964. At that time, it was reduced from 36.8 by 47 centimeters to its present size by the removal of added canvas strips and the tacking margin that had been extended during an earlier restoration to enlarge the composition. The paint film is in good condition. There is little loss, but certain worn or abraded details, such as the outlines of the green grapes in the center, have been retraced. The browns of the background and edges have also been retouched. Besides Korany's work in 1964, there are no extant records of previous treatment.

Provenance: Kunsthandel P. de Boer (dealer), Amsterdam. Acquired in 1935.

Exhibitions: Saginaw Art Museum, 1975.

References: Valentiner 1936: 49. Scheyer 1937: 59, fig. 30; 60. Detroit 1944: 18-19, no. 446. Whitcomb 1954: 50-51.

Gift of Anna Scripps Whitcomb (35.108)

Jan Brueghel the Elder

1568 BRUSSELS – ANTWERP 1625

THE second son of Pieter Bruegel the Elder, born the year before his father's death, Jan Brueghel the Elder achieved such fame as a painter of still lifes and landscapes that for centuries his name eclipsed that of his father, whose true stature has been recognized only in our century. Nor was Jan's reputation undeserved; in his specialties, he had hardly any peers. Rubens, who collaborated with him several times, was also on warm personal terms with him and conducted, in Jan's name, a correspondence in Italian (which Brueghel apparently knew less well than his colleague) with Cardinal Federico Borromeo of Milan. While in Italy between 1593 and 1597, Brueghel had found a great admirer in the cardinal, with the result that today one of the finest collections of Jan's paintings is in the Pinacoteca Ambrosiana, founded by Borromeo in 1618. Other museums that have significant groups of pictures by Jan Brueghel the Elder are the Alte Pinakothek in Munich and the Museo del Prado in Madrid.

Painted both on wood and on copper, his pictures

are marvels of detailed description of form, particularly of flowers that are botanically correct to the smallest petal and pistil; they are also faithfully colored, the aim of the artist having been to create a lively decorative ensemble in which each form retains its specific shape and pigmentation. Brueghel's landscapes are usually large vistas filled with figures and settlements, often located near the shoreline so that he could include busy scenes of maritime life. Only toward the end of his life did he turn to simpler arrangements, expressing—like his father, but in a minor key—the primitive life of the Flemish peasant. Jan Brueghel was so successful in his chosen style and subject matter that he was extensively copied and imitated, often with such skill that it is safe to say that only a fraction of the pictures carrying his name today were actually painted by him (indeed, some of these copies may have been produced in his own studio). He died a wealthy man, the owner of two houses and an art collection.

Still Life of Flowers

¶ This panel by Jan Brueghel the Elder is filled with a vast array of flowers issuing from the wide opening of a low bowl placed in the center of a smooth surface, which may be the floor or the top of a table. Even though the artist has bunched the flowers more closely together directly above the mouth of the bowl than at the periphery, as would normally be the case in such an arrangement, it is obvious that the bowl is no more than a device or a subterfuge to give to the whole composition a semblance of verisimilitude. The flowers depicted include both red and white roses, peonies, irises, Easter lilies, carnations, tulips of several varieties and colors, daffodils, narcissi, jonquils, daisies, hydrangeas, poppies, asters, sweet Williams, tiger lilies, and one crown imperial, along with other small flowers and greenery. The bowl itself is decorated with simulated scrollwork framing two fields, each of which contains a reclining nude—one symbolizing Water, the other, Earth—and, between the frames, a grotesque satyr herm. On closer inspection, one discovers a number of insects in the foreground: a fly, cockchafer, spider, butterfly, and dragonfly, among others; at the upper left is another butterfly.

It would be absurd to deny that delight in the beauty of flowers—primarily cultivated ones—was the artist's prime motivation for painting such pictures and the chief reason for his patrons to collect them. Yet we should not forget the notion of the impermanence of flowers and their symbolic association with the passing of human life, as spelled out by the prophet Isaiah (40:8) and repeated through the ages in ever-changing variations, an attitude still very much alive in the 17th century. It is likely that even in this seemingly decorative painting Brueghel intended to touch on this *Vanitas* theme by including, for instance, a few flowers lying forlornly, soon to wither, on the ground.

Another version of the same composition, with only very minor variations in the arrangement of the flowers, exists in the Koninklijk Museum voor Schone Kunsten, Antwerp (no. 643; oil on oak panel, 101 × 76 cm). The Antwerp and the Detroit versions seem to be of equal artistic quality, although neither can compare with Brueghel's similar but greatly superior example, the *Blumenstrauss* in the Alte Pinakothek, Munich (no. 824; oil on oak panel, 125.5 × 96 cm). A very similar bowl and arrangement of flowers appears in a still life in the Gemäldegalerie, Berlin-Dahlem (no. 688A; oil on oak panel, 64 × 59 cm).

Color plate I, page 17.

c. 1610

Oil on oak panel, 93 × 74 cm (36⅝ × 29⅛ in.)

Conservation: The single-membered oak panel is unbeveled and cradled with mahogany. There is an irregular crack about 33 centimeters from the left edge. The paint film reaches the edges of the panel, and there are also exposed and filled insect tunnels on both sides, suggesting that the painting has been trimmed. The paint film is in good condition. X-ray photographs show small losses, most of them occurring in the dark background, foreground floor or table, and along the above-mentioned crack. There is abrasion, however, particularly in the thin blue, red, and brown glazes employed by the artist. The use of thin, light scumbles over the dark background has caused a pentimento-like effect surrounding some of the flowers, such as the largest flower at the upper right. There is no underdrawing visible under infrared illumination. Examination under a microscope reveals the use of what appears to be an imprimatura that changes from a greenish tone in the center to a more brownish tone toward the edges. The panel was cradled and the central crack glued in 1936 by William Suhr, who also cleaned and retouched the painting at that time. In 1957 Suhr repaired scratches and damages incurred during transit and secured blisters; no cleaning was done.

Provenance: Kunsthandel P. de Boer (dealer), Amsterdam. Acquired in 1935.

Exhibitions: Milwaukee/Cincinnati 1956: no. 8. Philadelphia 1963: 105.

References: Valentiner 1936: cover, 48. Scheyer 1937: 56, fig. 27; 59. Detroit 1944: 19, no. 447. Whitcomb 1954: 52-53.

Gift of Mr. and Mrs. Edgar B. Whitcomb (35.105)

Jan Brueghel the Younger

1601 ANTWERP 1678

THE younger Jan Brueghel (also spelled Breughel) was the son and pupil of Jan Brueghel the Elder. Two years younger than Antoon van Dyck, with whom he was friendly, Jan left at about the same time as Van Dyck for Italy, where one of his patrons was his father's admirer Cardinal Federico Borromeo of Milan. Jan returned to Antwerp after the death of his father in 1625 and entered the artists' guild in the same year; in 1629 he was elected its dean. He was married in 1626 to Anna Maria Janssens, the daughter of the painter Abraham Janssens; after having borne 11 children, she died in 1668. Five of these children took up their father's profession.

Jan Brueghel collaborated with many other artists, for whom he painted landscape backgrounds or other subordinate areas, while they, in turn, occasionally painted the figures in his pictures. His own style was essentially shaped by that of his father, and his work is often attributed to the elder Jan. Of the many paintings ascribed to Jan the Younger in major galleries and private collections, only a few are signed and dated. Thus, the basis for a reliable reconstruction of his oeuvre is exceedingly limited, with the result that his works are not only apt to be attributed to his father, but that his own sons' and collaborators' works are apt to be given to him. There is no doubt that, in the case of Jan the Younger, we are dealing less with a clearly defined artistic personality than with the head of a busy and well-organized studio that provided the art market of Antwerp with rather impersonal variations of successful thematic and compositional formulas.

Studio of Jan Brueghel the Younger

Village Scene

This painting was formerly attributed to Jan Brueghel the Elder, but it belongs to a group of works that scholars have come to attribute to the younger Brueghel. That does not mean that they all were, in fact, painted by Jan Brueghel the Younger himself, but possibly by members of his workshop. The Detroit painting is a good example of a composition produced by juggling individual standardized motifs. These are its basic compositional elements: at the left, a house with a stepped gable and a low stable-like structure attached to it on the left side, and a few trees in

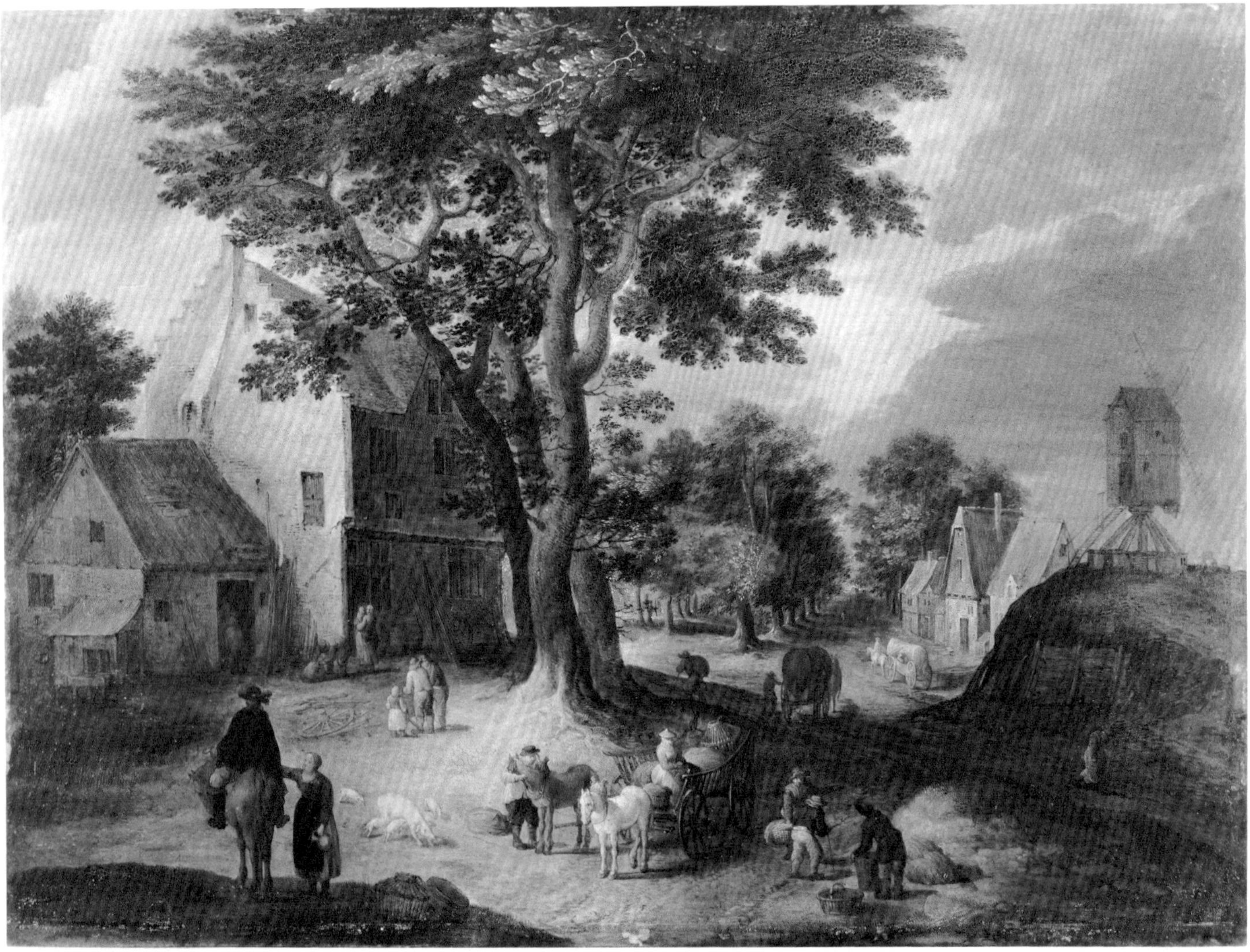

Studio of Jan Brueghel the Younger, *Village Scene.*

front; at the right, a windmill on a small knoll; and, between, a perspective view of trees flanking a road with a few houses lining it at the right. All these elements are also found in a painting attributed to Jan the Elder at the time of its sale at auction in Brussels on March 15, 1926 (lot 11; oil on panel, 27 × 37 cm). There are many more figures and vehicles in the foreground of the Brussels picture, yet the paintings are similar in that they both contain a foreshortened wagon, pulled by a white and a brown horse, with a woman who sits on some bundles just behind the empty driver's seat.

Even though the paintings are probably not by Jan the Elder, the formula of both pictures was almost certainly established by him. This same arrangement can be seen in four paintings on copper attributed to Jan the Elder: 1) 18 × 26 cm, signed and dated 1601, at the Kaplan Gallery, London, in 1956; 2) 18 × 25.4 cm, signed and dated 1603 or 1605, collection of Ferdinand Knecht, Zurich; 3) 18 × 25 cm, at the Galerie de Boer, Amsterdam, in 1963; and 4) 19 × 22.8 cm, signed and dated 1605, at the Slatter Gallery, London, in 1955. Other early versions, some signed and dated, are in the Niedersächsische Landesgalerie, Hanover (dated 1591); the Kunsthistorisches Museum, Vienna; the collection of the Princes of Liechtenstein, Vaduz (dated 1597); the Staatliche Gemäldegalerie, Kassel (dated 1597); the Musée du Louvre,

Paris (dated 1600); and formerly in the Perlman Collection, Stockholm. The Detroit painting and another version (with Leonard Koetser, London, in 1967) have both been attributed to Jan the Younger.

From the earlier versions of the composition, the painter of the Detroit copper took two motifs virtually without changing them: the horseman in the lower left corner, seen from the back, receiving a drink from a woman standing at his right; and the mother sow with her young, slightly to the right of the former group. Yet it is precisely by comparing the Detroit copper with the picture in Brussels by the elder Jan Brueghel, from which it is ultimately derived, that one becomes aware of the artistic shortcomings of the former—such as the disproportionate size and foliage of the trees in the center and the ill-defined differences in scale between the foreground figures and those farther in the distance. Moreover, the setting seems to call for the multitude of figures the elder Brueghel included in his composition; the Detroit picture, by contrast, strikes the beholder as bare.

c. 1640/50

Oil on copper, 23.5 × 31.2 cm (9¼ × 12¼ in.)

Conservation: Both the copper plate and the paint layer are in excellent condition. Infrared examination reveals another figure, not visible in normal light, standing to the right of the sow and piglets. This was painted out by the artist. The painting was last cleaned and inpainted by James L. Greaves (CSL) in 1971.

Provenance: Major Corbett-Winder, Vaynor Park, Berriew, Wales. Corbett-Winder sale, London, April 6, 1889. James E. Scripps, Detroit. Acquired in 1889.

Exhibitions: Detroit 1889: 28, no. 27 (as by Jan the Elder). Worcester/Philadelphia 1939: 62, no. 117.

References: Detroit 1930: no. 21 (as by Jan the Elder). Scheyer 1937: 52, fig. 23; 53-54 (as by Jan the Elder). Richardson 1938: 188, fig. 7; 193. Detroit 1944: 19, no. 21. London 1979: 66.

Gift of James E. Scripps (1889.57)

Gillis van Coninxloo

1544 ANTWERP – AMSTERDAM 1606

DESCENDED from an old Flemish family of artists, Gillis van Coninxloo was admitted to the painters' guild of Antwerp in 1570. He left his native city in 1585 when it was captured by the Spanish regent of the Netherlands, Alessandro Farnese; being an adherent of the Reformed faith, Coninxloo—like many of his coreligionists—preferred exile to conversion to Catholicism. He first went to Zeeland, but in 1587 settled in the south German town of Frankenthal, the home of many other Calvinist refugees. Here, he founded a school of landscape painting to which several other Flemish refugees belonged and which continued to flourish for some time after his departure in 1595 for Amsterdam, where he remained until his death. (Coninxloo's date of death is usually given as 1607; he actually died in late 1606 and was buried on January 4 of the next year.)

Coninxloo's manner of interpreting nature influenced several of the finest landscape painters active in the early 17th century, including Roelant Savery, David Vinckeboons, Jan Brueghel the Elder, and Adam Elsheimer. Although based on a careful study of nature, Coninxloo's landscapes are clearly the product of a highly personal and romantic imagination. In his earlier works he adhered to some of the complex compositional patterns of older Flemish masters, combining rocky mountain formations, winding rivers, and distant settlements, all seen in a rhythmic alternation of light and dark. Later, he closed off these distant views in favor of scenes in which the viewer loses himself among the densely placed trees of virgin forests. More concerned with establishing a poetic mood than with precise botanical exactitude, the artist developed an almost mechanical way of depicting foliage which became a hallmark of the work of his followers.

Circle of Coninxloo

Forest Landscape

This forest scene provides a good example of Coninxloo's style without necessarily being from his own hand. This is particularly true of the right half of the panel, with its accumulation of large trees—probably meant to be oaks—the crowns of which are so intertwined that no daylight can penetrate the dense foliage. The reeds and flowers growing near or in the water are also motifs often found in Coninxloo's work. Yet in the Detroit panel the individual elements are much less varied within the composition than in characteristic works by this artist: the manner in which the trees rise out of their individual mounds of earth or the way in which their branches separate from each other is repeated throughout. The painter of this panel evidently worked under the strong influence of Coninxloo and was possibly in his studio, but we know too little about Coninxloo's school to identify the picture as anything more than the work of a close follower.

c. 1600/20

Oil on oak panel, 50 × 82.5 cm ($19\frac{11}{16}$ × $32\frac{1}{2}$ in.)

Conservation: The single-membered panel has been planed to a 5-millimeter thickness and cradled. It is slightly beveled on the two sides; no bevels can be seen on the top and bottom. A rectangular oak insert (9 × 5 cm) is centered 17 centimeters up and 45 centimeters in from the lower left corner, corresponding to an area between two tree trunks in the lower center. The white-chalk ground and paint layer reach the edges of the panel.

Circle of Coninxloo, *Forest Landscape*.

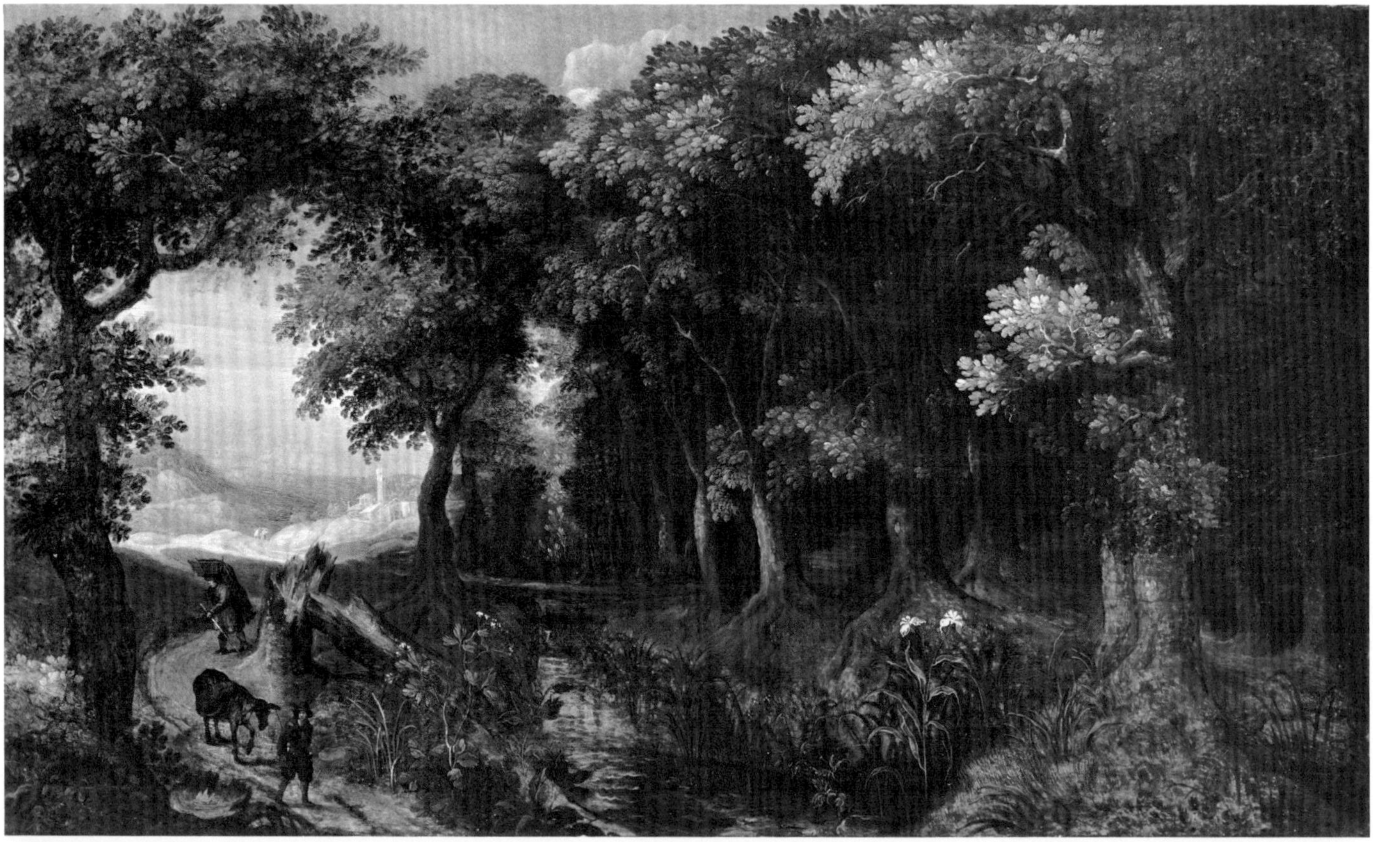

Beneath a thick varnish layer, the painting appears to be in fair condition. Notable areas of inpaint include the large insert mentioned above, much of the broken tree stump at center left, and a half-moon-shaped loss in the trees in the upper center. Later reinforcement of many of the dark elements, such as the outlines of tree branches, is apparent under ultraviolet light. The painting is very thinly worked and the underdrawing is easily visible under infrared illumination. Many of the semi-transparent glazes are abraded. There are no records of previous conservation treatment.

Provenance: Z. Birtschansky (dealer), Paris. Acquired in 1938.

Exhibitions: Los Angeles 1955. Colorado Springs 1955.

References: Detroit 1944: 29, no. 485. Bachrach 1978: 734.

Founders Society Purchase, William C. Yawkey Fund (38.70)

Jan Cossiers

1600 ANTWERP 1671

ONE OF THE most original colorists of 17th-century Flanders, Jan Cossiers was trained by his father, Antoon, and by Cornelis de Vos, but he appears to have come into contact early on with the Caravaggesque movement. This may have occurred in France: he is known to have resided in Aix-en-Provence between 1623 and 1626. What attracted Cossiers to work in the Caravaggesque manner may have been less its specific stylistic idiosyncracies than the themes of low life so popular with its artists. Back in Antwerp, he was received into the guild of Saint Luke in 1628, and in 1640-41 served as one of its deans. Cossiers was among the painters enlisted by Rubens to assist him in the execution of two major commissions of the 1630s: the decoration of the temporary structures erected for the triumphal entry into Antwerp of Cardinal-Infante Ferdinand in 1635, and the paintings for the Torre de la Parada, the royal hunting lodge near Madrid, in 1637. In his later years Cossiers appears to have been very active painting religious canvases for Flemish churches, particularly in Mechlin. A notable portraitist, he rendered his models in poses of casual elegance. He is also known for his excellent portrait drawings executed in black and red chalks.

Portrait of a Gentleman (Jan van Balen?)

Until 1979, when Cossiers' signature was discovered on this painting as it was being examined in the Art Institute's Conservation Services Laboratory, it was considered to be a work by Van Dyck. It had been accepted as such by Wilhelm von Bode, then director of the Berlin museums, and by W. R. Valentiner, who called it "an excellent work by Van Dyck" (certificates in the museum files). According to a letter of September 15, 1964, from Howard Young to Willis F. Woods (museum files), there were also certificates supporting this attribution from Max J. Friedländer and Adolfo Venturi, but these cannot be located. In a brochure apparently published when the canvas was on the New York art market, Alfred M. Frankfurter, then editor of *Art News*, went so far as to claim that "each line is unmistakably Van Dyck."

Besides demonstrating the fallibility of art experts, the former attribution of this picture to Van Dyck may also be taken as a strong affirmation of the superior artistic quality of Cossiers' work. Although it does differ stylistically from Van

Dyck's autograph works—contrary to some of the statements made about it—the painting is not unworthy of that master. The slight figure with his finely chiseled features and the somewhat affected pose of his hands, the use of a column as a prop to enhance the dignity of the setting, even a certain disdainful hauteur of expression, all recall Van Dyck's portraits, particularly those of his English period. Yet the brushwork in Cossiers' canvas is livelier and more forceful than that in works executed by Van Dyck in his later years, and the somber color scheme, dominated by grays and blacks, differs from the silvery sheen of Van Dyck's English portraits.

The picture's appeal depends a great deal on the intriguing physiognomy of the sitter. Still youthful in looks, he conveys an air of world-weariness; his dark eyes are deeply recessed and heavy-lidded, and his brown hair is flecked with gray. He is handsome but frail-looking; one would hardly rate him high on a life-expectancy chart. This impression may be used to lend support to an identification proposed here with due caution. (It ought to be noted here that Valentiner's suggestion that the sitter may be a Spaniard because of the shape of his collar is without foundation; it can easily be shown that the same collar was worn by Flemish burghers around the middle of the 17th century.) A considerable physiognomic likeness can be seen between Cossiers' subject and the painter Jan van Balen, son of artist Hendrik van Balen, as he appears in a print by Wenzel Hollar (De Bie 1661: 119). Not much is known about Jan van Balen; as a painter, he was of minor rank. Hollar's print was made from a lost self-portrait that, perhaps not accidentally, shows Van Balen in a pose similar to the one adopted by Cossiers for his model. We may even see in the print something of the mild arrogance of the figure in the Detroit canvas. The apparent frailty of Cossiers' sitter is not without significance here: Van Balen, born in 1611, died before he had reached his forty-third year. He was in Italy between 1639 and 1642, and the Detroit portrait, if it is his likeness, can only have been painted after his return to Antwerp; Cossiers' sitter looks even slightly older than Van Balen in Hollar's print. A date of around 1650, when Van Balen was about 40 years of age, would seem to fit the circumstances best, and it also agrees with the style of dress depicted. As regards Jan Cossiers, who was then around 50 years of age, the Detroit picture clearly shows him at the height of his artistic powers.

Color plate II, page 18.

c. 1650

Oil on canvas, 97 × 75.8 cm ($38\frac{3}{16} \times 29\frac{13}{16}$ in.)

Inscription: signed at base of column to left of figure: *COSSIERS F.*

Conservation: The canvas is lined. Three of its original tacking margins were cut off, and the one on the top was extended to enlarge the painting by a centimeter. There is a vertical tear about 10 centimeters long near the center of the painting, patched from the back. The paint film is in very good condition, except for minor abrasion and a wide area of loss around the tear. The coat is thinly painted, allowing the brown imprimatura to show through in certain places. The painting was cleaned in 1979 by the Conservation Services Laboratory, at which time a layer of reddish overpaint that obscured the signature was removed.

Provenance: Princes of Liechtenstein, Vienna, from 1767. Glückselig (dealer), Vienna, 1922. Countess de la Béraudière, Paris. Howard Young (dealer), New York, 1928. Grace Briggs Howenstein, Detroit. Acquired in 1979.

References: Liechtenstein 1767: 75, no. 373 (as by Van Dyck). Liechtenstein 1780: 217, no. 660 (as by Van Dyck). Liechtenstein 1873: 16, no. 123 (as by Van Dyck). Frankfurter n. d. [1934] (as by Van Dyck).

Gift of Grace Briggs Howenstein (79.14)

Antoon van Dyck

1599 ANTWERP – LONDON 1641

VAN DYCK alone of all the major Flemish painters appears to have been a true prodigy. Apprenticed to Hendrik van Balen at the age of ten, he painted a remarkably accomplished portrait in 1613, when he was only fourteen years old. We do not know if he was ever Rubens' pupil in the strict sense of the word; it is certain, however, that he was Rubens' principal assistant during the last years of the second decade. Van Dyck is singled out for mention in a contract of 1620 between Rubens and the prefect of the Jesuit church of Antwerp as the senior assistant responsible for the paintings for the building's ceilings. In November of that same year Van Dyck left for the court of James I in London, returning after four months, and in October 1621 he went to Italy, where he appears to have studied intensively the works of Venetian artists, especially Titian, as we can surmise from a sketchbook still preserved at the British Museum, London. He also painted a large number of portraits of Genoese nobles in that city, following a pattern developed by Rubens before him, but investing his works with an aristocratic refinement and psychological delicacy entirely his own. In 1624 he spent some time in Palermo, but left Sicily when an outbreak of the plague rendered a longer stay inadvisable.

From 1627 to 1632, Van Dyck was again in Antwerp, but soon proceeded to London where Charles I appointed him "principalle Paynter in Ordinary" and bestowed a knighthood on him. Restless by nature, the artist went again to the continent in 1634, returning to London one year later. When Rubens died in 1640, Van Dyck traveled in quick succession to Antwerp, Brussels, Paris, back to London, and once more to Paris. When he returned to London in November 1641, having failed to secure a commission from Philip IV of Spain and another for the decoration of the Grande Galerie of the Louvre, his health was broken. He died on December 9 and was buried in Saint Paul's Cathedral.

Despite his desire to be thought of as a painter of large religious and mythological compositions in the manner of Rubens, Van Dyck was most successful, and is best remembered, as a portraitist. Aided by great facility of execution and a shrewd understanding of the wishes and character of his models, he left behind an unparalleled record of the social group whose members were his patrons. It was he, above all, who shaped for posterity the image of the hapless Charles I and the English aristocracy during his reign; the graceful nonchalance Van Dyck preferred to stress in his portraits remained the ideal of British portraiture down to Gainsborough and Lawrence.

Portrait of a Married Couple

This painting was formerly attributed to Cornelis de Vos and identified as Frans Snyders and his wife, Margaretha de Vos, sister of Cornelis (although it bears little resemblance to that couple). It was correctly claimed for Van Dyck by W. R. Valentiner (1922), who cited the rapid, uneven technique, the brilliance of the brushstrokes, and the sensitivity of faces and hands. What is less certain, however, despite the fact that Gustav Glück (1931) accepted it, is Valentiner's theory that the models were the painter Jan Wildens (1586-1653) and his wife, Maria Stappart, whom he married in 1619. Wildens' features are well known from a print by Paul Pontius, based on a drawing by Van Dyck (Mauquoy-Hendrickx 1956: 233, no. 70), and from the portrait Van Dyck painted of him that was formerly in the Vienna Gemäldegalerie (no. 1053; oil on canvas, 75 × 58 cm; originally three-quarter length but later reduced to bust length). Wildens also appears in

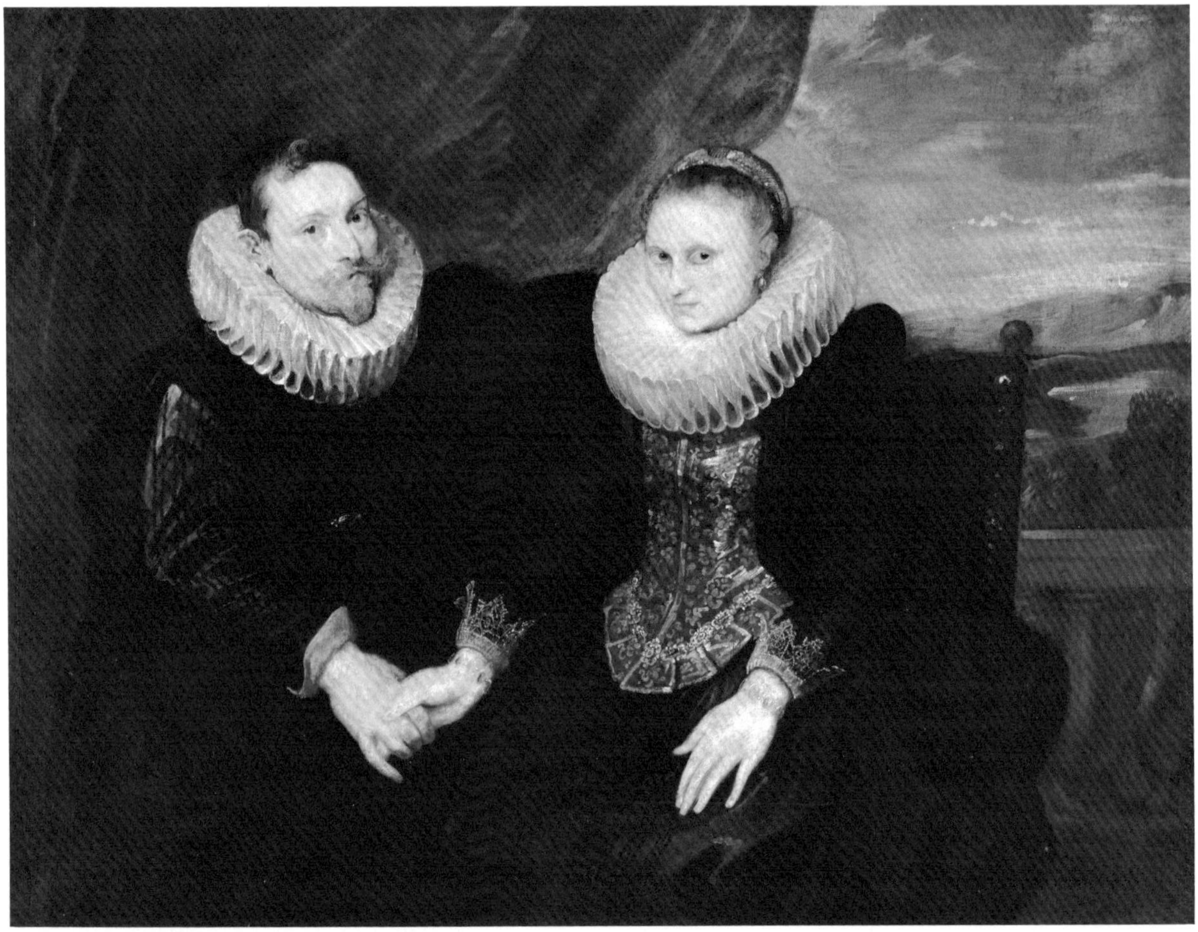

Van Dyck, *Portrait of a Married Couple.*

Willem van Haecht's painting of the gallery of collector Cornelis van der Geest (1628), now in the Rubenshuis, Antwerp.

In view of the fact that the Detroit canvas, for the stylistic reasons mentioned by Valentiner, must have been painted about the same time as Van Dyck's Vienna portrait of Wildens (and before the young Van Dyck left Antwerp in 1621), one has a right to expect a much closer physiognomic correspondence between the two portrayals than in fact exists. The only argument that might be quoted in support of Valentiner's theory is found in the joining of the couple's right hands—a motif that might refer to betrothal (the traditional *junctio dextrarum*) and hence perhaps to the 1619 marriage of Wildens and Maria Stappart. Yet the same motif was introduced by Van Dyck into a double portrait in Budapest (Glück 1931: 113) where it almost certainly indicates no more than the married state of the couple, obviously of advanced age, portrayed there.

c. 1618/20

Oil on canvas, 120 × 154 cm ($47\frac{1}{4} \times 60\frac{5}{8}$ in.)

Conservation: The painting has been glue-lined and extended on the right and left sides by inclusion of the original tacking margins. Approximately 2 centimeters of the lining canvas also add to the width of the composition on either side. There is a gray imprimatura over a light-colored ground. The painting appears to be in fair to poor condition beneath a heavy varnish layer. Ultraviolet examination shows rather extensive retouching along the edges and in the background, with smaller, scattered inpainting in the flesh tones. The faces of both figures are abraded, as is the background sky. The canvas grain has been impressed into the paint layer, and much of the impasto has been flattened during lining procedures. There are no records of conservation treatment.

Provenance: Henry Nugent Banks, London. James E. Scripps, Detroit. Acquired in 1889.

Exhibitions: Detroit 1889: 33-34, no. 33 (as by Cornelis de Vos). Detroit 1929: no. 7.

References: Valentiner 1922: 204-205, 208; reprinted in part in Valentiner 1922a: 10-12. Detroit 1930: no. 65. Detroit 1944: 42, no. 65. Glück 1931: 96, 529.

Gift of James E. Scripps (1889.66)

Portrait Sketch of Lucas van Uffele

Among the portraits painted by Van Dyck attributable on stylistic grounds to the years between 1620 and 1625 are two that most probably represent the same individual, a man not much older than 30 years of age. One of them is in the Städtisches Museum of Brunswick (oil on canvas, 109.5 × 90.5 cm; Glück 1931: 126); the other is in the Metropolitan Museum of Art, New York (oil on canvas, 124.5 × 101 cm; Glück 1931: 127). The New York portrait was also rendered in mezzotint by Wallerant Vaillant, and an impression of that print in the Rijksmuseum in Amsterdam bears the inscription: *DE HEER LUCAS VAN UFFEL* (Wessely 1865: 211, no. 35). Lucas van Uffele (I owe to Margaretta Salinger the information that this is the preferred spelling of his name) was a well-to-do banker and art collector who settled in Venice (not Genoa, as had been stated earlier). The scion of a Flemish family, he was said to have been born a citizen of Amsterdam, so his birth could not have been earlier than 1591 (Vaes 1924: 178 ff.), when his father acquired Amsterdam citizenship. He died in 1637.

P. J. Mariette knew of another impression of Vaillant's print, inscribed *Mr de Nys Amatoor* (now in the Bibliothèque Nationale, Paris; see Chennevières and Montaiglon 1853-54: 205). This probably referred to Daniel de Nys, also established in Venice, whom Van Dyck visited in 1622 (Vaes 1924: 181, 206). Yet it is most unlikely that De Nys was Van Dyck's model for these portraits since he was born in 1572 and therefore was at least 50 years old when the portraits in question were painted—an age surely not matched by the appearance of the sitter. (For some of the data on Van Uffele and De Nys presented here I am indebted to the discussion of the New York canvas in the catalogue of the Flemish paintings in the Metropolitan Museum of Art, kindly made accessible to me in manuscript form.) That Van Dyck had close contacts with Van Uffele is proved by the elaborate dedication that the artist placed on the print known as *Titian and his Mistress*: *Al molto illustre, magnifico et osservandis.mo Sig.r il SIG.r LVCA VAN UFFEL, in segno d'affectione et inclinatione amorevole, como Patrone et singularis.mo amico suo dedicato il vero ritratto del unico Titiano Ant. van Dyck* (Mauquoy-Hendrickx 1956: 179).

What we know about Van Uffele agrees well

Van Dyck, *Portrait Sketch of Lucas van Uffele*.

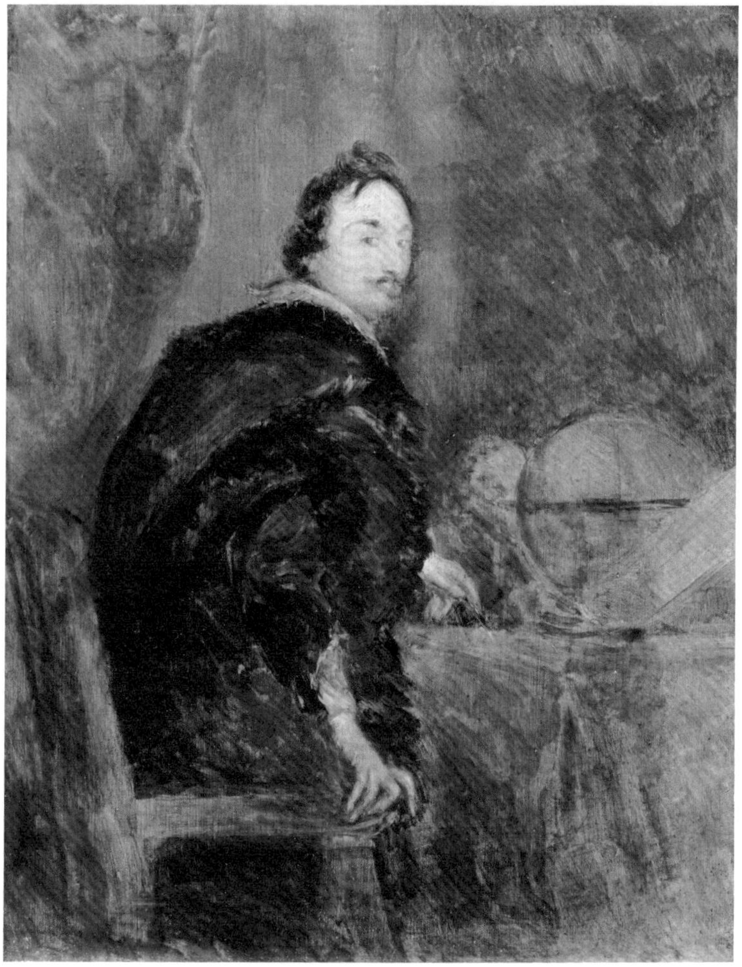

with the appearance of the gentleman depicted in Van Dyck's Brunswick, New York, and Detroit canvases, who was an elegant and youthful individual with interests in learning and art, judging from the New York picture, where a marble head (probably Roman) and a globe are placed before him on the table. His commercial activities might be alluded to in the background of the Brunswick painting, where an estuary and a seagoing vessel are seen outside a window.

A small grisaille sketch in the collection of C. Embiricos, London (Jaffé 1967: fig. 6; oil on panel, 20.3 × 16.2 cm) may have been painted by Van Dyck to be included in his *Iconographie*, but was in the end not so used; it was clearly based on the Brunswick portrait, rather than made as a study for it. The Detroit sketch, on the other hand, is closely related to the painting in the Metropolitan Museum, and is generally accepted as the sketch for that canvas. It was praised effusively by Jaffé ("the essentials of energy and tension were determined at a brilliant pace on the small scale"). While not denying outright that the Detroit sketch might be Van Dyck's preliminary study for the New York picture, I consider its present condition so unsatisfactory that the work does not, in my opinion, permit unqualified acceptance as a study for the picture in the Metropolitan.

There is, in fact, an argument that definitely weakens the claim of chronological priority for the Detroit panel. When the New York canvas was photographed with x-rays, it was found that Van Dyck had painted Van Uffele first with his left hand pointing—palm upwards—to the objects on the table. It was only in a revision of this first thought that Van Uffele received the compasses he now holds with that hand. While this represents no final proof (Van Dyck may have tried out a variant of the position of the hand in the Metropolitan canvas before returning to his "original" thought), it clearly gives rise to some serious doubts that the Detroit panel preceded the New York portrait.

c. 1622/25
Oil on oak panel, 30.4 × 23.7 cm (12 × $9\frac{5}{16}$ in.)

Conservation: The panel is uncradled and unbeveled with a slight convex warp following the vertical grain of the wood. The paint film and light-colored ground reach the edges of the panel, which, nevertheless, does not appear to have been trimmed. The paint film is in rather poor condition with extensive overglazing in the background, cloak, globe, and curtain. There is a horizontal inpainted scratch running through the face of the figure at eye level, as well as losses in the right eye and left cheek. The painting was cleaned and inpainted in 1948 by William Suhr. In 1966 the scratch was repaired by Edward O. Korany.

Provenance: Thomas Agnew and Sons (dealer), London. Acquired in 1930.

Exhibitions: Hartford 1935: no. 38.37. Los Angeles 1946: no. 47. Genoa 1955 (not in cat.).

References: Heil 1930: 79, 81. Detroit 1930: no. 67. Scheyer 1937: 49-51. Detroit 1944: 42, no. 67. Jaffé 1967: 158-161.

Founders Society Purchase, General Membership Fund (30.91)

Portrait of a Genoese Lady

While there has been a reassuring unanimity about the attribution and date of this canvas as a work by the young Van Dyck, painted in Italy around 1625/27, the identity of the model has not been established. When still with the dealer Sedelmeyer in Paris, the portrait was said to represent Marchesa Spinola, a member of one of the leading families of Genoa, and this name was taken over in most of the publications of the Detroit Institute of Arts, as well as in the Genoese exhibition of 1955 to which it was lent by the Art Institute. Yet even as early as 1909, in the first edition of the *Klassiker der Kunst* volume on Van Dyck, Schaeffer pointed out that "Spinola" appears to be a *Sammelname* for all unknown models in paintings from the artist's Italian period and that the model had more recently been identified as a Marchesa Gropallo. It has also been overlooked that there seems to have been some uncertainty all along, since in an exhibition of 1910 in Brussels, to which the picture had been lent by Dr. James Simon, it was shown merely as a *Portrait de Femme*. Glück (1931) preferred the identification with Marchesa Gropallo, but admitted that it remained uncertain; Scheyer (1937) prudently called her *A Young Genoese No-*

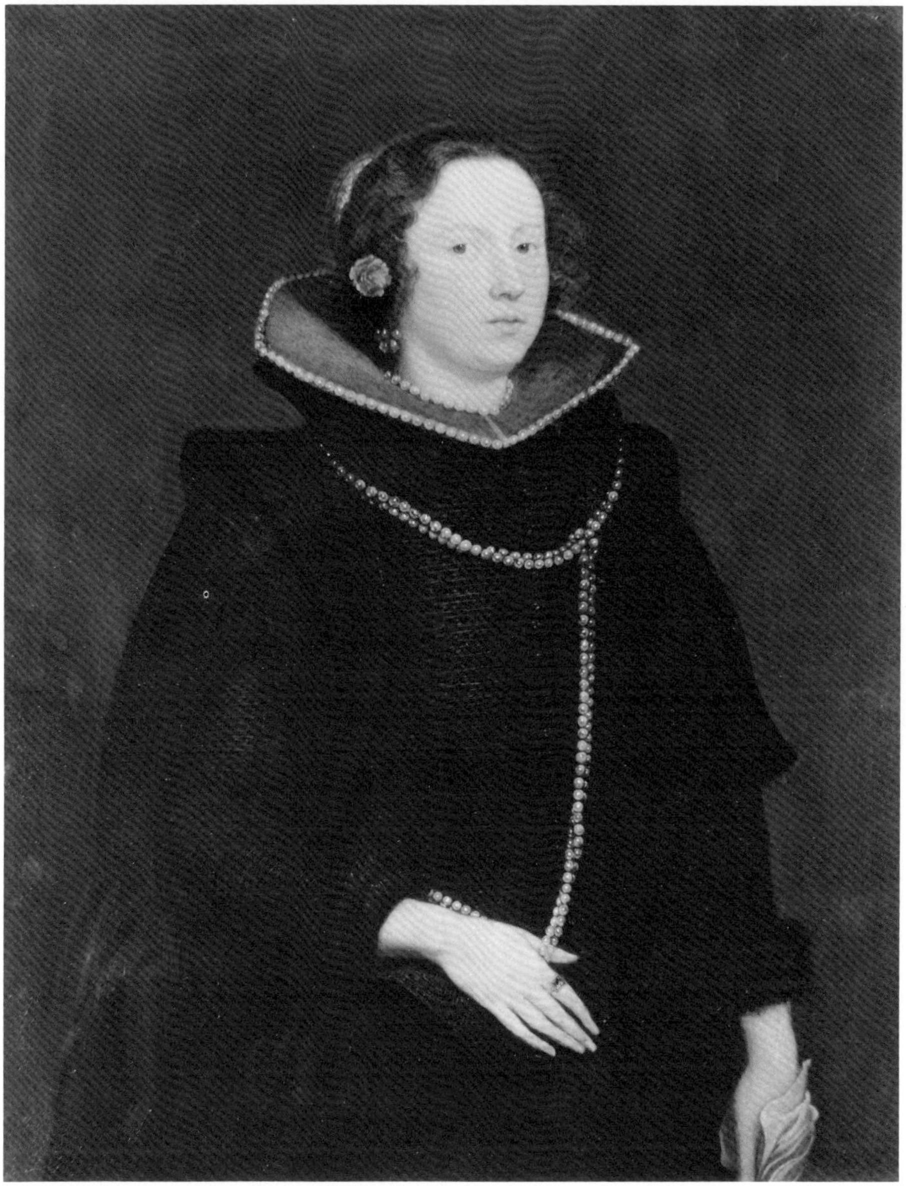

Van Dyck, *Portrait of a Genoese Lady.*

blewoman, but then added "of the house of Spinola or Gropallo." At one point in 1928/29, Valentiner thought he had discovered a companion piece representing a man in armor and identified as "a Genoese officer" (then at M. Knoedler and Co., New York; oil on canvas, 99 × 73.5 cm; Glück 1931: 209), but later (1929) he was content to say that the latter looked "almost like a companion piece"—which it evidently was not.

The identity of the sitter, which remains uncertain, is not the only problem presented by this portrait, however. In view of the fact that Van Dyck was active in many parts of Italy—Milan, Florence, Rome, Mantua, Venice, and even Palermo—there is no reason at all for thinking that the portrait was painted in Genoa, even though the artist appears to have resided there longer than anywhere else. The costume, in fact, does not accord with the fashion seen in his identifiable portraits of young Genoese ladies of this period. Most similar to it—though not identical—is the costume of a Genoese woman seen with her daughter (now in the Musées Royaux des Beaux-Arts de Belgique, Brussels; Glück 1931: 168), where an equally dark costume also serves as foil for a long chain of pearls, and the shape of the collar is similar—though fringed with lace rather than pearls—to that in the Detroit canvas.

Another question is whether or not the painting has been preserved in its original dimensions. In half-length figures Van Dyck strove for the impression of ease, almost informality, while his full-length portraits were apt to be more formal and rigid. This latter impression is precisely the one created by the Detroit canvas. In addition, there is something distinctly unsatisfactory in the manner in which the left hand—holding a handkerchief(?)—is cut off. Both hands, in fact, are treated in a perfunctory manner, the right hand being surprisingly feeble and attenuated even by Van Dyck's standards; such weaknesses might have been less noticeable in a full-length portrait than in a half-length one.

The red flower provides a welcome contrast to the restrained color scheme and to the cool, distant countenance of the model. One may doubt, however, whether it really does give, as Valentiner also wrote, "a hint of the fiery temperament which is hidden behind the veil of sombre colors."

c. 1625/27

Oil on canvas, 106.2 × 81.6 cm ($41\frac{13}{16}$ × $32\frac{1}{8}$ in.)

Conservation: The canvas has been glue-lined and the original tacking margins removed. In an attempt to confirm Professor Held's suspicions that the painting had been cut down at the bottom, the upper and lower canvas edges were x-rayed. Scalloping caused by pulling the original canvas was equally pronounced on the top and bottom. It would appear from this either that the canvas was not cut down, or that it was cut down and restretched before the ground and paint were entirely dry. Although hidden beneath a heavy layer of discolored varnish, the paint layer appears to be in rather poor condition. The impasto has been flattened due to excessive pressure during linings. The flesh tones are abraded and heavily retouched; x-rays show many small losses in these areas. The background has been overglazed with a lighter pigment that is easily visible under strong illumination. Highlights have been added to the sitter's black gown. The left hand, especially, has been extensively overpainted. The painting was revarnished by William Suhr in 1946, 1959, and 1961. There are no records of previous treatment.

Provenance: Charles Sedelmeyer (dealer), Paris. Dr. James Simon, Berlin, 1910. Camillo Castiglioni, Vienna. Castiglioni sale, F. Müller and Co., Amsterdam, November 17-20, 1925, lot 57. Acquired in 1926.

Exhibitions: Berlin 1906: 13, no. 27 (as Marchesa Spinola). Berlin 1909. Brussels 1910: no. 153. Detroit 1929: no. 21 (as Marchesa Spinola). Genoa 1955: no. 22 (as Marchesa Spinola).

References: Freiherr von Hadeln 1909: 297 ("thought to be a Spinola"). Schaeffer 1909: 185, 503 (as Marchesa Gropallo). Valentiner 1926: 4-7 (as Marchesa Spinola). Valentiner 1928: 7-8 ("a Genoese lady"). Detroit 1930: no. 66 (as Marchesa Spinola). Glück 1931: 172, 538 (as Marchesa Gropallo, "not certain"). Scheyer 1937: 48, fig. 20; 49 (*A Young Genoese Noblewoman* "of the house of Spinola or Gropallo"). Detroit 1944: 42, no. 66 (as Marchesa Spinola).

Gift of Ralph Harman Booth (26.102)

A Family Group

This portrait of seven children is a puzzling work in more than one respect, and its mystery is far from being solved. This is surprising since, until Richardson's study (1953), all the essential facts about the picture were thought to be known; according to the entry printed in two different catalogues of the Saltram collection, to which the work once belonged:

The following account of the Bolingbroke family, and of this picture, is taken from an antient [sic] chronicle. "Oliver St. John, created by James 1st. in 1624 Earl of Bolingbroke, married Elizabeth Poulett, sister to John Lord Poulett.—They had four sons and three daughters. Oliver bore arms against the king, and was killed in 1642, in the battle fought near Kineton, in Warwickshire. Poulett (made a Knight of the Bath, at the coronation of Charles 1st) Francis (died unmarried) Anthony; Elizabeth (died unmarried) Dorothy (married to John Lord Rochford, eldest son of Henry Earl of Dover) and Barbara (died unmarried). Van Dyck has here painted Barbara in the act of reciting to her brothers and sisters. Poulett is represented in the collar of his order." This picture was presented to John Lord Boringdon, by his uncle, the Honourable Anne Poulett, whose great aunt Elizabeth Countess of Bolingbroke was mother to the persons here represented.

The entry in Cust (1900) is slightly different:

Bolingbroke, Children of the First Earl of. The seven children of Oliver St. John, first Earl of Bolingbroke, and Elizabeth Paulet, his wife. 1. Oliver St. John, Baron St. John, killed during the Civil War, 1642; 2. Sir Paulet St. John, K.B., died 1638; 3. Francis St. John, died young; 4. Anthony St. John; 5. Dorothy, married John Cary, afterwards Earl of Dover; 6. Elizabeth; 7. Barbara. Presented to John Parker, Lord Boringdon, by the Hon. Orme Paulet. Exhibited, S.K., 1866.

On the strength of these circumstantial data and the inscription on the canvas proper, it had always been believed that the painting portrayed the seven children of Oliver St. John, created Earl of Bolingbroke in 1624, and Elizabeth Poulett, sister of John Lord Poulett. This seemed all the more probable since not only did Oliver St. John in fact have seven children but, just as in Van Dyck's picture, three of them were girls, and the others boys. This historical edifice collapsed, however, when Richardson pointed out that Oliver St. John married in 1602, and that his oldest child was a boy, Oliver, born in 1603. Since the picture cannot have been painted before the 1630s for a number of reasons, including the costumes, the children of Oliver St. John would have been much too old to be the ones portrayed here. Further, Richardson claimed that the dress worn by the girl at the extreme left is Flemish and, in fact, that it dates the picture "quite exactly in 1634-1635." He also stated that the bangs over the foreheads of the two older girls were a fashion that appeared only during the year 1634, again, primarily in Flanders. He concluded, therefore, that the children were from a Flemish, not an English, family, and that Van Dyck must have painted the portrait during his stay in the Netherlands between March 1634 and the spring of 1635. As for the evidence of the inscription, it should be pointed out that in a letter of March 18, 1952, to Richardson, Ellis K. Waterhouse stated that it "cannot be earlier than 1781 since it is in the same characters as that on the Northcotes and Gilbert Stuarts still at Saltram, which date from 1781 onwards" (museum files).

At any rate, there is no reason to doubt the provenance as recorded in the Saltram catalogues, to wit, that the Honourable Anne Poulett (1711-1785)—a man who had come by his curious name because Queen Anne had been his baptismal sponsor—had owned the painting and had passed it on to his nephew, John Parker, Lord Boringdon, and that it remained in the possession of Boringdon's heirs, the Earls of Morley. In an effort to explain the presence of the picture in an English collection, Richardson considered the possibility that it was purchased on the art market by Anne Poulett. He admits, however, that it may very well have been in England long before: in the 1682 sale of Sir Peter Lely's collection in London, two group portraits by Van Dyck were listed: "The Family of Endymion Porter, many Figures. Another Family of seven Figures." The anonymous writer of an editorial in the *Burlington Magazine* (83 [Aug. 1943]: 187) had already suggested that the second item might have been the Saltram picture. That there should have been two different group portraits of seven figures by the same artist, besides being almost identical in size (the dimensions of Lely's picture were given as 3 feet, 7 inches, by 5 feet, 3 inches), is hard to believe. We may then assume that the Detroit picture was indeed owned by Lely before it came into the collection of Anne Poulett. Richardson also argued, not unreasonably, that the identification of the children with those of Oliver St. John is weakened when we see that as early as 1682, the names of the models had been forgotten.

However, this possibility leads to another, more puzzling, coincidence. If we accept the claim that the children in the Detroit canvas are not those of Oliver St. John, we must assume that in the circles likely to have commissioned Van Dyck to paint such a portrait there happened to be another family that not only had seven children, but in exactly the same distribution by sex: three girls and four boys. And if we accept the premise that the family was not English, we must also accept the facts that, relatively soon after it was painted, the picture was imported into England, placed on the market, acquired by Sir Peter Lely, and, after the sale of his collection, bought by a distant relative of the English noble family that happened to have exactly the same number and distribution of children, so that for close to 200 years it was regarded, without question, as a true ancestral portrait. The odds against such a sequence of events would seem to be astronomical.

Nor are Richardson's reasons for his chronological placement of the canvas in 1634/35 as conclusive as he would have liked us to believe. Arguments based on costumes and hairdos have only a limited validity; certainly, dating this portrait because the fashion of bangs first appeared in the year 1634 is not only risky, given the small number of samples on which it is based, but also is demonstrably wrong. In Rubens' portrait of Hélène Fourment in Munich (Alte Pinakothek; no. 340), painted no later than 1631, his young bride has precisely that same hairdo. Moreover, styles at that time rarely developed as casually or as irrationally as they do today. More often than not, they were started by personages who by their rank were conspicuous and deserving of imitation. Richardson in fact realized this when he pointed out that under the influence of Queen Henrietta Maria of England, the ladies of her court wore little ringlets of curls framing their foreheads. The fashion of bangs over the forehead may well have originated in the Netherlands with the visit of Maria de' Medici to Antwerp between September 4 and October 16, 1631. This was indeed the hairdo worn by that lady in the years of her political decline, as may be seen from the portrait Van Dyck painted of her in that same year (Glück 1931: 316), a picture that was frequently copied and widely distributed as a print.

The time span for the origin of the Detroit painting can be extended forward as well as backward. It hardly needs stating that even if it were correct that the fashion for bangs originated in 1634, there is no reason to assume that they also disappeared again in that year. The same, I believe, goes for the costume of the young woman on the far left of the portrait; no one who has seriously tried to date a painting by costume—in this case, by a single one, worn by one out of seven people—no matter how striking, would agree that it could be used to date the picture "quite exactly in 1634-1635." Richardson may well have unintentionally overstated his case from a desire to date the picture in the period—probably no more than a year—during which Van Dyck was in Antwerp and Brussels (a year in which he painted a large canvas of the Brussels magistrates that was unfortunately destroyed in the French bombardment of the city in 1695), and thus could easily have portrayed the children of a Flemish family. What Richardson apparently failed to consider is that Flemish families resided in London in large numbers, and that a group portrait like this one could well have been commissioned by such expatriates. In fact, one item of fashion not mentioned by Richardson might point in that direction: the silk and lace collar of the young boy at the right. This style of collar is not known to me from Flemish portraits, but rather is characteristic of English ones. An almost identical example appears in Van Dyck's portrait of the children of Charles I in the Pinacoteca, Turin (Glück 1931: 375), where it is worn by the future Charles II, born May 29, 1630; the picture was probably painted in 1635, after Van Dyck's return to England. Also, contrary to Richardson's opinion (expressed in rather general terms), I find the technique of the picture perfectly compatible with Van Dyck's later period, nor can I see a difference from the work of "his last Flemish year"—the key work of which has unfortunately disappeared, as I mentioned above.

Although Richardson was chiefly interested in the history of this painting, he also addressed himself to one detail that involves the possible meaning of the painting: the herm of Mercury, placed centrally and in a dominant position, albeit partly hidden by rocks and foliage. Richardson ends his article with two questions: "Is it Mercury, the god of Commerce, and these the children of some

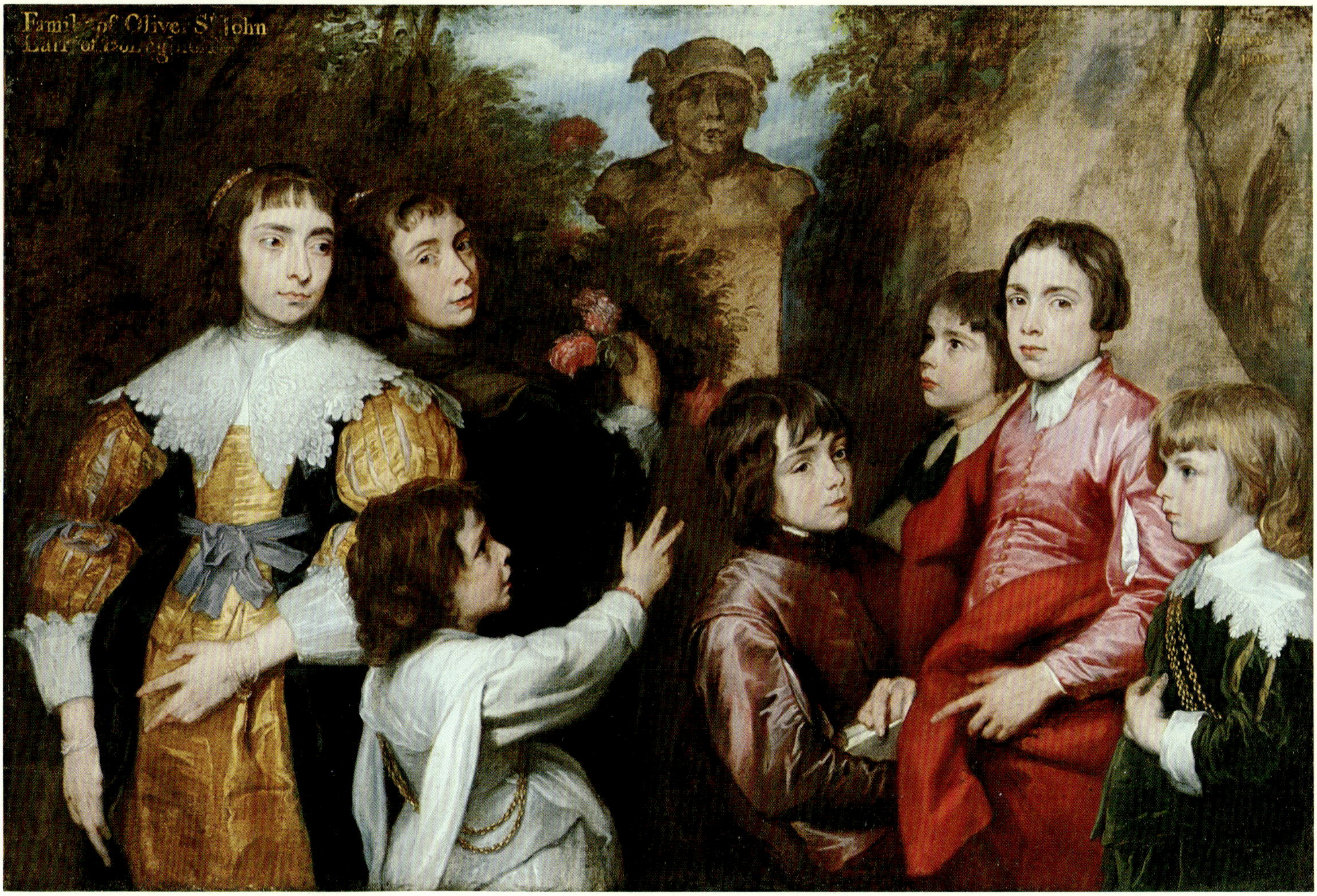

PLATE III. Van Dyck, *A Family Group.*

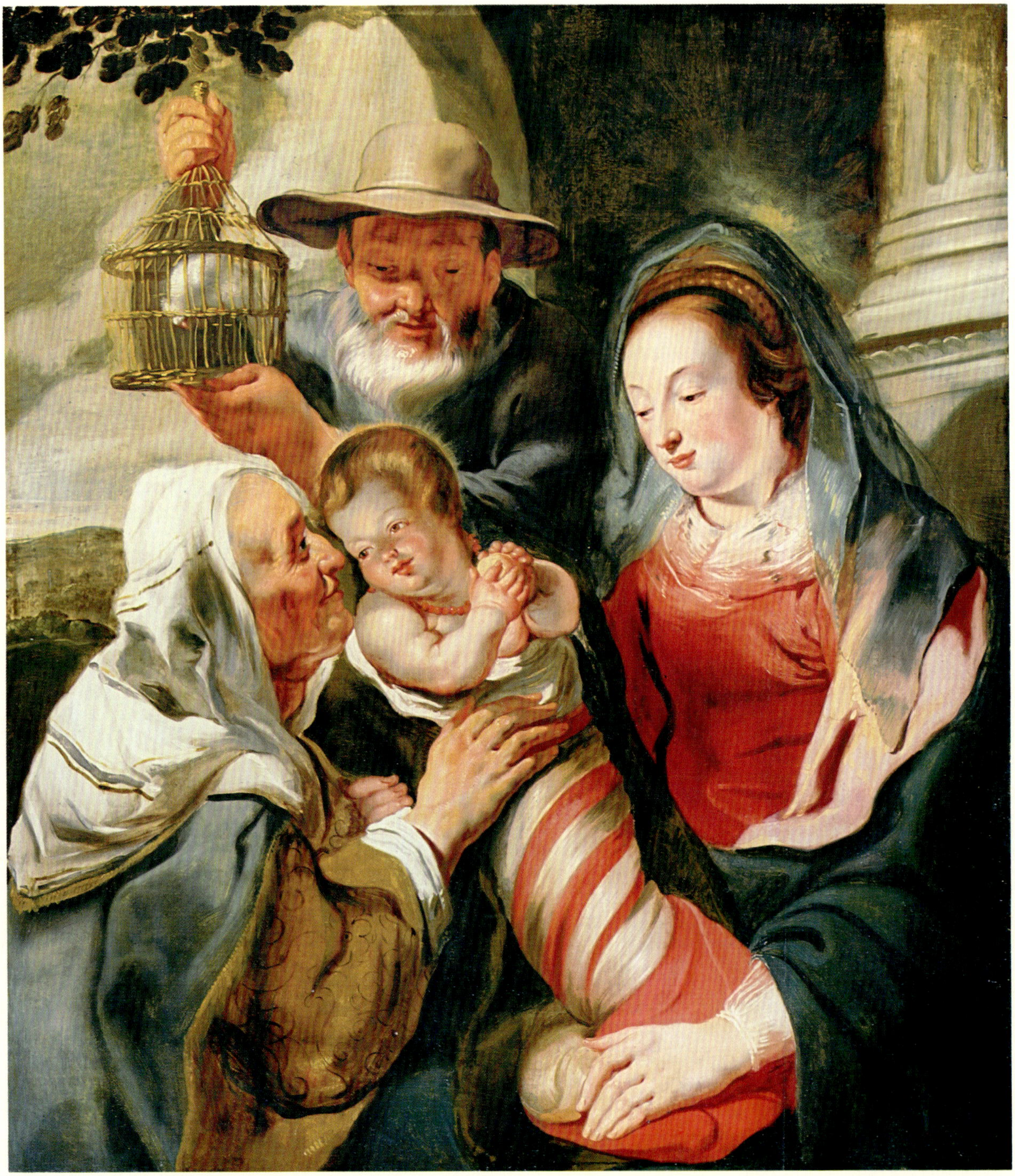

PLATE IV. Jordaens, *The Holy Family with Saint Anne.*

great Antwerp merchant banker? Or is it Mercury Psychopompus, the conductor of the souls of the dead, and these children orphans?" The last is indeed a tempting possibility in view of the fact—surely most unusual in such a picture (unless it is of royal infants)—that the children are portrayed alone, and all wear serious, if not somber, expressions. Their arrangement is also peculiar; although physically close to one another (albeit segregated by sex), there is no psychological contact between them. The most active pose is struck by the youngest, a girl to the left of center. In the Saltram catalogues, where she is identified as Barbara, the youngest child of Oliver St. John, she is said to be shown "in the act of reciting to her brothers and sisters." This may be so, but none of them is paying any attention to her. Perhaps her gesture is meant to point to the Mercury herm. The boy beside her turns his back to her; he holds a book, presumably as an indication of his interest in study, and the pointing finger of the tallest boy at the right insures that we do not overlook this detail. The littlest girl and the princely looking boy at the extreme right wear gold chains; whether they are endowed with a specific meaning remains unclear. Finally, there is the older girl who looks back at the viewer across her right shoulder; she is seen in the act of picking (or just holding?) a red rose from a bush on which there are two other red roses. This unquestionably is a symbolic act although its meaning remains obscure.

The setting is a rocky grove, painted very sketchily and, notwithstanding the herm placed amidst the shrubbery, provided as the merest backdrop. Aside from one of the girls reaching into the flowering shrub, the children might just as well be in an interior. They are quite crowded; the form of the girl looking at us over her shoulder can barely be disengaged from the figure of her frontally seen sister with the harsh, shining eyes. At the right, too, the two taller boys lack space between them; the one looking up is hardly more than a head. Were these two figures afterthoughts? Van Dyck may not have been the most imaginative designer of group portraits, but I do not know a single case in which the spatial arrangement is as unsatisfactory and unresolved as in this canvas. Since the inscription in the upper left corner has been deprived of all historical reliability, should we perhaps question also the value of the inscription in the upper right that acclaims Van Dyck as the painter? I am not ready to do so, although much remains to be accounted for in this painting.

An old copy of the Detroit canvas is in the collection of the Akademie der Bildenden Künste, Vienna (oil on canvas, 111 × 156 cm; Vienna 1927: no. 759). Accepting Glück's original attribution of the Detroit canvas, then in the collection of Baron Louis Rothschild in Vienna, to Adriaen Hanneman—an attribution Glück later repudiated—Eigenberger (Vienna 1927) also listed the Vienna copy under Hanneman's name.

Color plate III, page 35.

c. 1634

Oil on canvas, 111.8 × 162 cm (44 × 63¾ in.)

Inscriptions: upper left corner: *Family of Oliver St. John/ Earl of Bolingbroke*; upper right corner: *Vandyke/pinxit.*

Conservation: The painting is glue-lined and supported on a stretcher from the early part of this century. The original tacking margins have been removed. The paint film, on a light-colored ground, is in fair condition. However, it is extremely abraded, especially in the blacks, browns, and sketchily painted background. The faces of the boy holding the book and the girl holding the roses are also very abraded. The only sizeable paint losses occur in the lower right corner along the edges. One major pentimento can be seen with infrared illumination beneath the red cape over the tallest boy's right shoulder and continuing through the torso, hand, and arm of the boy with the book. The form of this pentimento is indecipherable. In 1953 and 1957 the painting was treated for varnish bloom by William Suhr. It was cleaned (except for the inscriptions) and inpainted in 1978 by Barbara Heller (CSL). At that time, the previously overpainted collar and green coat of the third boy from the right were revealed.

Provenance: The Honourable Anne Poulett, grand-nephew of Elizabeth, Countess of Bolingbroke. By gift to John Parker, Lord Boringdon, Poulett's nephew. The Earls of Morley, Saltram House (John Parker's eldest son was created first Earl of Morley in 1815). Sold c. 1875 (perhaps through Asher Wertheimer, a London dealer) to Baron Alfred Rothschild, Vienna. Baron Louis Rothschild, Vienna. Last recorded in the Rothschild Collection in 1931. Acquired in 1951.

Exhibitions: London 1842: no. 153. London 1866: no. 732. Vienna 1930: no. 94; pl. 100. Detroit 1978: no. 10.

References: Saltram 1819: 22, no. 96. Smith 1829-42: III, no. 691 (as "Portrait of Oliver St. John, Earl of Bolingbroke, with his Countess and four Daughters"). Saltram 1848: 24, no. 97. Cust 1900: 270, no. 30. Vienna 1927: 186, no. 759 (as by Adriaen Hanneman). Baldass 1930: 135-136. Glück 1930: 171; pl. 100. Glück 1931: 503, 576 (Glück was unaware that the Saltram and Rothschild pictures were one and the same and mentioned them as two separate examples). Richardson 1953: 228-234. Richardson 1953-54: 6-8. Comstock 1954: 71. Gerson and Ter Kuile 1960: 192, n. 59. Hertford 1981: 129-130, nos. 101-102.

Founders Society Purchase, General Membership and Donations Funds (51.230)

Attributed to Van Dyck

Portrait of a Young Gentleman (The Earl of Downe?)

The question of whether or not this portrait represents a "Lord Downe," and, if so, which one, has overshadowed a more pertinent matter: whether it is indeed the work of Van Dyck. On June 21, 1944, when W. R. Valentiner recommended its purchase to Edgar B. Whitcomb, then the President of the Detroit Institute of Arts, he wrote: "there cannot be the slightest doubt that the painting is an outstanding example of Van Dyck's great English period" (museum files). Valentiner also was confident that "it will always be considered one of [the museum's] most distinguished portraits." To judge from the virtually complete critical silence about the canvas during the subsequent decades (and perhaps even from the fact that a paper by E. P. Richardson on this picture was never published), Valentiner's high hopes for it have not materialized. Moreover, in the course of a lengthy correspondence carried on in 1972 about the identity of the sitter, Oliver Millar ended a letter of June 30, 1972 (museum files), to Richard G. Williams, then at the Detroit Institute of Arts, with the significant question: "Has the attribution to Van Dyck ever been contested?" Since the inquiries originally addressed to Millar had nothing to do with the problem of attribution of this painting, one may safely conclude that Millar, surely one of the finest connoisseurs of the work of Van Dyck, had serious reservations about this picture's authorship.

Any judgment in regard to this question is made difficult by the condition of the painting. It seems that, during the process of relining, the paint film was flattened out to such a degree that the picture has the smoothness of a mirror. Thus, it is no longer possible to observe the "life" that the surface of a picture obtains from the minute variations in thickness and direction of the brush strokes. Allowances must obviously be made because of this condition. Compositionally, the painting is unimaginative, but still well within the range of comparable portraits generally accepted as Van Dyck's work. The sharp vertical behind the figure, dividing the background into a flat dark area and an open view, is found in several canvases—for instance, the portrait of Sir Edmund Verney at Claydon House (Glück 1931: 448). Nevertheless, the balance among all the compositional elements seems to lack the felicitousness that marks most, and certainly the best, works of the master. The dead space all along the left side, the awkward placing of the model's left arm, the perfunctory treatment of the wall, sky, and darker area between them at the right also detract from the effectiveness of the whole. Even the dank masses of hair descending on either side of the face, with nary a curl adding a bit of grace or whimsy, contribute a negative element to the canvas.

None of these observations—even if all are taken together—seem sufficient to strike the painting from Van Dyck's own oeuvre, yet they are enough to suggest that the attribution to the master should not be accepted without serious reservations. When the picture was acquired in 1944, it came with a letter from its previous owner, Anthony F. Reyre, quoting a Miss Ure, from whom he had bought it, to the effect that it represented a Lord Downe and that it had originally come from the collection of the Earl of Pembroke at Wilton House. In his unpublished paper, Rich-

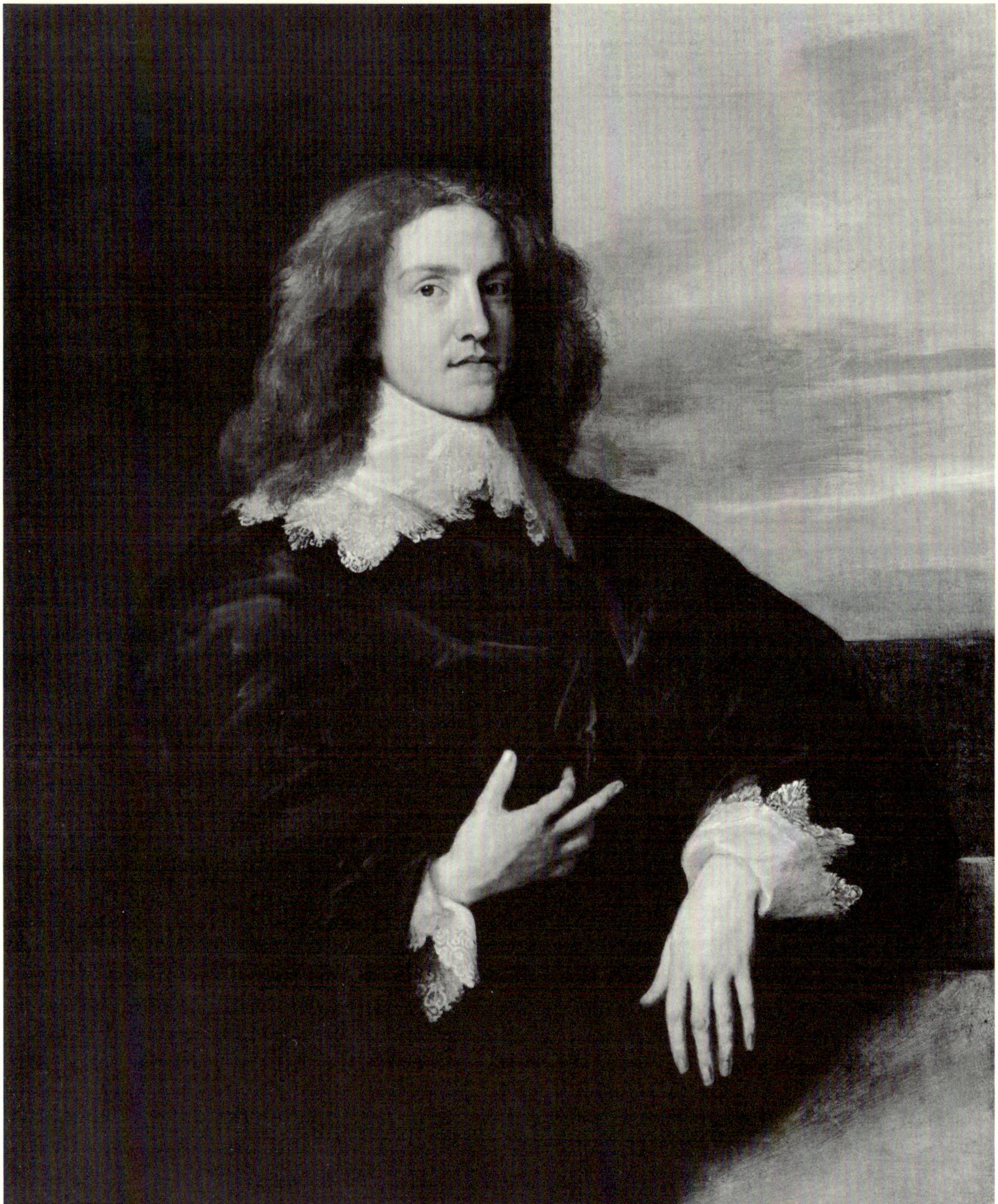

Attributed to Van Dyck, *Portrait of a Young Gentleman* (*The Earl of Downe*?).

ardson denied on historical grounds that the sitter could be a Lord Downe; accepting the Wilton House provenance, however, he suggested that the portrait might be of James Herbert, one of the sons of the fourth Earl of Pembroke. The Downe thesis again gained strength when it was found that there had indeed been Earls of Downe in the early 17th century (the title became extinct in 1668; see J. B. Burke, *A Genealogical History of the Dormant, Abeyant, Forfeited and Extinct Peerages of the British Empire*, London, 1883: 442). In the catalogue of the Whitcomb Collection (1954) the sitter was identified as Sir Thomas Pope, second Earl of Downe (1622-1660).

The question was again revived in 1972 in correspondence initiated by J. R. S. Guinness, British High Commissioner in Ottawa, Canada. In the course of that correspondence, Guinness pointed out that a trustworthy likeness of Sir Thomas Pope existed in a double portrait (with Sir Thomas Penyston) by William Sheppard (collection of the late Rt. Hon. Harold Arthur, Viscount Dillon, C. H., Ditchley, Oxfordshire; sold at Sotheby's, London, May 24, 1933 [lot no. 84], and there incorrectly identified as "Sir William Pope Bt."). Another portrait, supposedly of the second Earl, executed by Cornelius Johnson in 1641, in Guinness' opinion more likely depicts the third Earl (letter of August 18, 1972; museum files). It is quite obvious, at any rate, that the second Earl of Downe, as portrayed by Sheppard, is a very different man from the young gentleman in the Detroit canvas; Oliver Millar, in the letter previously referred to, pointed out that the second Earl "had a longer and thinner face."

Since, in addition to the uncertainties about the authorship of the picture and the identity of the sitter, even its Pembroke collection provenance (as asserted by Miss Ure) may well be doubted, the picture's interest, then, relies entirely on what we see before us: a portrait of a well-dressed, serious, possibly strong-willed young man who almost certainly belonged to the upper stratum of British society. Even if not by Van Dyck, the painting strongly reflects the casual elegance introduced by him into English portraiture.

c. 1640

Oil on canvas, 114 × 91 cm ($44\frac{7}{8} \times 35\frac{13}{16}$ in.)

Conservation: The painting has been glue-lined and its original tacking margins removed. It is supported on a five-member, mitered keyable stretcher. The paint film, on a white lead ground, has been severely abraded. This is particularly notable in the sky, lace cuffs and collar, and hair. It has also been flattened, through various relinings, obliterating a once lively impasto. The varnish is yellowed. In 1951 the painting was varnished by William Suhr. There are no prior treatment reports.

Provenance: Miss Ure, Allenbury Lodge, Forest Hill. Anthony F. Reyre (dealer), New York. Hammer Galleries, (dealer), New York. Acquired in 1944.

Exhibitions: Chattanooga 1952. Fort Wayne 1953. Grand Rapids 1959.

References: E. P. Richardson, "A Portrait of a Young Englishman by Sir Anthony Van Dyck," unpub. manuscript (museum files). Whitcomb 1954: 58-59.

Gift of Mr. and Mrs. Edgar B. Whitcomb (44.167)

Style of Van Dyck

Portrait of a Man

As late as 1920, this painting was still a full-length portrait, as can be seen in a sales catalogue from that year. The dimensions of the canvas were then 172 by 114 centimeters (measurements were probably taken inside the frame, which explains the slight discrepancy in width; it is thus also likely that the canvas was actually 2 to 3 centimeters taller). The gentleman stood in a relaxed attitude, the right leg crossed over the left. The reduction of the canvas to its present size must have occurred between the sale of 1920 and the donation of the picture to the Art Institute in 1929.

That this cannot be the work of Van Dyck has been recognized since the publication of the Art Institute's 1944 catalogue. Yet the suggestion made at that time that it might be the work of Caspar de Crayer is untenable and actually contradicts the attribution of the work to the "school of Van Dyck," since De Crayer, 15 years older than Van Dyck, can hardly be identified as a member of the master's "school." The restrained con-

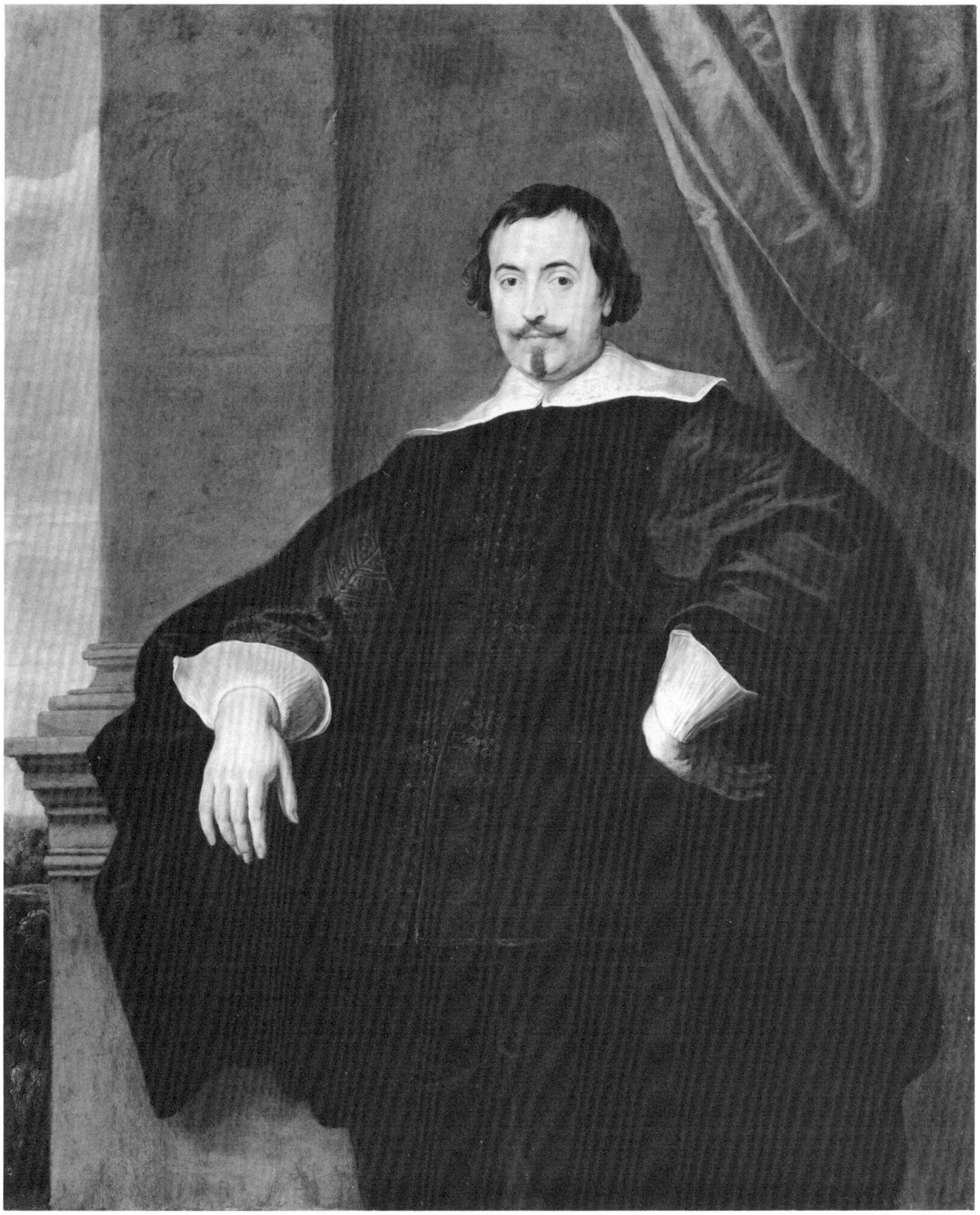

Style of Van Dyck, *Portrait of a Man*.

ception of the painting, the precise modeling of all forms, and the absence of the psychological animation so characteristic of Van Dyck would seem to indicate the hand of a competent but prosaic artist, working more in the style of Philippe de Champaigne than of the Antwerp masters. The form of the large, flat collar worn by the sitter is found in only one of Van Dyck's portraits, that of the Marquis Francisco de Moncada (Musée du Louvre, no. 1971), which presumably was painted before 1635, the year in which Moncada died.

c. 1630/40

Oil on canvas, 145.5 × 116 cm (57¼ × 45⅝ in.)

Conservation: The painting is glue-lined. The original tacking edge has been removed on all four sides. Approximately 2.5 centimeters of the paint layer are folded over the bottom stretcher member. The portrait was originally full-length and was cut down during a previous restoration. Because of the thick and discolored varnish, the condition of the painting is difficult to ascertain. X-ray photographs of the face and hands show little paint loss. The background, however, has a considerable amount of inpainting, particularly in the upper part of the wall and pilaster. Foliage, resembling grape leaves, can be seen in the x-rays in this area. A low wall-like architectural element can also be vaguely seen in the x-rays to the left of the figure. The present background is contemporaneous with the figure and the change of background appears to be the artist's own. In 1947 the painting was "surface polished" by William Suhr. No prior treatment is recorded.

Provenance: Leroy frères (dealer), Brussels. Sale, Brussels, March 7, 1920, lot 191. Galerie Van Diemen (dealer), Berlin, 1929. Acquired in 1929.

Exhibitions: Brussels 1910: no. 172 (as "a magistrate").

References: Detroit 1930: no. 69 (as by Van Dyck). Detroit 1944: 42, no. 69 (as by "school of Van Dyck ... perhaps by Caspar de Crayer").

Gift of the Van Diemen Galleries (29.294)

Copy after Van Dyck

Martyrdom of Saint George

Any discussion of the Detroit sketch of the *Martyrdom of Saint George* must also take note of two other sketches of the same subject, both unquestionably works of Van Dyck. The finer one is a panel in the Musée Bonnat, Bayonne (no. 934; 51.5 × 40 cm; formerly in the Hoschek Collection [sale, Vienna, March 24, 1909, no. 13]; Glück 1931: 253). The other panel belongs to the Library of Christ Church, Oxford (43.5 × 35.7 cm; Oxford 1916: no 324; Glück 1931: 252). All three sketches have been discussed by Vey (1956) who placed the Bayonne sketch chronologically (with sound arguments, I believe) before the one at Oxford; I am also in complete agreement with his removal of the Detroit sketch from Van Dyck's authentic oeuvre, but I part company with him when he dismisses it, without further study, as the work of an imitator. In the catalogue of the 1979 exhibition in Princeton, the phrase "by an imitator in Van Dyck's studio" does not clarify the situation; "imitators" were not normally suffered in artists' studios. Actually, I believe that the Detroit panel is a fairly skillful copy of an original, lost sketch by Van Dyck. The same artist who painted the Detroit panel copied another sketch by Van Dyck, and it is fortunate that both the copy and the original have been preserved. The subject of that sketch is the *Ecstasy of Saint Augustine*, executed in preparation for the celebrated painting of around 1628 for the church of the Augustinian friars in Antwerp (Glück 1931: 237); the original is now in the Mauritshuis, The Hague, the copy in the Ashmolean Museum, Oxford (Vey 1956: fig. 7). Vey accepted the Oxford sketch as the original—understandably, since the better version had not yet become known; it is surprising, however, that he failed to see how close the Oxford panel was to the Detroit sketch, which he justly rejected.

I cannot agree with Vey when he suggests that Van Dyck might have painted the sketches for the *Martyrdom of Saint George* for their own sake, without intending them for a specific project. It is true that no large painting of this subject is known or may ever have been painted, yet it is unlikely that a master of Van Dyck's standing during this period (the late 1620s) would have made three elaborate studies without a commission or at least a good chance of obtaining one.

Since I take the Detroit panel to be a faithful copy of a lost original, the place of the original of that sketch in the development of the artist's ideas must be faced anew. The Bayonne sketch must certainly retain its standing as the earliest version; it alone does not yet include the two steps that raise the saint to a higher level. More difficult is the question of whether the composition recorded in the Detroit copy was an intermediate one, or whether it was the final solution and, therefore, followed the Oxford sketch. There is one argument favoring the latter possibility: the

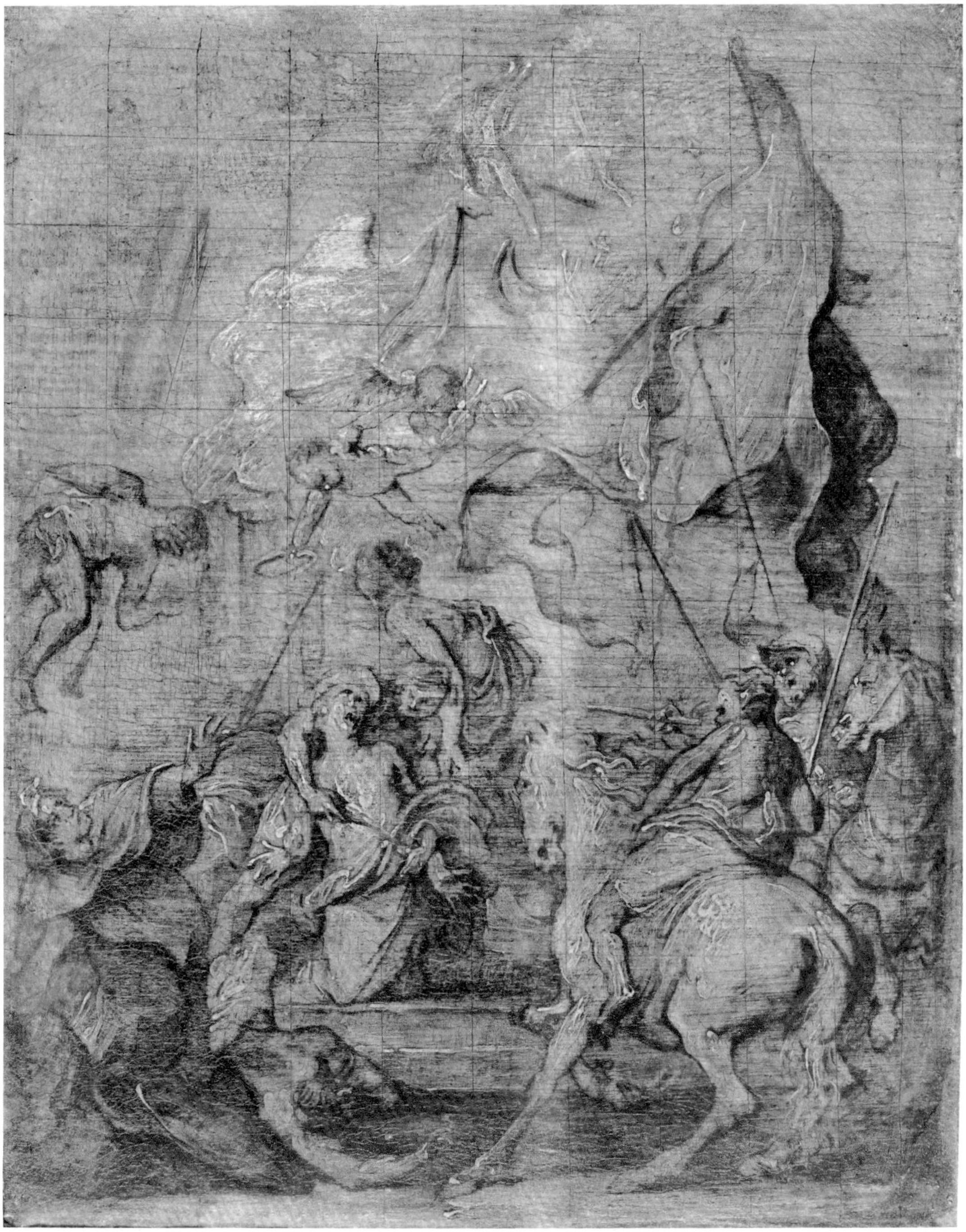

Copy after Van Dyck, *Martyrdom of Saint George*.

Detroit sketch has a grid pattern laid over it—the normal device for facilitating the transfer of a design to a larger format. Yet we obviously cannot know if the lost original version also had that grid; the copyist may have added it for reasons of his own (it is not, in fact, carefully applied; its lines rarely cross each other at exact right angles). The strongest argument against the Detroit composition as Van Dyck's final idea was put forth by Vey: it is most unlikely that the artist, after achieving the lucid and balanced formula of the Oxford sketch, would have again reverted to a confused and markedly asymmetrical arrangement. Moreover, it is difficult to believe that the smallest (that is, Detroit) version was painted at the end; I prefer to see it as an intermediate stage. Finally, the theory that there must have been a similar, but superior, version, now no longer traceable, finds additional support in the fact that the composition was engraved by Peeter Clouwet and etched in 1658 by Willem Paets, a dealer in Rotterdam.

In the inventory of the collection of Alexander Voet, dated July 12, 1685, a sketch by Van Dyck representing the *Martyrdom of Saint George* is mentioned: "Item, een schetsken, Onthalsinghe van Sint Joris, van van Dyck gl. 6" (Denucé 1932: 315). It is obviously impossible to say to which of the three sketches this entry may refer.

Oil on oak panel, 23.2 × 17.7 cm (9⅛ × 7 in.)

Conservation: The panel is beveled and uncradled. It has a slight convex warp following the horizontal direction of the wood grain. The paint film reaches the edges of the panel, which does not, however, appear to have been trimmed. The thinly applied glazes are somewhat abraded beneath a heavy varnish. However, there appear to be few actual paint losses and the paint film seems to be in fair condition. In 1947 dirt and old varnish were removed by William Suhr. There are no other conservation treatment records.

Provenance: E. Warneck, Paris. Sale, G. Petit, Paris, May 27-28, 1926, lot 39. A. S. Drey (dealer), Munich. Acquired in 1929.

Exhibitions: Detroit 1978: no. 9.

References: Detroit 1930: no. 68. Heil 1930: 80. Glück 1931: 252, 546. Scheyer 1937: 45, fig. 18; 47. Detroit 1944: 47, no. 68. Vey 1956: 206, n. 38 ("the work of an imitator"). Antwerp/Rotterdam 1960: 162, under no. 128 (as "the work of an imitator"). Princeton 1979: 142, under no. 38 (as by "an imitator in Van Dyck's studio").

Gift of A. S. Drey (29.446)

Copy after Van Dyck

Virgin and Child

As was noted by W. R. Valentiner and L. J. Walther, the authors of the 1929 Detroit exhibition catalogue, the composition of this painting owes much to a work by Titian formerly in the Palazzo Ducale, Venice, a partial copy of which was included by Van Dyck in his Italian sketchbook (Van Dyck 1940: pl. 9v.). The position of the Christ Child is particularly reminiscent of Titian's infant, while the pose of the Virgin is much closer to that in another painting by Titian, two versions of which still survive in the Louvre and in the Kunsthistorisches Museum, Vienna (no. 93; Fischel n. d. [1906]: 7-8; neither of these paintings, however, is fully accepted by all scholars, and some authors, like Hans Tietze [1936: II, 305, 315] are inclined to consider them both copies of a lost painting by the master).

Judging from the exceptionally large number of versions and copies extant, Van Dyck's picture of the Virgin affectionately gazing at the playful child on her lap was one of his most successful compositions. It is generally and, I believe, correctly, assumed that the version in Buckingham Palace, London (oil on canvas, 117 × 98 cm) is Van Dyck's original (Glück 1931: 225, 543). It can be traced back through the collections of Queen Anne and William III to that of King James II and hence has an excellent pedigree. It was exhibited in 1946-47 at the Royal Academy of Arts in London; in the catalogue, after the introductory remark, "Other versions, most of them of inferior quality," is the following list:

1. Wallace Collection; 2. Hampton Court, no. 431; 3. Formerly Hope Collection, Deepdene (this picture was sold in 1898 to C. Wertheimer); 4. Harrington

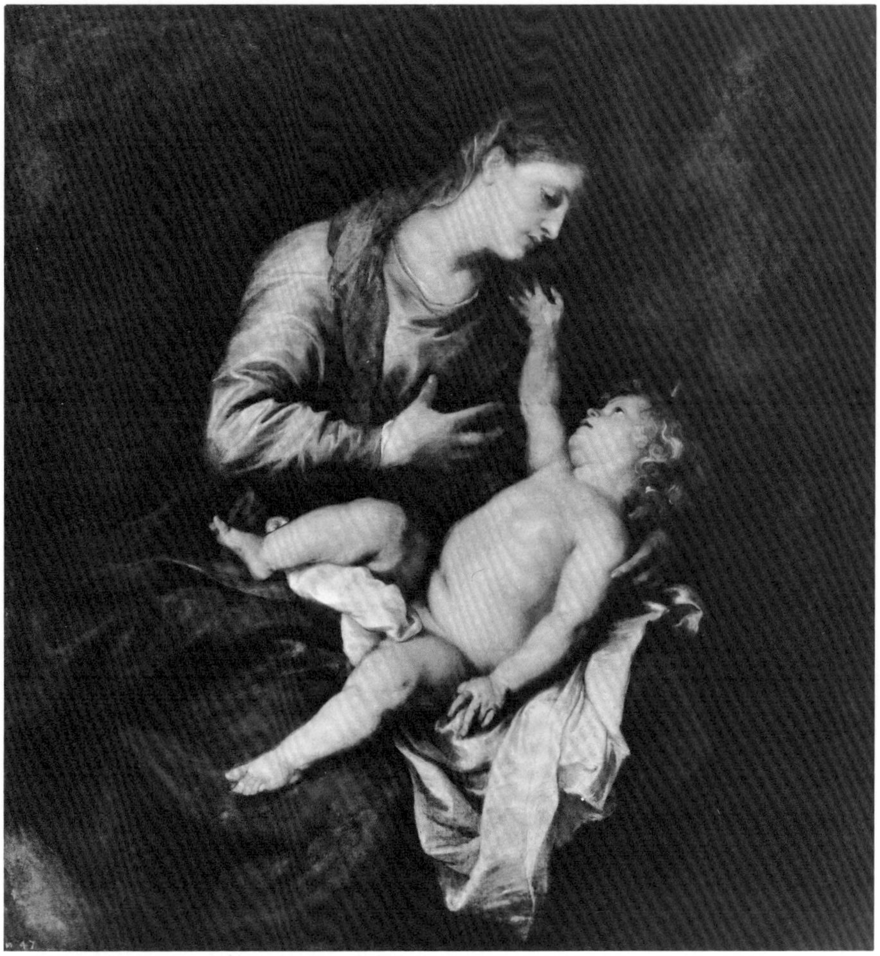

Copy after Van Dyck, *Virgin and Child.*

House, Kensington; 5. Hoschek Collection, Prague; 6. Talon Sale, Brussels (Fiévez), March 10, 1927, no. 17, pl. 11; 7. Ross Hall Collection, sale Glasgow, February 27, 1908, no. 61; 8. Van Dyck Exhibition, Detroit, April 1929, no. 15 [the picture discussed here].

To these can be added a ninth, in the collection of Mrs. T. P. Howell, Cleveland. To the best of my knowledge, there is no duplication in this list, each painting being, in fact, a different version.

In addition, there exists a small grisaille version (oil on panel, 39 × 32 cm), which in the upper left corner contains the figure of Joseph walking with a donkey in a wooded landscape. Formerly in the collection of A. Schindler, Vienna, it was sold by F. Müller in Amsterdam on July 13, 1926 (lot 664); it was later with the firm of Cassirer in Amsterdam, but its present whereabouts are unknown to me. This version served as the model for an engraving by Hendrik Snyers.

Oil on canvas, transferred from panel, 125 × 113 cm ($49\frac{1}{4} \times 44\frac{1}{2}$ in.)

Conservation: The presence of vertical join cracks at 18, 39, 66, and 84 centimeters from the left edge indicates that the painting was originally executed on panel. It was transferred to canvas using a glue-paste adhesive. The paint layer is in poor condition due to damages that occurred both before and after the painting's transfer. The background, the Virgin's brown scarf, and the darkest glazes of the blue mantle over her left shoulder are particularly abraded. The flesh tones and more opaque pigments are in better condition though they do show extensive minor flaking. Major losses occur along the join running through the child's head, in the lower right background, and around the child's right hand. Various pentimenti are visible in the infrared photograph. There is a diagonal line crossing the chest of the Madonna, and there are some changes in the folds of her mantle. The child's left forefinger, right hand, and right forearm have been reworked, as has the Madonna's left hand. The painting was cleaned and inpainted by Barbara Heller (CSL) in 1977. There are no records of previous treatment.

Provenance: Count Alessandro Contini, Rome. Howard Young (dealer), New York, 1926. William T. Fisher, Detroit. William A. Fisher, Detroit. Deeded to Founders Society, December 29, 1960, although Mrs. William A. Fisher retained life interest until her death in 1972.

Exhibitions: Detroit 1929: no. 15. Detroit 1978: no. 8.

References: London 1946: 104, under no. 292.

Bequest of Mr. and Mrs. William A. Fisher (F60.5)

Flemish Artist

An Elderly Woman on Her Deathbed

This panel, which came to the museum with an attribution to Jean Bellegambe the Younger, was attributed to Marcus Gheeraerts the Younger by W. R. Valentiner, on the basis of a painting of a similar subject (a deathbed portrait of a man) signed with the initials, *M.G.F.*, and dated 1607 (Rijksmuseum Kröller-Müller, Otterloo; Collins Baker and Constable 1930: 31; pl. 23). There are, however, hardly any similarities between the two works (except for the fact that in both cases the pillow on which the head is propped is edged with a strip of lace, though the patterns are different). The Detroit panel is executed in a much more hard-edged manner, with a marked tendency to simplify all three-dimensional modulations. Nor does any one of the few portrait attributions to Gheeraerts accepted by Collins Baker and Constable (six at the most, one of which they characterize as a "repainted wreck") show any stylistic kinship with the Detroit picture. (We are really much in the dark about the style of the younger Gheeraerts, as was neatly summarized by Ellis Waterhouse [1953: 27] when he said, "In short, the personality of Gheeraerts remains an enigma.")

What Valentiner and, following his lead, Richardson failed to consider is the large number of portraits of deceased people painted precisely in this manner, depicting the head resting on a pillow, while the arms and the rest of the body are hidden under a linen sheet turned at the top over a darker blanket. Such pictures date as early as the beginning of the 16th century, and usually depict men of high rank or great distinction (Emperor Maximilian, Luther, Melanchthon, William of Orange, Duke William IV of Bavaria, Henry IV of France, and Richelieu, to name but a few). Even children were occasionally commemorated in this way; one example is the depiction, dating from around 1650, of the young child of Johan Honich, alderman and member of the city magistracy of Middelburg, Holland, and a resident of the Château Steenhove (Mauritshuis, The Hague, no. 603). The formal pattern of these representations loosened up considerably in the 17th century; a miniature painting by Jacob II de Gheyn depicts a dead woman inside a bed-alcove, from which the curtains have been drawn, and a man standing at the right (perhaps the painter himself) who points at her. In this case, her arms are also visible, with the hands crossed. A candle, symbol of the passing of life, stands in front of the bed. In the Van Dyck portrait of Lady Venetia Digby on her deathbed (Dulwich Picture Gallery, London, no. 194), the reference to death is provided only emblematically by a rose that is losing its petals on her coverlet, while she rests her head on her hand as if only

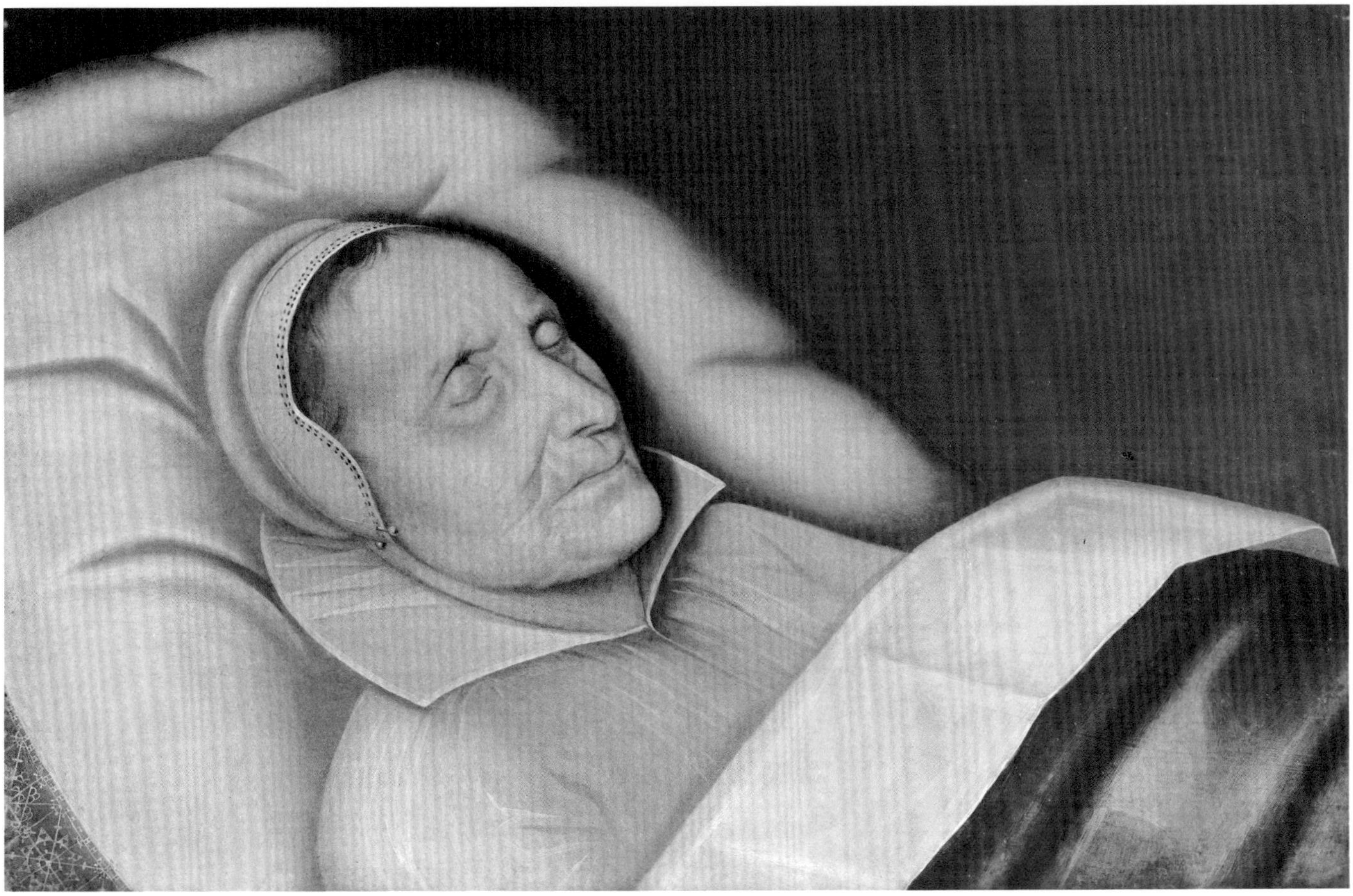

Flemish Artist, *An Elderly Woman on Her Deathbed.*

asleep. (This subject has been studied by Andor Pigler [1956: 1-75]; reference kindly provided by E. Haverkamp Begemann).

Besides suggesting that the model for the Detroit picture may well have been a woman of rank, a study of the formal and iconographic tradition of this theme makes it likely that the panel has been cut off at the bottom, a surmise supported by technical evidence (nowhere else, as far as I know, is the body cut off in this way, which makes it impossible to determine whether or not the protective linen covers the near arm). An x-ray photograph taken in 1979 revealed that there is the portrait of a living woman, who may or may not be the same as the one now seen in death, in the lower right corner of the present composition and at right angles to it. It is likely that the panel was cut down (on the right side of the original portrait, which is now the bottom of the picture), since otherwise the first face would have been placed asymmetrically in the upper right corner of the painting.

Early 17th century

Oil on oak panel, 38.1 × 57.8 cm (15 × 22¾ in.)

Conservation: The cradled, two-membered panel is horizontally joined (at 26 centimeters from the top edge). Open insect tunneling on the reverse indicates that the panel has been planed (to a 5-millimeter thickness). The right side shows a small part of a bevel: no beveling is present on the left, top, or bottom. The paint layer and chalk ground reach the edges of the panel on all four sides. The bottom edge appears to have been trimmed. The paint layer is in fair condition beneath a discolored varnish. There are inpainted losses along the join, in the green coverlet, and in the face and neck. The shadows in the face have been reinforced with glazes. X-ray photographs reveal a portrait of a living female beneath the present figure. Her head is horizontally placed, top to the right, beneath the folded sheet. She wears a white cap similar to that of the dead woman. In 1953 William Suhr laid down numerous small blisters and restored small paint losses.

Provenance: André de Hévésy (dealer), Paris. Acquired in 1939.

Exhibitions: Richmond/Detroit 1964: 21 (as by Marcus Gheeraerts the Younger).

References: Richardson 1940: 85-86 (as by Gheeraerts). Detroit 1944: 52, no. 541 (as by Gheeraerts).

Gift of Mr. and Mrs. E. Raymond Field (39.662)

Flemish Artist

Portrait Study of a Man

The attribution of this painting to Van Dyck, which seems to have been proposed first in 1924 by Hofstede de Groot (certificate in the museum files), has been accepted within the Art Institute, but not outside it. There should be no doubt about the inadmissibility of such an attribution; while the study is painted with a certain bravura, the head lacks the clear anatomical articulation and the subtle interplay of light and shade characteristic of even the most hastily executed productions of Van Dyck. To some degree, the fault may lie with the picture's state of preservation, since it appears to have been cleaned rather harshly; yet, even after making allowances on that account, this painting remains in every respect below the level of Van Dyck's portraiture.

I am unable to suggest another name for the artist of the work; there are points of similarity with portraits painted by Cossiers and Franchoys, but they are insufficient to permit an attribution to either of these masters. It seems likely, however, that the painter must be sought among the Antwerp artists of the second quarter of the 17th century and, more specifically, toward the latter part of that period.

There is, finally, good reason to think that the

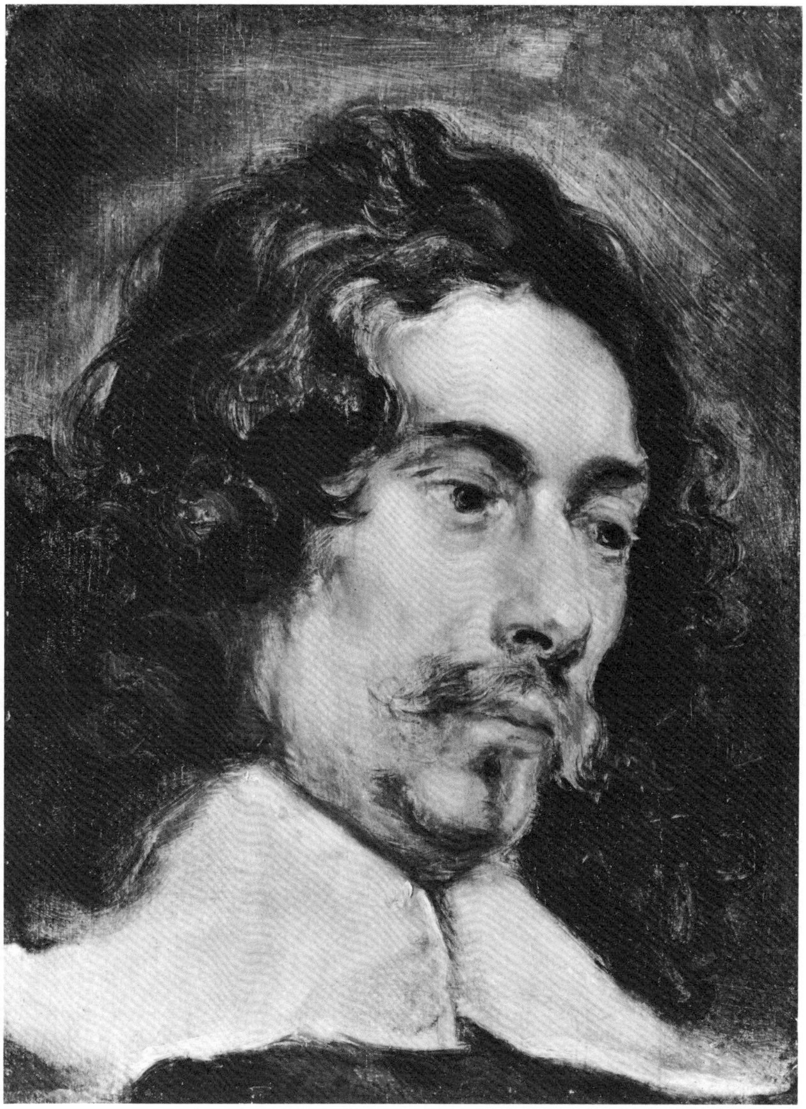

Flemish Artist, *Portrait Study of a Man.*

picture, as it now exists, is a fragment of a larger panel. The head is much too large for the size of the panel, and both at the left and the bottom the forms are awkwardly cut off. A clearly beveled edge (on the reverse of the panel) is seen only at the top (it can also be partly seen at the bottom, but this may be the result of an effort to hide the fragmentary character of the work).

c. 1625/50
Oil on oak panel, 37.2 × 27.2 cm (14⅝ × 10$\frac{11}{16}$ in.)

Conservation: The uncradled panel is slightly beveled on the top and bottom edges. The left side is broken and uneven due to insect tunneling. There are no inpainted margins; the paint film reaches to the edges on all four sides. Except for the thick impasto highlights, the paint is rather thinly applied and in good condition. There are inpainted losses to the left of the mustache, in the collar area, and near the edges (especially the lower right and center left). The painting was last cleaned and inpainted by William Suhr in 1954.

Provenance: Private collection, England. Mr. and Mrs. Edgar B. Whitcomb, Detroit, 1924. Acquired in 1953.

Exhibitions: Detroit 1926: 39 (as by Van Dyck).

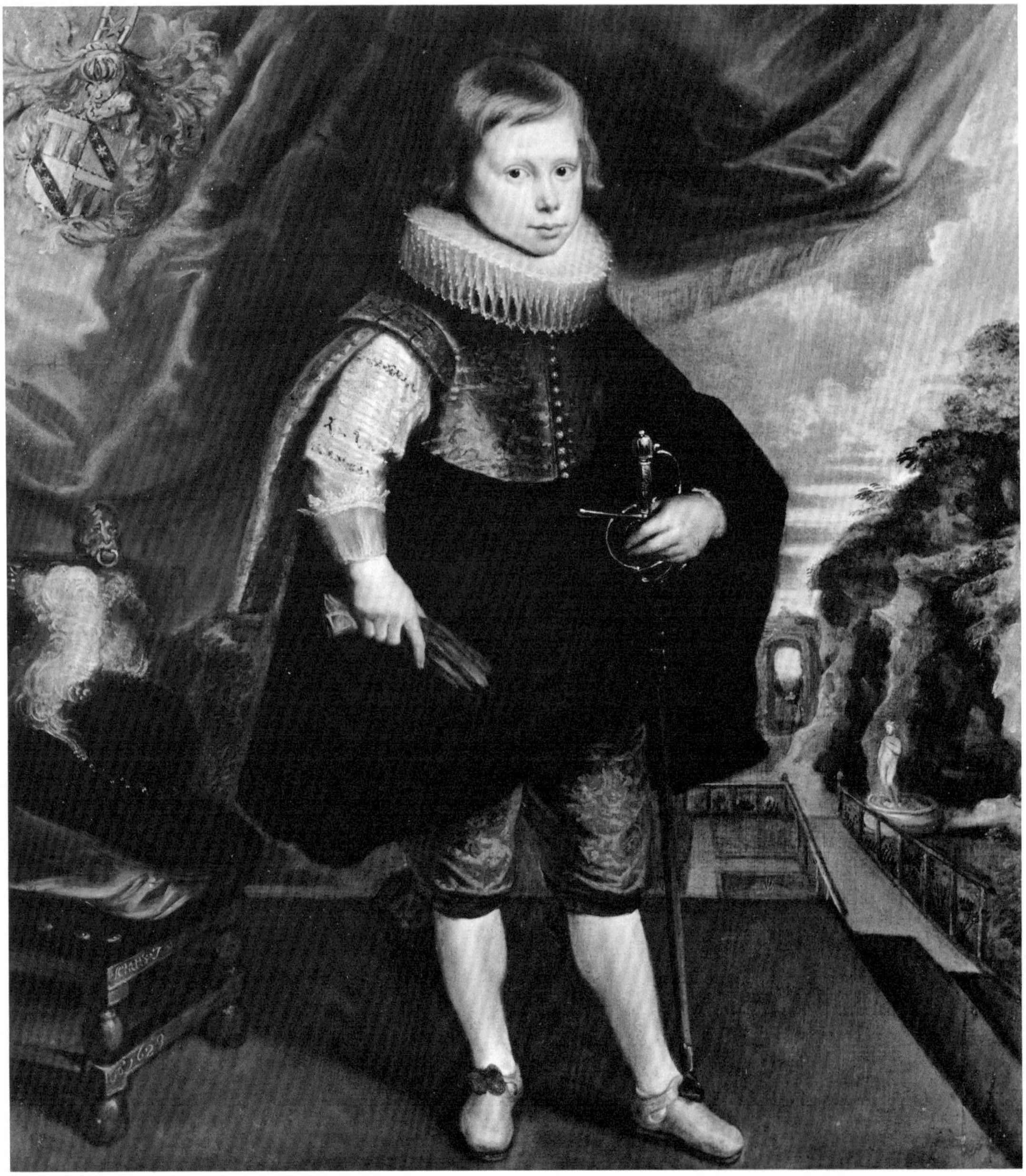

Flemish Artist, *Portrait of a Young Prince.*

Detroit 1927: 32, no. 53 (as by Van Dyck). Detroit 1929: no. 38 (as by Van Dyck). Los Angeles 1946: no. 60 (as by Van Dyck). Albion 1959 (as by Van Dyck).

References: Heil 1928: 50; fig. 1 (as by Van Dyck). W. Heil, "Catalogue of the Works of Art in the Collection of Mr. and Mrs. Edgar B. Whitcomb," unpub. manuscript (Detroit Institute of Arts Research Library), 1931: 24-26 (as by Van Dyck). Whitcomb 1954: 56-57 (as by Van Dyck).

Gift of Mr. and Mrs. Edgar B. Whitcomb (53.357)

Flemish Artist

Portrait of a Young Prince

The status of this seven-year-old boy as a member of a noble house is attested not only by the elegance of his dress, including the large hat, with its two proud ostrich feathers, placed on the chair at the left, and the sword in his hand, but also by the escutcheon superimposed on the red curtain (if it is indeed part of the original design). The background, too, with its fountain figure possibly representing Venus, and a tall archway marking the entrance to a formal garden, suggests an aristocratic milieu. Yet the quality of the picture does not correspond to the artistic expectations such a social background would suggest. An attribution to Cornelis de Vos, under whose name it has hitherto been catalogued (a certificate of January 16, 1928, from Gustav Glück attributing the work to De Vos is in the museum files), can hardly be maintained, nor is the canvas listed in Edith Greindl's standard work on that master (1944). The work is reminiscent of the manner of Pieter van Lint, but he would seem to be excluded from consideration by the date 1629. Even though, by that year, he had ten years of training behind him, Van Lint was not formally admitted to the painters' guild in Antwerp as a master until 1633, and no known work by him can be dated as early as 1629.

1629

Oil on canvas, 116.2 × 99 cm (45¾ × 39 in.)

Inscriptions: on base of chair seat at left: *Aetatis 7*; on rung of chair: *A 1629*. At the upper left is a heraldic shield, quartered per cross, surmounted by a grated helmet with wreath and mantling supporting a star or, between vertical elements. The dexter chief and sinister base are divided per fess, a fess gules in chief above, above paly of five, sanguine and argent. Sinister chief and dexter base have bend sable, three stars or, on field argent.

Conservation: The painting has been glue-lined to a loosely woven canvas. The original tacking margins remain on the top and bottom edges. On the two sides, they have been removed, and painted canvas has been folded over the stretcher, suggesting that the painting has been narrowed by at least 4 centimeters. Beneath a yellowed varnish the paint film appears to be in good condition, although somewhat abraded, particularly in the sky area and brown glazes. There is only minor inpainted loss. The painting was varnished in 1959 and 1961 by William Suhr. There are no previous conservation records.

Provenance: Mr. and Mrs. Benjamin Siegel, Detroit. Acquired in 1961.

Gift of Mr. and Mrs. Bernard F. Walker in memory of Benjamin and Sophie Siegel (61.31)

Flemish Artist(s)

Two Jesters

This curious panel, depicting two men looking straight at the viewer, appeared, without any previous record, on the Paris art market in 1935. Friedländer (1936) somewhat hesitantly attributed it to Lambert Lombard, an attribution retained in the English edition of Friedländer's work (1975). W. R. Valentiner is reported to have considered an attribution to Antonio Moro, due to a tentative identification of one of the figures (see below). Ever since Richardson (1939) published the new acquisition as "a capital work of Frans Floris," the painting has been catalogued in Detroit as a work by that master.

Unfortunately, Carl van de Velde, the author

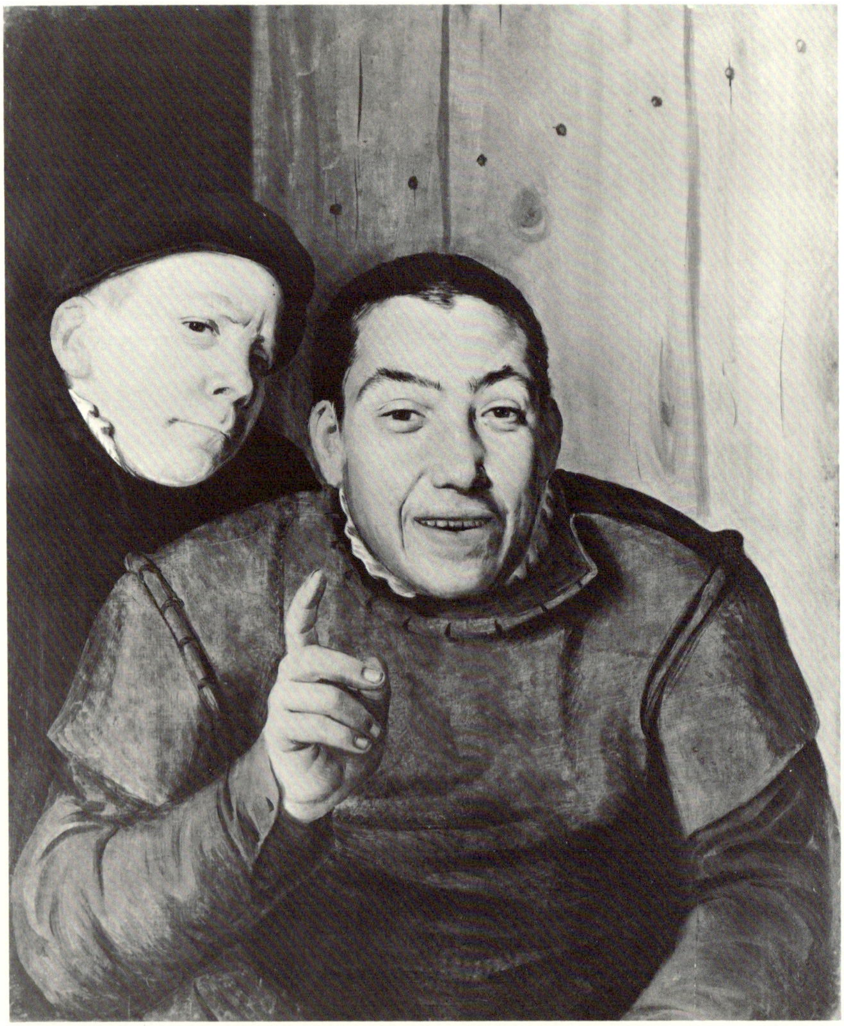

Flemish Artist(s), *Two Jesters.*

of the fundamental and probably definitive catalogue of Floris' oeuvre (1975), does not even mention the Detroit panel, apparently considering its attribution to Floris not even worthy of refutation. The attribution is clearly untenable. I see no more merit in Friedländer's notion that Lombard might be the author, nor in Valentiner's suggestion of Moro. However, it should not reflect on the quality or importance of the painting that it must be regarded, for the time being, as the work of an anonymous artist; as such, it is in good company.

In fact, there is good reason to think that the panel is not the work of one single artist. In technique and conception, the background head seems to be the work of a hand different from that responsible for the smiling figure. The latter is treated more conventionally, and its solid, traditional modeling of forms shows up clearly in the x-ray photograph. The former is painted much more thinly but at the same time more spiritedly, with a freedom of brushwork not seen in the foreground figure. In addition, the sly and suspicious expression of the frowning man, together with his highly individualized features, are likely to attract our attention and intrigue us much more than the mask-like, slightly imbecile face of the smiling one. To this must be added the strange arrangement in space: the second figure seems to have been inserted as an afterthought; it is hardly likely that the off-balance composition was planned from the outset as it appears today. This suspicion is substantiated by the x-ray photograph. The foreground figure is built up somewhat academically with a calculated use of lead white for a maximum three-dimensional effect. The second head appears only indistinctly in the x-ray, as an egg-shaped area of white with very little discernible modulation. The reason for this may well derive from a decision by the "second" painter to provide for *his* head a solid and light-colored foundation so that he would not have to contend with the paint film—a relatively dark one—that the "first" painter had applied.

It is not only the attribution of the painting that is open to question but also the title under which it has been exhibited ever since its acquisition by the Art Institute: *Two Court Jesters*. The basis for the assumption that the figures might be court jesters was the observation that the background figure looks very much like Cardinal Granvella's jester, known from a famous portrait by Antonio Moro, showing the dwarf full-length, accompanied by a huge dog (Musée du Louvre, Paris; Friedländer 1975: pl. 185). There is indeed a certain similarity of physiognomy and expression, but it is not compelling enough to warrant an identification, nor is there any indication in the Detroit panel that the frowning man is a dwarf. The height of Granvella's dwarf, calculated in comparison with the mastiff standing next to him in the Louvre portrait, probably did not exceed three feet, and his head was proportionate to his size, that is, quite small; this is not at all true of the figure in the Detroit picture. Moreover, Granvella's dwarf is dressed, as was appropriate even for such members of a princely household, in fashionable and richly embroidered garments, with a gold chain around his neck, and a sword—surely specially ordered to fit his size—at his side. The fellow in the Detroit panel, on the other hand, is dressed very plainly, like his companion, and wears only a simple black beret on his head. Whatever the meaning of this picture, it was certainly not painted as a portrait of *court* jesters. The background to the figures consists of three rough vertical panels with nails inserted in a diagonal line, giving it the appearance of a door held ajar, especially since it recedes into shadow.

Stylistically, a date in the third quarter of the 16th century appears to be indicated, at least for the work of the "first" master, and to that extent I agree with all suggested attributions, since they agree with each other in regard to the period to which the picture should be assigned. Technically, the style of the "second" master evokes Dutch rather than Flemish tradition, however, and I am inclined to think that an interval of time passed before this part of the picture was added.

c. 1550/75

Oil on oak panel, 64.8 × 53.3 cm ($25\frac{1}{2}$ × 21 in.)

Conservation: The panel has been planed on the reverse (to a thickness of about 4 millimeters) and cradled. It has an incomplete vertical crack beginning at the bottom of the panel 44 centimeters from the left edge. The paint reaches the edges of the panel with no inpainted margin and could therefore have been trimmed. The paint film is in very good condition. X-ray photographs show one notable loss above the foreground figure's right eye and a scratch in his left cheek. An indentation in the center of his chest does not represent a paint loss. The x-rays also show a change in the underpainting of the figure on the left: the right contour of his face was first painted about one-half centimeter to the left, placing the head somewhat more in profile. There are no records of previous conservation treatment, except that the painting was "surface polished" in 1947 by William Suhr.

Provenance: Paris art market, 1935. Alexander Popoff (dealer), Paris, 1938. Acquired in 1939.

Exhibitions: Pittsburgh 1954: no. 6 (as by Frans Floris).

References: Friedländer 1936: 57-58; 151, no. 109; pl. 29 (as by Lambert Lombard). Richardson 1939: cover, 2-4 (as by Floris). McVan 1942: 103, fig. 5 (as by Floris). Detroit 1944: 47, no. 531 (as by Floris). Tietze-Conrat 1957: 101 (as by Floris). Puyvelde 1962: 339 (as by Floris). Friedländer 1975: 83, no. 109; pl. 55 (as by Lombard).

Founders Society Purchase, General Membership and Donations Funds (39.1)

Flemish or German Artist

Still Life with Strawberries

The main object in this breakfast piece is a large blue and white bowl with a fluted rim, filled with strawberries. Around the bowl are plums, a hazelnut husk, several varieties of cherries, and a glass vase filled with roses. Above the bowl hover two butterflies.

This panel was acquired as a work by Osias Beert, an Antwerp still-life painter who excelled in the minute rendering of the shapes and textures of fruits and flowers, and the dishes, bowls, and glasses in which they were arranged. Beert often assembled objects in the foreground of his compositions on a plain wooden surface, occasionally, but not always, identified as a tabletop; his backgrounds are generally dark. Thus, the attribution of the Detroit still life to Beert is understandable, but it is by no means assured. It was not even mentioned by Edith Greindl in her list of that artist's work (1956: 149-150), even though she was surely acquainted with it.

The hesitation on the part of two eminent experts on the Flemish 17th-century still-life painters, Greindl and Marie-Louise Hairs (1951), to accept the attribution of the picture to Beert is also shared by this author, primarily because the picture lacks Beert's extreme subtlety of expression, a lack most evident in the primitively rendered strawberries and the lifeless butterflies, which look as if they had been mounted by a lepidopterist. The unclear spatial relationship of the roses (which, moreover, are out of proportion to the vase that contains them) to the bowl of strawberries also argues against the attribution to Beert, who always kept his forms neatly separated. In this respect, the Detroit painting comes closer to the early works of Jacob van Hulsdonck, who was most likely trained under Ambrosius Bosschaert the Elder of Middelburg. There are two paintings on copper, both signed by Van Hulsdonck, that depict a blue and white bowl of strawberries, with pinks and a butterfly also in the bowl, and cherries, white currants, and nuts arranged in the foreground (28.6 × 36.3 cm, in 1967 with Leonard Koetser, London; illustrated in *Connoisseur* 164 [Apr. 1967]: 253, fig. 3; and 29 × 38 cm, in 1969 at the H. Terry-Engell Gallery, London; illustrated in *Burlington Magazine* 111 [June 1969]: suppl., pl. 22). However, although there are undeniable similarities between the two signed works and the Detroit picture, they only prove that this type of still life, in terms of both its subject and its compositional arrangement, was very popular. Such pictures were produced by several artists, representing in a broad sense the school of Antwerp, even when the painters themselves were active elsewhere.

A good argument could be made for ascribing the picture to yet another circle of painters. It certainly is much closer to the works of Isaak Soreau, an artist active in Hanau and Frankfort whose oeuvre has been studied most thoroughly by Gerhard Bott (1961-62: 27-93). Isaak was the son of Daniel Soreau, a native of Antwerp who settled in Hanau. He often placed a bowl with fruit in the center of his compositions. These were generally grapes, but in each of two examples (Bott 1961-62, figs. 9 and 10) there is a bowl of strawberries in front of which are randomly scattered hazelnuts, cherries, and flowers; in addition, in several paintings Soreau included a glass container with cut flowers to the right of a bowl. Even the pattern on the bowl in the Detroit picture appears quite similar to those in some of Soreau's works. While it is instructive to point out these connections, it should also be stressed that, just as in the case of Osias Beert, the quality of the Detroit panel remains distinctly below that of Isaak Soreau's paintings. A classification as an anonymous work seems to me the only one that can be justified at this time.

c. 1600/25
Oil on oak panel, 27.9 × 41.6 cm (11 × 16⅜ in.)
Conservation: The vertically grained panel is slightly beveled on all four sides and uncradled. There is a hori-

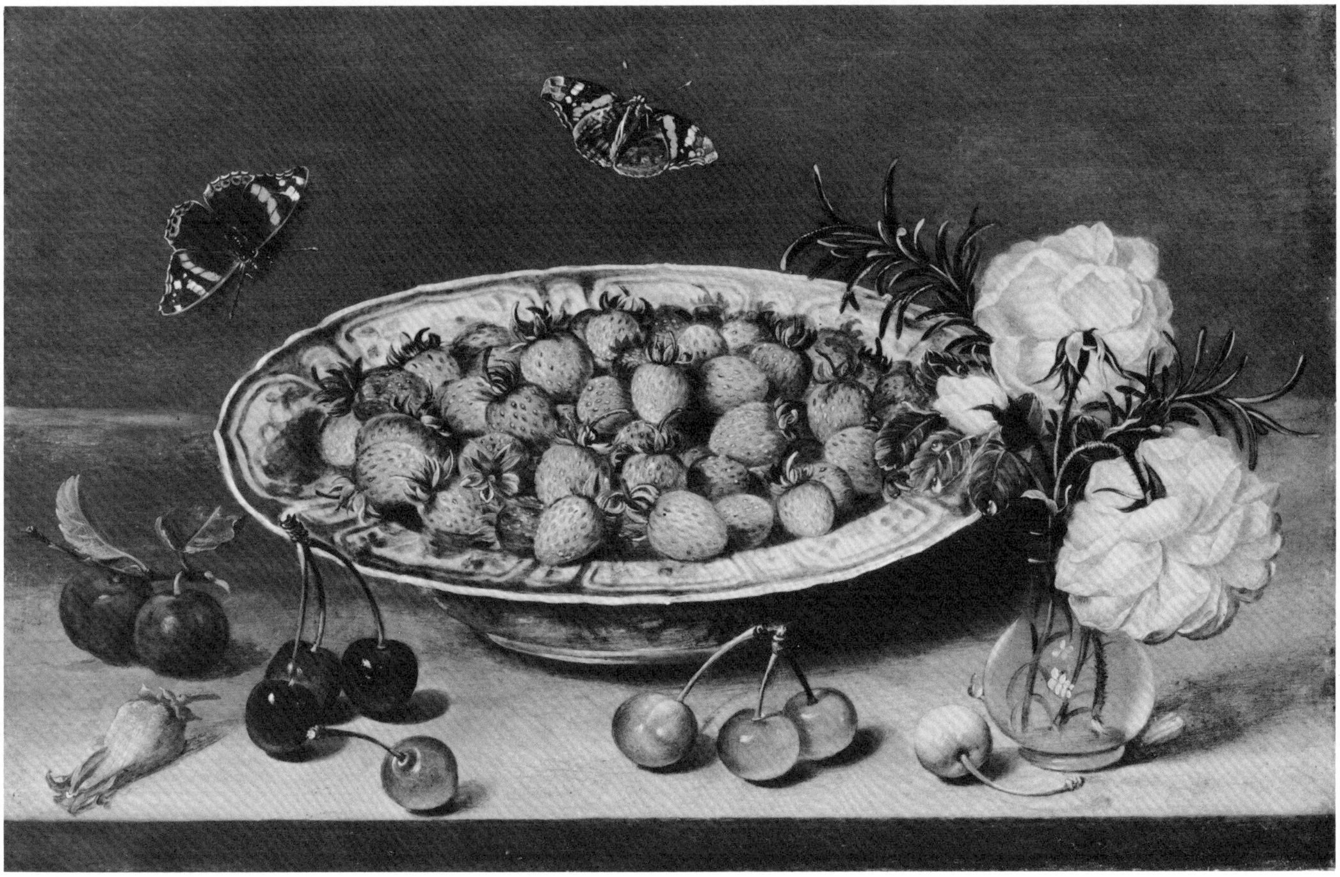

Flemish or German Artist, *Still Life with Strawberries.*

zontal convex warp. The paint film reaches the edges of the panel, which nevertheless does not appear to have been cut down. The paint film is in very good condition. X-ray photography shows only minor loss in the background. Under ultraviolet light, these losses can be seen to have been broadly retouched, especially in the upper right corner and to the upper right and left of the central butterfly. There is a pentimento of a pod-like fruit (or flower) beneath the two plums and hazelnut husk on the left side. This can be seen most clearly with infrared illumination or in the x-ray. There are no records of previous conservation treatment.

Provenance: Sale, "Baumann et autres amateurs," The Hague, April 28, 1930 (attributed to Ambrosius Bosschaert). Kunsthandel P. de Boer (dealer), Amsterdam, 1935. Acquired in 1935.

Exhibitions: Amsterdam 1935: no. 14. Santa Barbara 1958: 15, no. 7. New York 1961. Windsor/London (Ontario) 1969-70: no. 3.

References: Valentiner 1936: 49 (as by Beert). Scheyer 1937: 58, fig. 29; 60 (as by Beert). Detroit 1944: 10-11, no. 426 (as by Beert). Hairs 1951: 251 ("oeuvre douteaux"). Whitcomb 1954: 50-51 (as by Beert).

Gift of Mrs. Anna Scripps Whitcomb (35.106)

Lucas Franchoys the Younger

1616 MECHLIN 1681

LUCAS FRANCHOYS was a member of a family of painters. His brother Peter was primarily active as a portraitist. Both had been trained by their father, Lucas the Elder, but Lucas the Younger appears to have been decisively influenced during the years he spent in Rubens' studio until the master's death in 1640. Before he settled again in his home town in 1654, Franchoys appears to have been active in Tournai (1649-50) as well as in France, although little is known about his actual movements during this period. In his later years he was a successful and esteemed artist, and in 1663 he served as dean of the artists' guild. He was appointed court painter to Archbishop Alphonsius de Berghes, a post that resulted in many commissions for churches and monasteries. He married at an advanced age (1668) and had eight children with his much younger wife, Anna Theresa van Wolschaeten; according to J. F. van den Branden (1883: 810), she was a peasant woman who had served as his model.

Except in lexica and general surveys of Flemish art, little notice has been taken by modern scholars of the work of this master, who enjoyed a considerable reputation in his own time. None of his sketches had been identified before the attribution of the Detroit panel to him in 1951. It is characteristic of the neglect of minor masters that their best works are fated to be absorbed into the oeuvre of their greater contemporaries—in this case, no less a one than Rubens. Even the fact that Franchoys belonged to the school of Mechlin may have contributed to his neglect: the historiography of Flemish art of the 17th century is primarily concentrated on the school of Antwerp, followed—distantly—by those of Brussels and Ghent. Mechlin still remains a terra incognita.

Saint Michael in Combat with the Rebel Angels

This spirited little sketch, also known as *Saint Michael Overcoming Lucifer*, was apparently connected with Rubens only after the Budapest sale of 1917. It is actually the bozzetto for the left wing of a triptych (the central panel is lost) in one of the shallow chapels off the ambulatory of the Cathedral of Tournai. The right wing depicts the *Conversion of William of Aquitaine*, and the sketch for this subject has also been preserved; formerly in the Gustav Neuerburg Collection in Hamburg, it is now presumably in the possession of another member of the family. On the reverse of the Tournai wings is the *Annunciation to the Virgin*, carrying the artist's signature and date: *L. Franchoys Pinxit 1649.*

The two scenes on the inside of the wings correspond iconographically: Saint Bernard of Clairvaux humbling the rebellious William of Aquitaine, who supported the antipope Anacletus II against Pope Innocent X, is the terrestrial equivalent of the archangel's victory over the mutinous angels. Both scenes express vividly the aims and methods of the Counter Reformation: the legend of Saint Bernard's chastisement of William is an example of the supremacy of the Church over secular authority; the martial figure of Saint Michael is a symbol of the Church's new militancy in fighting heresy.

Franchoys did not follow the Detroit sketch literally when painting the larger version. Some changes were made necessary by the difference in format, the Tournai wing being both higher and narrower than the sketch. He also replaced Michael's straight sword with a "flaming" one, and

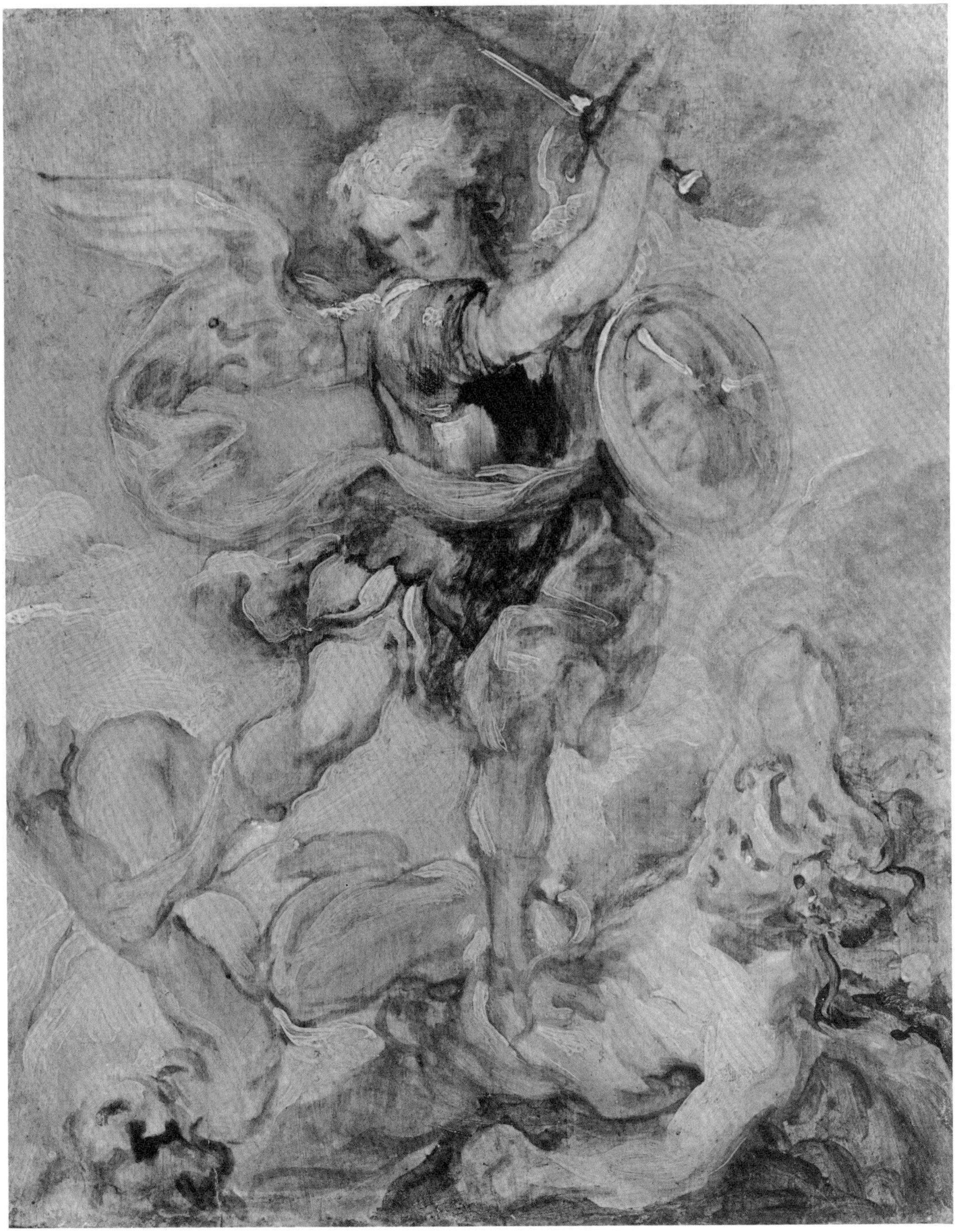

Franchoys, *Saint Michael in Combat with the Rebel Angels.*

he turned around the fallen figure at the left so that it would be seen from the back, thus emphasizing the impression of a headlong fall. In general, however, Franchoys' style as seen in the finished panels is surprisingly smooth and idealizing, and thus contrasts considerably with the free and spontaneous brushwork of the sketch, which had reminded some competent observers of Rubens' own manner. Yet, even in the sketch, the underlying classicism of Franchoys' art can be noted in the slightly theatrical elegance of Saint Michael's pose—a pose ultimately derived from Guido Reni's *Saint Michael* (1630s) in Santa Maria della Concezione, Rome.

c. 1648/49
Oil on oak panel, 25.2 × 19.2 cm (9 15/16 × 7 9/16 in.)
Conservation: The panel is uncradled and beveled on all four sides. It has a convex warp. The paint film reaches the edges of the panel but does not appear to have been trimmed. It is in excellent condition despite the very thin and sketchy application. There is only minor paint loss near the margins of the painting. Blisters were laid down by William Suhr in 1955. The painting was last cleaned and retouched in 1966 by Edward O. Korany.

Provenance: K. von Kilonyi sale, Budapest, September 26, 1917, lot 13 (as by Jan Boeckhorst). Galerie Haberstock (dealer), Berlin. J. Böhler (dealer), Munich, 1930. Acquired in 1930.

Exhibitions: Detroit 1936: no. 43 (as by Rubens). Brussels 1937: no. 26 (as by Rubens). Los Angeles 1946: no. 25 (as by Rubens). Detroit 1978: no. 12.

References: Heil 1930: cover, 80 (as by Rubens). Scheyer 1937: cover, 45, 47 (as by Rubens). Valentiner 1946: 160, no. 73 (as by Rubens). Goris and Held 1947: 52, no. A. 70 (as by a "classicizing follower of Rubens"). Held 1951: 46-49, 53-55. Saligny 1967: 224, no. 34.

Founders Society Purchase, Membership Fund (30.90)

Jan Fyt

1611 ANTWERP 1661

RENOWNED above all for his paintings of small game and birds bagged by hunters and displayed with seeming artlessness, Fyt also painted some of the finest flower-pieces produced in Flanders during the 17th century. He was trained by Frans Snyders, but his paintings are easily distinguished from those of his master by a darker tonality and a subtler concern for variations in texture and coloristic patterns. The difference between these two artists was perfectly summarized by Charles Sterling (Paris 1936: 63) when he said that their relationship was comparable to that of Rubens and Van Dyck: "La vie robuste et sensuelle d'un côté, la poésie de l'élégance et de la rareté de l'autre" (in Rubens and Snyders "a robust and sensual life," in Van Dyck and Fyt, "the poetry of elegance and singularity").

Fyt entered the painters' guild in Antwerp as a master in 1630 and traveled considerably in the 15 years that followed, going to Paris (1633-34), Italy (1641), and the northern Netherlands (1642 and 1645). He had several pupils, among them Pieter Boel (who imitated his style closely); various authors have pointed out that his influence extended to some of the major French masters of the 18th century (for example, François Desportes and even Chardin). The figures in his paintings were often contributed by other artists, but he alone was responsible for the delicate landscape backgrounds found in a number of his works.

Dead Game with Weasels

In contrast to the large still lifes by his teacher Frans Snyders, Fyt's own compositions tended to

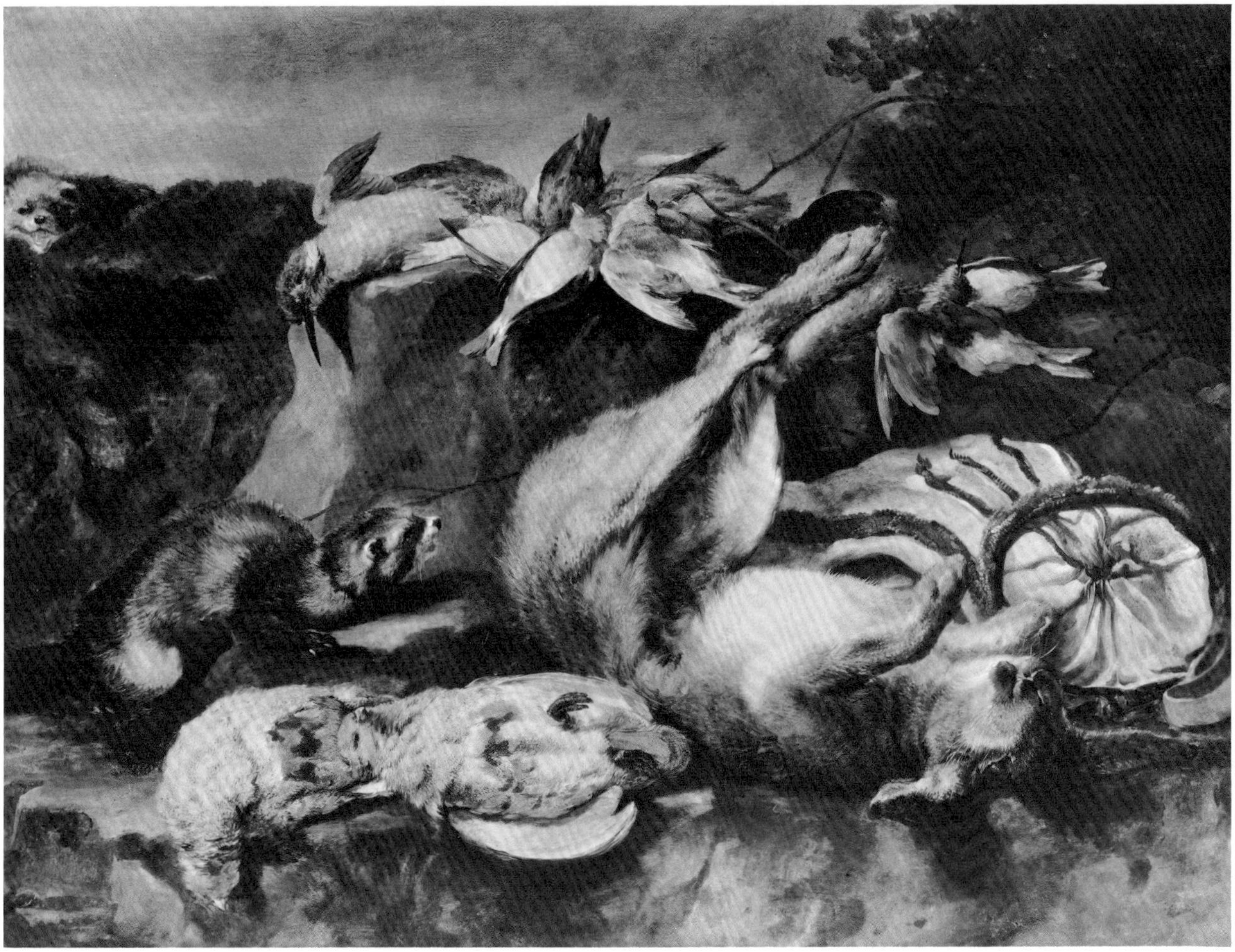

Fyt, *Dead Game with Weasels.*

focus on fewer objects, observed more closely and rendered with great attention to minute differences in surface and tone. This painting, although not signed, is a good example of his work, demonstrating especially well his skill at imparting a tactile quality to the plumage of birds and the fur of various small animals. It was also characteristic of Fyt to combine dead birds and game with live animals, attracted to the spoils left unattended by the hunter (who is referred to by the game bag at right). Scott Sullivan (1981) has pointed out that weasels, the natural enemies of rabbits and hares, were often used by hunters to flush these animals out of their holes and into the hunters' nets.

A variation on this theme, *Dead Game with a Cat* (oil on panel, 68 × 93 cm), dated 1642, has been identified by Sullivan in a Belgian private collection.

c. 1642

Oil on oak-veneered masonite panel, 73.7 × 93.5 cm (29 × 36$\frac{13}{16}$ in.)

Conservation: The painting has been transferred to oak-veneered masonite and given an oak cradle. The original white-chalk ground and warm brownish imprimatura remain; the original oak panel was removed. A strip approximately 10 centimeters in height across the top of the composition appears to be an old addition, which was transferred along with the rest. There are two major horizontal cracks from the original oak panel (at 13 and 23 centimeters from the top edge). The paint film is in fair condition. There are inpainted losses along the cracks, in the lower right and left corners, and along the four sides and bottom. The entire top 10-centimeter addition is repainted. The painting was first treated for blisters by William Suhr in 1936 and again in 1955. In 1965 further blistering, cleavages, and cracking prompted removal of the previous pine cradle and transfer of the painting to a 5/16-inch, tempered masonite presswood panel. It was also cradled, cleaned, and inpainted at that time by Suhr.

Provenance: Arthur Sambon (dealer), Paris. Acquired in 1928.

References: Detroit 1930: no. 81. Valentiner 1936: 49-50. Detroit 1944: 49, no. 81. Sullivan 1981: 35-36.

City of Detroit Purchase (28.94)

Jan Joseph Horemans the Elder

1682 ANTWERP 1759

THE SON of a notary, Jan Joseph Horemans was first apprenticed to a sculptor, Michiel van der Voort, whose daughter he later married; he received his instruction as a painter from Jan van Pee, a specialist in genre painting. In 1706 he was received as a master into the guild of Saint Luke. Horemans specialized in genre scenes of peasants and tradespeople, and was known for the somber scale of his colors. His son and pupil, Jan Joseph the Younger, continued the tradition of genre scenes, but in a lighter coloristic vein. The most successful member of the Horemans family was a younger brother of Jan Joseph the Elder, Peter Jacob, who moved to Munich and became court painter to the Elector of Bavaria.

The Sculptor's Studio

While the locale of this modest genre scene is clearly—as the title proclaims—a sculptor's studio, the action is only marginally connected with the artist's craft. A workman is shown putting some last touches on an outsized decorative urn of marble dominating the center of the composition; it is probably intended for the adornment of a formal garden. Smaller pieces of sculpture (relief panels?) can be made out dimly on a shelf in the upper right background. In a second room at the left, another assistant, wearing a three-cornered hat, wields a wooden mallet as he works on a figure placed prone on a workbench. In front of him sits a student engaged in drawing on a sheet of paper.

The master of the studio, standing at the left, turns to listen to a visitor leaning on the back of a chair in which sits a woman, presumably the sculptor's wife. Wearing a wig of long curls, wrapped in a flowing cloak, and holding his hat in his hand, the visitor may well be a customer, if not actually the patron who ordered the urn. The woman turns to him—in a pose paralleling that of her husband—while holding a pitcher of pewter and a filled glass (perhaps of beer). It is not clear if she has been interrupted while taking refreshment herself, or has poured the drink to offer it to the guest. Her action is watched intently by a dog sitting at her feet.

Too little is known about the organization of Horemans' studio to be sure that the Detroit canvas is indeed a work of the master's own hand; it lacks both signature and date. The quality of

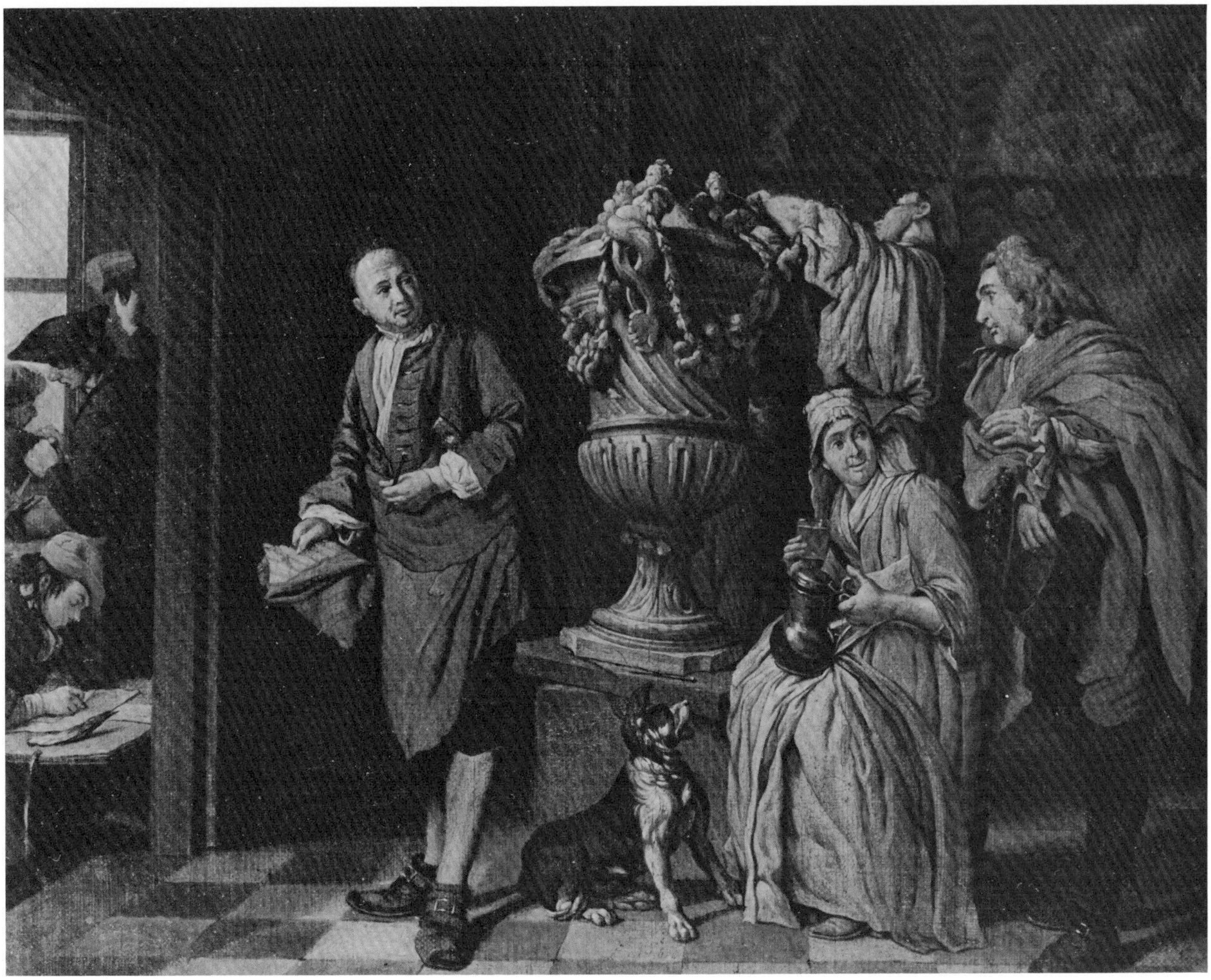

Horemans, *The Sculptor's Studio.*

Horemans' oeuvre, unless we have been mislead by false attributions, is rather uneven, bearing witness to the general decline of Flemish genre painting in the 18th century. While the artistic level of the Detroit canvas is not particularly high, there is no sufficient reason, given the present state of our knowledge, to question the attribution.

Oil on canvas, 34 × 41.5 cm (13⅜ × 16⅜ in.)

Conservation: The original canvas, with its tacking margins removed, has been glue-lined. There is a canvas patch in the upper center reinforcing a hole, and another hole exists beneath the right hand of the figure at left. A light reddish brown ground color shows through in most of the abraded areas. The paint layer has overall abrasion but few losses. These include the above-mentioned holes and an area in the lower left corner. Many highlights, particularly in the faces of the four main figures, have been reinforced during restorations. There are no records of previous treatment.

Provenance: Acquired in 1966.

Gift of Mrs. Henry Patten and Marc T. Patten (F66.3)

Jacob Jordaens

1593 ANTWERP 1678

JORDAENS, the son of a prosperous Antwerp linen-draper, received his artistic training in the studio of Adam van Noort, who had also been one of Rubens' teachers. At the age of 22, he was inscribed in the Antwerp painters' guild as a master, with an emphasis on his work as *waterschilder* (painter in tempera and watercolor). One year later, he married Catherine, the eldest daughter of Van Noort; she died in 1659. Although both were raised in the Catholic faith, they had apparently embraced Calvinism, which forced the artist, after his wife's death, to have her interred in a cemetery in Putte, a small town just over the Dutch border. Jordaens and his eldest daughter, Elisabeth, who died the same night as he, were also buried there.

A painter of large-scale religious canvases, Jordaens continued to supply works for Catholic churches even after his own conversion. He also painted mythological subjects and designed cartoons for tapestries, among them scenes from rural life and illustrations of Flemish proverbs. After Rubens' death (1640), Jordaens was considered the foremost painter in Antwerp (Van Dyck, who was still living, resided in England). He received the lion's share of the commissions for the monumental decoration planned for Huis ten Bosch (1651-52) outside The Hague, the private residence of Amalia van Solms, the widow of Frederick Henry, Prince of Orange; ten years later, he furnished three paintings for the new Amsterdam town hall as part of the same project to which Rembrandt contributed the ill-fated canvas of Claudius Civilis.

In Jordaens' early years he combined influences from Caravaggio and Rubens with his own robust talent into works of great vigor and originality. The plain, occasionally even coarse, characters in his narratives are kept close to the foreground and each other. During the 1630s and 1640s, he avoided the harsh contrasts of his earlier works, and his palette became subtler and more mellow; his famous family feasts (often depicting the celebration of Twelfth-night) belong to this period. He never developed a distinct "late" style, being content to exploit his own earlier inventions and end his career as his own plagiarist.

The Holy Family with Saint Anne

¶ *The Holy Family with Saint Anne* was first introduced into the literature by Ludwig Burchard; in his effort to support the attribution of the painting to the young Jordaens, Burchard relied chiefly on an exceedingly detailed description of the colors of the picture. His conclusion regarding its date remained somewhat tentative; he felt it was certainly an early work of the master, but that it might "be closer to 1615 than to 1618."

Burchard's commentary stressed what he took to be signs of the artist's immaturity, most noticeable in the head of the child, modeled, as he said, "with a mixture of cold and warm colors, with the result that a dull (*trüb*) reddish gray stands alongside a dirty gray-green." This head indeed differs from the others; Burchard accounted for this difference by assuming that Jordaens lacked a live model and had to fall back on his imagination—alas, without success ("es ist ihm nicht recht geglückt"). A more adequate explanation might be the persistence in Jordaens' early style of a mannerist tradition, both in its smooth modeling and its artificial illumination from below.

Following another line of reasoning, the present author gave the picture a date of 1617, pointing out that the model for the Virgin was obviously Catherine van Noort, the artist's wife, whom he had married in 1616. Their first child, Elisabeth, was born on June 26, 1617, and it is tempting to think that the painting reflects to some extent this new domestic situation—all the more so, since the model for the elderly Saint Joseph was, with great likelihood, Catherine's father, Adam van Noort, Jordaens' former teacher. The features of Catherine van Noort are known with certainty from Jordaens' *Self-portrait with Catherine van Noort* in the Prado, Madrid (Held 1940: fig. 8), and those of Adam van Noort from an engraving by Hendrik Snyers (ibid.: fig. 2). Although accepting the identification of the Virgin and Saint Joseph as Catherine and Adam van Noort, respectively, Jaffé (in the Ottawa exhibition catalogue) reverted to Burchard's dating in the text of his entry by placing the picture around 1615/16 (although in the caption for the illustration on page 255, he did date it 1617).

The setting, with its suggestion of stately columnar architecture, may indicate Jordaens' familiarity with similar subjects treated by Rubens around 1615, such as the *Virgin and Child with Saints Elizabeth and John the Baptist* in the Palazzo Pitti, Florence (Oldenbourg 1921: 65). While the actions of the three foreground figures are clear—the infant Jesus holds a roll or piece of bread, presumably given to him by Saint Anne—the function of Joseph within the context of the picture would seem to be in need of explanation. Wearing a broadbrimmed hat, and leaning forward under an open arch, he has evidently just arrived from the open spaces beyond. With a gesture of presentation, he holds in both hands a rustic wicker birdcage containing a white bird sitting on a perch. The same type of cage with a bird either inside or escaping from it appears in several of Jordaens' paintings, including one of the earliest works by the master, *The Holy Family with Saints Elizabeth and John the Baptist* (Musées Royaux des Beaux-Arts de Belgique, Brussels; Puyvelde 1953: fig. 64), in which a cat, eager to get at the bird, has overturned the cage so that it is about to tumble from the socle on which Joseph had placed it. The motif is found again a few years later (but not before 1620) in a signed painting, *The Virgin and Child Visited by Joachim, Elizabeth, and the Young Saint John*, in the North Carolina Museum of Art (Raleigh 1956: 63, no. 117; a slightly inferior version is in the National Gallery, London [no. 3215], and a larger and much later variant, in which Saint Joseph was added at the right, was sold in Brussels on December 10, 1928 [lot 32], and was later in the Ehrich Galleries, New York). In this composition, the bird has been allowed to fly from the cage and approach the infant Christ. The same type of cage, also with a white bird in it, is carried by a child who accompanies his mother in the *Adoration of the Shepherds* in the Koninklijk Museum voor Schone Kunsten, Antwerp (no. 221).

Before speculating on the possible symbolic associations of the birdcage, one should realize that in all these paintings it is offered as a gift. Bringing a bird in a cage to a small child appears to have been a practice not uncommon at Jordaens' time. Attached to strings, such birds became playthings, as we can tell, for instance, from Rubens' painting of a small child, probably his nephew Philip, in the Gemäldegalerie in Berlin-Dahlem (Berlin-Dahlem 1978: 20-29). In fact, whatever symbolic meaning may have been associated with the motif of a caged bird offered to the infant Jesus, it should be remembered that it was recognized as a common practice to occupy and amuse infants (Jongh 1967: 42-49).

The Detroit painting has so far escaped the danger of being the victim of arbitrary speculations as to its symbolism. This is not the case with similar works by Jordaens or by Rubens. The bird in the Raleigh and London paintings mentioned before, identified by Jaffé as a goldfinch, is said by him (Ottawa 1968-69: 74, no. 9) to be symbolic "both of the Passion and of the longing of the soul for God." It is not clear whether he thinks that the bird in those paintings has only one of these meanings or both simultaneously. Gregory Martin (London 1970: 89-90) quotes George W. Ferguson (1954: 17) as the source for the first of these interpretations, and H. W. Janson (1952: 181) for the second. Martin also relies on Herbert Friedmann (1946: 55-56), quoting from his study that "a bird in a cage was an old symbol of the soul imprisoned in the body" and that the bird, "homing," as it were, to the Christ Child, "presaged the salvation of souls from their physically mortal habiliments." There are other possible interpretations, as was pointed out by Kelch (Berlin-Dahlem 1978) when he—again with reference to Janson (1948: 137-138)—cited the *Reductorium morale* of Petrus Berchorius, who interprets the image of a captive songbird as the symbol of man "captive" to a system of Christian education who thus learns to "sing" the praise of God (VII, chap. 26). The image was later used to depict emblematically the benefits of poverty for members of the Jesuit order (*Imago primi saeculi Societatis Iesu*, Antwerp, 1640: 179). Birds in cages can have still more very different and completely secular meanings, as has been demonstrated by E. de Jongh (1967: 42-49).

Nor should it finally be forgotten that for a valid symbolical explanation, one should be certain about the ornithological identity of the caged birds. The bird in the Detroit Jordaens may be a dove, although I am not certain; it certainly is not a goldfinch. For the time being, it would seem to be advisable not to press the symbolical interpretation too far, particularly in the work of a master who was hardly given to sophisticated intellectual constructs.

A small version of this composition (oil on panel, 45 × 41 cm) was in the collection of Chanoine H. Misonne (Turnhout) in 1968. It may be either a study for the Detroit panel or a reduced copy.

Color plate IV, page 36.

c. 1617

Oil on oak panel, 111.5 × 95.2 cm (43⅞ × 37½ in.)

Conservation: The four-membered oak panel is joined at 24, 50, and 75 centimeters from the left edge. It has been planed (to a 6-millimeter thickness) and cradled. The top and bottom edges are beveled but were reinforced with wedges to support the cradle (the two sides are hidden by cradle members). The paint layer, a gray striated imprimatura, and light-colored ground reach the edges of the panel. The paint layer is in good condition. Scattered inpainted losses occur along the joins and in the Madonna's red robe (especially in the darkest glazes). There are relatively large inpaints above the Virgin's ear, in the sky behind Saint Anne's head, along the top edge, and in the lower left corner. The painting was treated for blisters by William Suhr in 1953 and for scratches by Edward O. Korany in 1966. No prior treatment is recorded.

Provenance: Paul Bottenwieser (dealer), Berlin. Ralph Harman Booth, Detroit. Acquired in 1946.

Exhibitions: Ottawa 1968-69: 74, no. 8. Detroit 1978: no. 11.

References: Burchard 1928: 214-216. Held 1940: 78-79; fig. 9. Richardson 1947: 56-58. *Art News* 1947: 38-39. *Art News Annual* 1947: 140. Puyvelde 1953: 92, 188; fig. 65. D'Hulst 1953: 89-138; fig. 12. D'Hulst 1953a: 211. D'Hulst 1956: 51; fig. 18.

Gift of Mrs. Ralph Harman Booth (46.300)

Job

With its bold brushwork and almost crude realism in the rendering of the old man's haggard, grizzled head and scrawny neck, this study is a characteristic product of Jordaens' early period. One of his most original stylistic ideas is particularly well represented in the panel: the expression of powerful contrasts of light and shade resulting from bright sunlight on the human form. Other Northern painters who emulated Caravaggio's emphasis on such contrasts either failed, like the Italian, to account for the light source or depicted the highlights and shadows as the result of artificial illumination. No one before Jordaens—not even Rubens—achieved as convincing an "outdoors" effect in his work. In paintings done precisely in the years to which the Detroit panel belongs (that is, shortly before and after 1620), we recognize the light of a hot summer day when the skin glistens with sweat, and even shadows are bright with reflected light.

The model that posed for Jordaens here was Abraham Grapheus (De Graef), often referred to as a "servant" or "messenger" of the guild of Saint Luke, the artists' professional organization in Antwerp. In 1620, just about the time that Grapheus posed for Jordaens, Cornelis de Vos painted a formal portrait of him surrounded by silver and gold vessels and decorated with the guild's medals and badges.

Grapheus had been trained as a painter and accepted as a member of the guild in 1572; 20 years later, however, he gave up the profession to devote himself to the many organizational tasks of the guild, including the planning and supervision of auctions for the benefit of the families of deceased guild members. He also kept the books and seems to have been in demand as a calligrapher, a skill he also taught. He was a favorite model of Antwerp's painters, his first recognizable appearance being in Marten de Vos' *Madonna with Saint Luke* of 1602 (Koninklijk Museum voor Schone Kunsten, Antwerp), where he is seen grinding pigments for the Evangelist. He later appears in paintings by Van Dyck and, particularly frequently, by Jordaens. In a pose rather like the one in the Detroit panel, he can be seen in the so-called *Ferryboat of Antwerp* (actually depicting Saint Peter finding the tribute money in the mouth of a fish) in the Statens Museums for Kunst, Copenhagen (no. 350; oil canvas, 281 × 468 cm), dated around 1620/25. Grapheus died in 1624, but Cornelis de Vos' portrayal, exhibited in the main chamber of the painters' guild, reminded generations of artists of

Jordaens, *Job*.

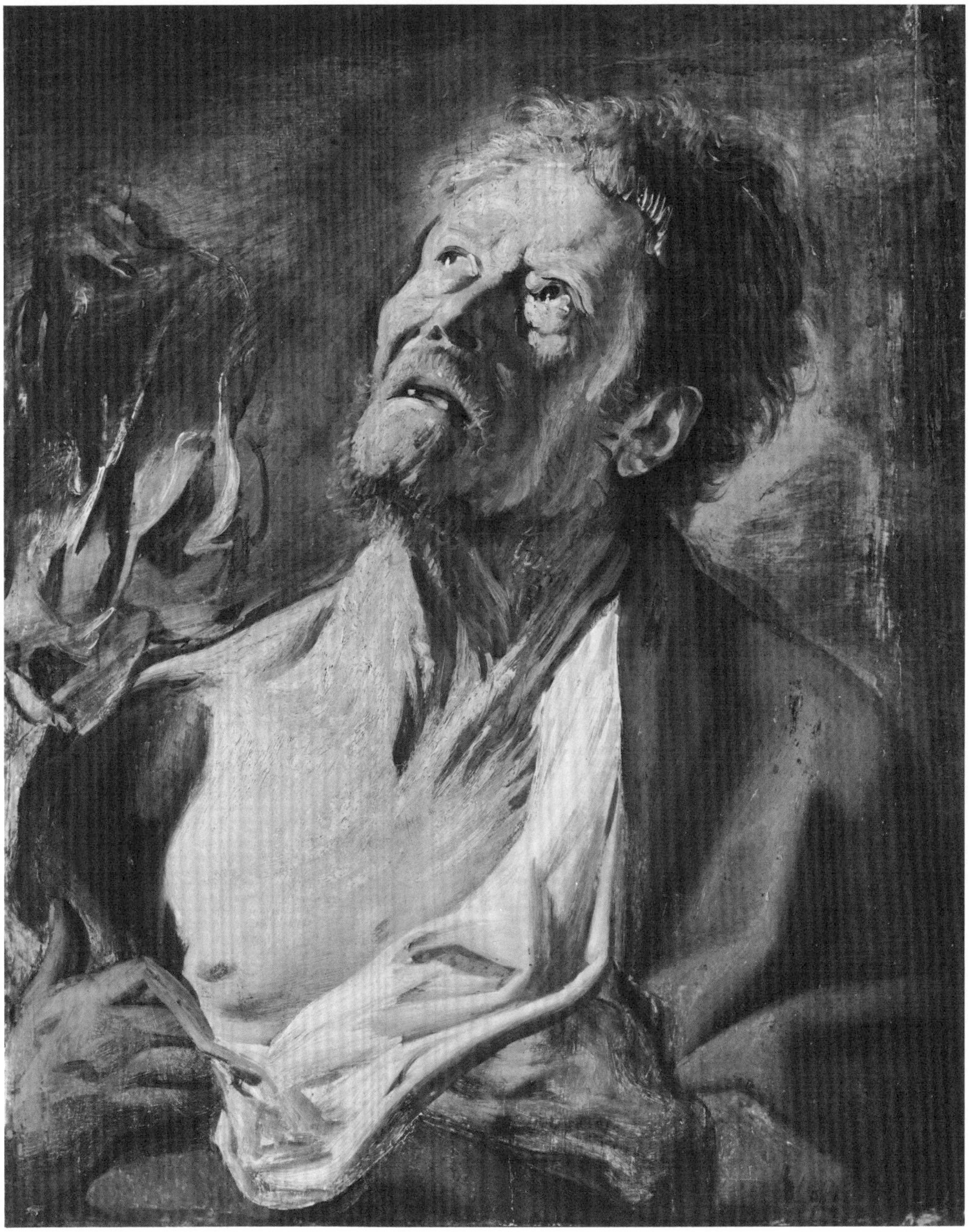

the modest *knap* who had faithfully served some of their greatest masters.

The original purpose of the Detroit study is not known. Although Valentiner (1944) suggested that it might depict the penitent Saint Peter, more recently the panel has been listed simply as *An Apostle*. Yet the pose of the old man, with his chest bared and an expression of anguish as well as piety visible on his face, makes it likely that Jordaens was thinking of a particular subject. The penitent Saint Peter is indeed a subject frequently depicted in Flemish art, but as a rule the apostle is shown folding his hands in prayer, and his gown is not disheveled as it is here. Before it came to Detroit, the panel was known under the title *Job*, and the entry in the catalogue of the Haro sale of 1892 in fact states: "On lit en haut, à droite: *Job*." That inscription is no longer visible, which means that it was probably of recent date and was removed when the picture was cleaned. Yet Job in his misery would seem to be a perfectly appropriate identification for the painting and is surely preferable to the rather colorless one of *An Apostle*.

An unresolved mystery is presented by the shape at the upper left, above the figure's right shoulder. Since in the x-ray photograph this form appears much less forcefully modeled than those of the old man, it may be no more than part of a preliminary sketch done in single, long lines painted with lead white. Parts of the form are painted over to make them less conspicuous, but whether this was done by the artist himself or by a later painter, we cannot say; there is also the possibility that Jordaens intended to cover it up entirely, and that what he had covered was later laid bare, possibly out of respect for the artist's work.

c. 1620

Oil on oak panel, 67 × 52 cm (26⅜ × 20½ in.)

Conservation: The panel originally consisted of two members joined at 25.5 centimeters from the left edge. Additions, 3 centimeters in width, were glued to the top and right sides during a later restoration. The panel was subsequently thinned (to a 3-millimeter width), adhered to an oak backing, and cradled. X-rays show that the core panel has several vertical cracks as well as insect damage. The chalk ground and paint layer reach the edges of the original panel. The condition of the paint layer, considering that the work is a study and therefore sketchily painted, appears fairly good. The x-rays show scattered paint losses, particularly where the original panel meets the additions on the right, on the top, and along the bottom edge. Other losses exist along the cracks and at the back of the head. Many areas in the painting have been reworked, but whether these are pentimenti or roughly contemporary changes by another hand is uncertain. A layer of red lies beneath the figure's orange-brown cloak; the white garment has been roughly painted over most of the left and part of the right hand; and the blue background color roughly covers the form to the left of the head. Blisters were treated and the painting was surface cleaned and inpainted by Edward O. Korany in 1966. There are no records of earlier conservation treatment.

Provenance: Haro père et fils sale, Galerie Sedelmeyer, Paris, May 30-31, 1892, lot 26. Paul Mersch, Paris. Marcel Nemes, Budapest. Warneck Collection. Baron Leon Pitteurs Hugaerts d'Orange, 1927. Alberto J. Pani, Mexico City. Pani sale, Kende Galleries, New York, December 17, 1942, lot 33 (with certificates from C. Hofstede de Groot, 1929, no. 5973, and W. R. Valentiner). Acquired in 1943.

Exhibitions: Antwerp 1905: no. 2. Brussels 1910: no. 229. Brussels 1927: no. 69. New York 1967: no. 51.

References: Album 1905: pl. 1 (2). Rooses 1906: 38, 265. Held 1939: 11. Pani 1940: 63-64, no. 21. Detroit 1944: 71, no. 594. Valentiner 1944: 16-19. Puyvelde 1953: 84, 232. D'Hulst 1956: 86, n. 1. Leningrad 1963: 94, 151. Held 1969: 272.

Gift of Frederic A. Gimbel and Dr. Armand Hammer (43.418)

Jan van Kessel the Elder

1626 ANTWERP 1679

THE SON of a portrait painter, Hieronymus van Kessel, and the grandson of Jan Brueghel the Elder, Jan van Kessel was clearly destined to be a painter; at the tender age of nine, he was apprenticed to Simon de Vos, a painter of genre and historical subjects. It can also be assumed that he received instruction from his uncle, Jan Brueghel the Younger. In 16/45 he was recognized as a master by the Antwerp artists' guild. In 1647 he married Maria van Apshoven with whom he had two sons, Ferdinand and Jan, both of whom also became painters. He collaborated with other painters, such as Erasmus Quellinus (or Quellin), who painted the human figures in some of his paintings, and David Teniers the Younger—another uncle—each of whom cosigned a painting with Van Kessel in 1664. Although a skillful technician in the tradition of Flemish still-life painting, Van Kessel relied to a great extent on the invention of other artists, frequently combining in his compositions elements lifted from several different sources. He also repeated his own compositions in response to a demand for painstakingly executed, "scientific" pictures of animals in outdoor settings, often enclosed in frames composed of allegorical scenes.

Water

℃ The title of this painting is based on the assumption (for which no evidence has been adduced) that it is one of four related paintings, each depicting one of the four elements, the others being Earth, Fire, and Air. Except for the background, the composition is closely related to two other paintings on copper that form part of the large series of the *Four Continents* painted by Van Kessel around 1660. A version of the complete series is in the Alte Pinakothek, Munich, where each continent is emblematically depicted in a central field, surrounded by 16 small landscapes replete with a melange of domestic, wild, and occasionally even fantastic creatures. The composition related to the Detroit copper is number eight of the group representing the *Allegory of Europe* (Munich 1973: 9 ff.). Another series, without the central emblematic composition, is in the Prado (Madrid 1975: 169-170, no. 1554); one of the paintings in this series is dated 1660. The size of each individual panel in Munich is approximately 14.5 by 21 centimeters; those in the Prado measure 17 by 23 centimeters. Both Ulla Krempel (Munich 1973) and Matías Díaz Padrón (Madrid 1975) mention that various other European museums possess individual examples of these compositions, which may indicate that Van Kessel executed still other sets of the entire series. Van Kessel's son Ferdinand also painted a set of the *Four Continents* and replaced it when it was destroyed by fire (Munich 1973: 9). Only a thorough examination of all the existing examples can tell us whether the Detroit copper was part of a larger allegorical set—be it the *Four Continents* or the *Four Elements*—or was painted as an individual work. The difference in the setting, which in the series of the *Continents* is normally a city view (in one case, the city of Copenhagen), gives weight to the latter possibility, as does the fact that the Detroit picture is signed; of the 40 pictures in the Prado, only two are signed, while of the 64 pieces in Munich, none carries a signature (the name of the artist is inscribed on the frames instead).

The "action" depicted in the Detroit picture involves two otters at the left, one of which emerges from a cave, while the other, standing over a dead fish, snarls at a seal approaching from the right. There are various dead fish, two eels, and a ray in the foreground; in the water, further back

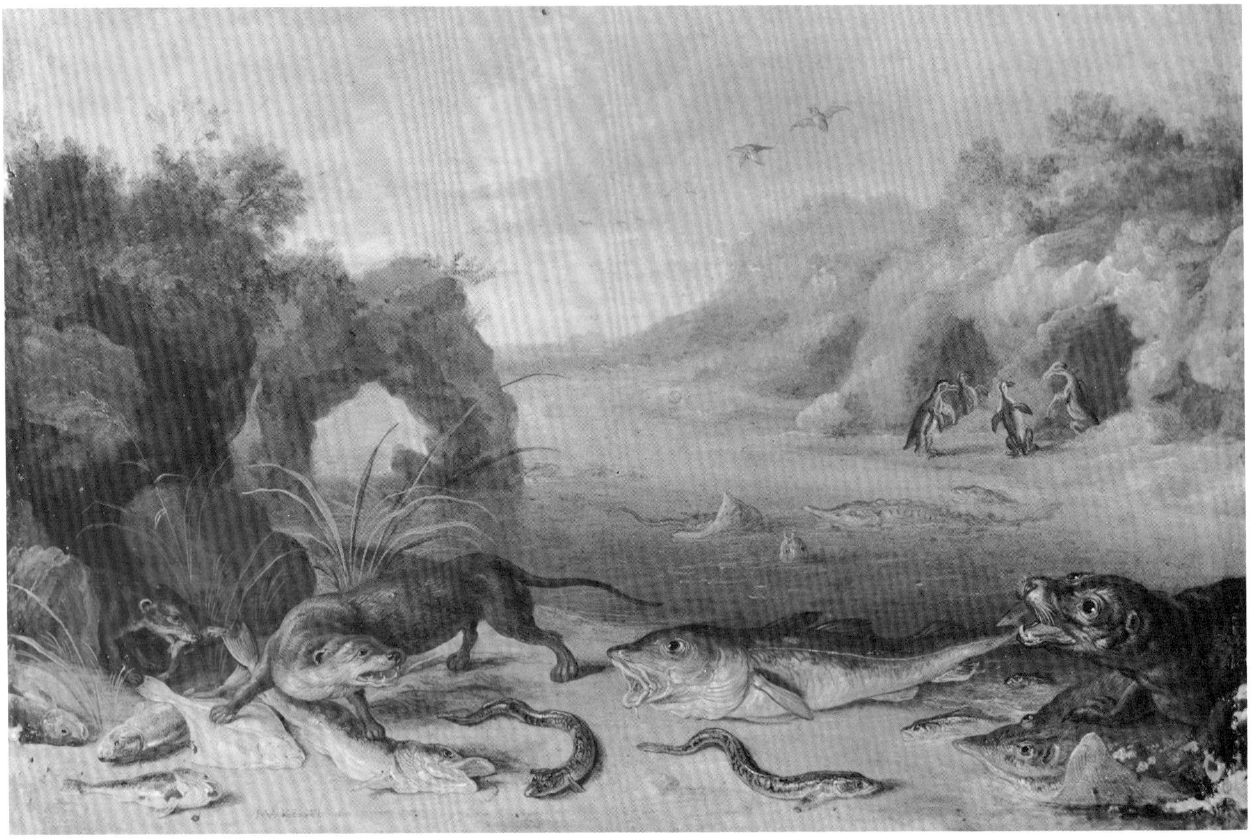

Van Kessel, *Water.*

between rocky embankments, swims a crocodile amid several oddly shaped fish and another ray, while, on the shore beyond, four penguins seem to be performing a lighthearted quadrille. Few of these animals appear to be based on actual observation.

c. 1660/70

Oil on copper, 20 × 29 cm ($7\frac{7}{8} \times 11\frac{7}{16}$ in.)

Inscription: at bottom edge to left of center: *I. V. KESSEL F.*

Conservation: The copper panel is damaged in the lower right corner. The paint layer is in good condition. There are losses connected with the damaged lower right corner, in the lower left corner, and along the upper edge. The varnish is discolored. There are no records of conservation treatment.

Provenance: Major Corbett-Winder, Vaynor Park, Berriew, Wales. Corbett-Winder sale, London, April 6, 1889. James E. Scripps, Detroit. Acquired in 1909.

Exhibitions: Detroit 1889: 56, no. 65.

References: Scripps 1897: 10-11, no. 26. Scripps 1900: 14, no. 38. *BDMA* 1909: 47. Detroit 1944: 74, no. 602. Paris 1977: 120, under no. 81.

Gift of Mrs. James E. Scripps (09.15)

Gysbrecht Leytens

1586 ANTWERP 1643/56

LITTLE is known about the life of Leytens, who only in recent times has been identified as the painter of winter scenes, most of which had been either attributed to other painters such as Momper or Keirincx—as this one was—or assembled as the oeuvre of an anonymous "Master of the Winter Landscapes." Leytens was a pupil of Jacques Vrolyck and may have gained admission to the guild of Saint Luke as a master in 1611.

His style is easily recognized not only because of his preference for snow-scenes, but even more so on account of the intricate and curiously "fuzzy" patterns made by the bare branches and twigs of the generally large trees that dominate the foreground. Compositionally, he appears to have followed works by Paul Bril and Jan Brueghel the Elder, and like the latter he adopted the method of juggling, with relatively minor variations, a limited number of motifs, rarely based on concrete observation. At a time when Dutch artists were revolutionizing landscape painting by revealing the poetry of modest rural settings, this single-minded Flemish artist perpetuated mannerist concepts of nature into the middle of the 17th century. The figures in his paintings were often inserted by other artists, such as Frans Francken the Younger, Vincent Malo, and Sebastian Vrancx.

Winter Landscape

Although this landscape (formerly attributed to Alexander Keirincx) resembles several other works by Leytens (Greindl 1973: 254-263), there is only one in which the painter depicted the same scenery and even several of the same figures. It is a panel in a private collection in Brussels, exhibited in 1965 (Brussels 1965: no. 142). By placing the largest tree closer to the center than in the Brussels panel, the artist was able to add a second tunnellike opening between trees at the left.

Leytens used the right part of the Detroit composition in yet another painting, a *Winter Scene with Gypsies* in the Musée des Beaux-Arts, Nantes (Greindl 1973: fig. 9), and, on a smaller scale, in the background of a painting in the collection of Comte Marc d'Oultremont, Château de Xhos, Belgium (ibid.: fig. 5).

Color plate V, page 77.

Oil on oak panel, 45 × 77.7 cm (17 11/16 × 30 5/8 in.)

Conservation: The two-membered oak panel is joined at 26.4 centimeters from the top edge. The reverse has been planed and cradled; however, shallow bevels are still visible on the right and left sides (the top and bottom are hidden by cradle members). The paint layer and ground (white chalk) reach the edges of the panel, which does not appear to have been reduced in size. The paint layer is in good condition. There is minor inpainted loss along the join, and there is reinforcement of the darks and shadows, particularly in the trees and to the left of the arborway. There is no record of any conservation treatment.

Provenance: Windschmidt Collection, Paris. F. Kleinberger Galleries (dealer), New York. Acquired in 1939.

Exhibitions: Los Angeles 1955 (as by Keirincx). Colorado Springs 1955 (as by Keirincx).

References: Detroit 1944: 73, no. 599 (as by Keirincx).

Founders Society Purchase, General Membership and Donations Funds (39.672)

Joos (Jodocus) de Momper the Younger

1564 ANTWERP 1635

THE most prominent member of a family of painters, Joos de Momper the Younger was the foremost representative of the rustic and mountainous landscape tradition derived from Pieter Bruegel the Elder, in contrast to the romantic and Italianate trends represented by Gillis van Coninxloo and Paul Bril, respectively. Momper was inscribed in the artists' guild of Antwerp in 1581. He subsequently visited Italy for a number of years, but there is little documentary evidence that would permit us to plot his itinerary in time as well as in space. He was back in Antwerp in 1590, when he married Elisabeth Gobyn. In 1594 he participated in the decoration of triumphal arches erected for the solemn reception in Antwerp of Archduke Ernest of Austria and in 1611 served as dean of the artists' guild. Since only a few of his paintings are signed, and still fewer are dated, it is difficult to establish a stylistic development, though it is likely that the more precisely articulated paintings belong to the beginning of his career, the more atmospheric and freely painted ones to his later years. A special problem is presented by a group of Italian scenes (including views of Rome) that, according to some scholars, belong to the last period of the master's life. These works suggest either that Momper made a second trip to Italy or was influenced by paintings by Paul Bril accessible to him in the North. Although Momper was capable of painting, and indeed often did paint, the figures in his landscapes, he also employed other artists (among them Sebastian Vrancx, Jan Brueghel the Elder, and David Teniers the Elder) to provide the "staffage."

Circle of Momper, *Mountainous Landscape with a Distant Seaport.*

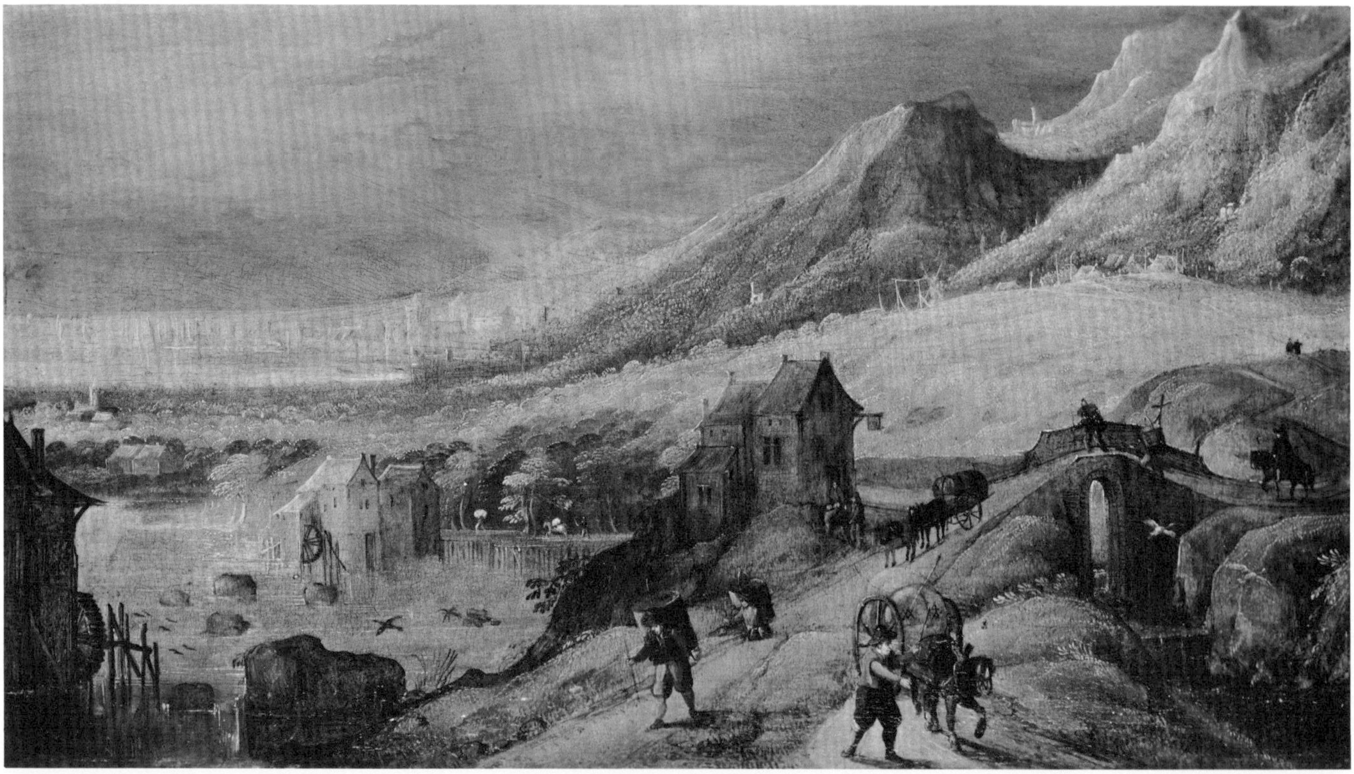

Circle of Momper

Mountainous Landscape with a Distant Seaport

The aspect of nature depicted in this panel, with its hazy view in the distance and the mountains rising to craggy peaks at the right, is very much in the manner of Momper; nevertheless, it is doubtful whether he painted it himself. The rendering of details is too schematic for the master, and the assembly of motifs in the foreground lacks cohesion and spatial clarity. Above all, the figures are weakly painted and poorly integrated with the setting, something Momper would hardly have found acceptable in a work of his own. Thus it is likely that we have here the work of a follower, perhaps one of Momper's sons.

c. 1620/30
Oil on oak panel, 43.8 × 77 cm ($17\frac{1}{4}$ × $30\frac{5}{16}$ in.)

Inscription: on wagonload (right foreground) are the markings xx 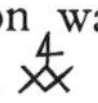

Conservation: The panel has been planed (to a 4-millimeter thickness) and cradled. It is composed of two members joined horizontally at 30 centimeters from the bottom edge and originally reinforced with dowels. The top edge is slightly beveled; the sides and bottom are unbeveled. The paint layer and chalk ground reach the edges of the panel. A discolored varnish layer obscures the condition of the paint layer; however, x-ray photographs reveal only minor paint loss, particularly along the join and in the hill in the right middleground. Under ultraviolet illumination, a large inpaint can be seen in the central sky above the lowest mountain range. The painting is abraded overall, but particularly in the thin brown and green glazes. Infrared examination shows that the foreground figure, horse, and cart were executed after the landscape features were painted. Pentimenti of the outline of the hillock can be seen through the figure and cart. There are no records of prior conservation treatment.

Provenance: Private collection, Scotland (?). Lilienfeld Galleries, Inc. (dealer), New York. Acquired in 1938.

References: Richardson 1938: 184-186. Detroit 1944: 91, no. 647. Whitcomb 1954: 59.

Gift of Mrs. Anna Scripps Whitcomb (38.32)

Pieter Neefs the Elder

C. 1578 ANTWERP 1656/61

PIETER NEEFS (also spelled Neeffs) is believed to have been trained by Hendrik van Steenwijck the Elder; in style and choice of subject, his works indeed show a marked similarity to those of both Steenwijck and his son. Neefs was accepted as a master in the painters' guild of Antwerp in 1609 and in 1612 married Maria Lauterbeens.

Church interiors that permitted a comprehensive view of the central nave and side aisles were his specialty. While few of these views can be considered exact portrayals of existing structures, many of them appear to have been inspired by the High Gothic forms of Antwerp Cathedral. Neefs was also adept at rendering the effects of artificial illumination in crypt-like spaces.

Like the Steenwijcks, Neefs collaborated with other artists who painted the figures in his interiors; in later years he also employed his sons, Pieter the Younger and Lodewijk. As in the Steenwijck workshop, the contributions of the older and younger artists are difficult to distinguish, but those dated before 1640 are most likely by the elder Neefs alone. His works are found in many major museums and are often signed by him even if the figures were clearly contributed by other artists, a fact that demonstrates that the painter of the architecture had aesthetic priority and that his name carried commercial weight.

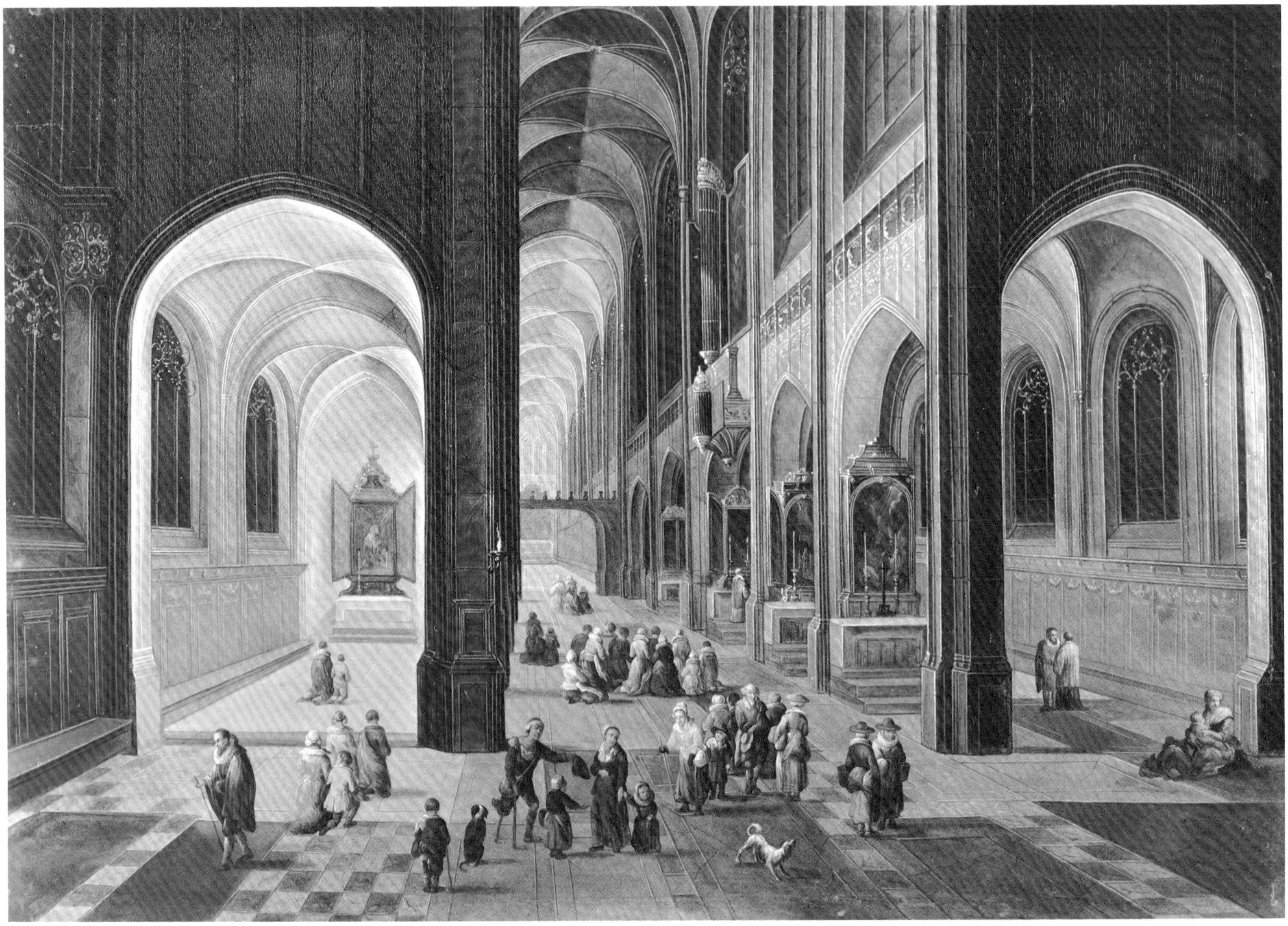

Style of Neefs, *Interior of a Gothic Church.*

Style of Neefs

Interior of a Gothic Church

With its emphasis on a dark foreground foil on either side, and its rapidly receding perspective, particularly of the nave as seen through the central opening, this picture is a typical product of the Antwerp school of architectural painters of which the elder Steenwijck and the elder Neefs were the leaders. Equally characteristic is the contrast between the rigidly outlined architecture and the random distribution of the human figures (and two dogs). These figures were added after the church itself had been painted, as can be seen in many places where orthogonal or horizontal lines can be discerned underneath them.

Thus, while the painting is perfectly representative of a particular trend, and is, in fact, related to the manner of Neefs' paintings of church interiors, it is most unlikely that Neefs himself is its author. It may actually be a copy of one of Neefs' works, or a free imitation of such a picture, but it contains such weaknesses that it is unworthy of an artist of Neefs' stature. One of the details most revealing of the painter's incompetence or carelessness is the manner in which the tracery of the windows has been treated. In the first window of the side aisle at the left, the tracery has emancipated itself from its structural function and has become a free, decorative—and entirely meaningless—play of curlicues. In fact, all similar sections of the architecture, while not always as irrational, have been treated as purely ornamental lacework. Nor is the perspective constructed with the care that one would expect from Neefs; the various points of convergence of the arches of the nave do not lie on one orthogonal, but move up and down. The cross-section of the pier at the left does not correspond to that at the right, and the perspective of the foreshortened left side of that pier is most carelessly constructed. Thus, the picture can at best be characterized as the work of a follower of Pieter Neefs.

c. 1630/40
Oil on oak panel, 26 × 36.5 cm (10¼ × 14⅜ in.)

Inscription: Remnants of what may have been a signature are seen at the bottom of the pillar at the center left but are indecipherable even if examined with the help of infrared or ultraviolet photography.

Conservation: The panel is uncradled and beveled on all four sides. It is very slightly bowed vertically. The paint film and white-chalk ground reach the edges of the panel, which does not appear to have been reduced in size. The paint layer is in excellent condition with only a few small losses along the lower edge. No previous treatment is reported.

Provenance: Major Corbett-Winder, Vaynor Park, Berriew, Wales. Corbett-Winder sale, London, April 6, 1889. James E. Scripps, Detroit. Acquired in 1909.

Exhibitions: Detroit 1889: 33, no. 31. Hartford/Andover 1949-50: 19, no. 30; pl. 19.

References: Scripps 1897: 14, no. 34. Scripps 1900: 18-19, no. 50. *BDMA* 1909: 48. Richardson 1937: 106-107.

Gift of Mrs. James E. Scripps (09.21)

Philipp Peter Roos ("Rosa da Tivoli")

1655 OR 1657 FRANKFORT – ROME 1706

PHILIPP ROOS is one of the best known of the many members of a family of painters. Trained by his father, Johann Heinrich, he soon attracted the attention of the Count of Hesse-Kassel, who provided the young artist with the means to go to Italy (1677) on the condition that he would return to his court. However, once in Rome, Roos married the daughter of the painter Giacinto Brandi and settled first in Rome and then, in 1685, in Tivoli, developing as his specialty the painting of farm animals. He joined the Dutch *Schilderbent* (artists' association) and in accordance with the custom of that group assumed (or was given) a pseudonym *Mercurius* because of the speed at which he worked and his facility in drawing as well as painting. Roos' style reflects his method of working; it is marked by a bold, occasionally almost coarse handling of the brush, and strong contrasts between light and dark. This personal mannerism was apparently popular and attracted imitators; as a result, many works executed by other animal-painters have been attributed to Roos. The confusion is increased by the fact that the same range of subjects was treated by Roos' brothers and sons. Works in the art market attributed to "Rosa da Tivoli" should always be regarded with caution.

Attributed to Roos

A Military Encampment

¶ The main interest of this large canvas lies in its vivid portrayal of military life in the late 17th or early 18th century. In front of three large tents, one of which stands out in size and sumptuousness of decor, a motley group of horsemen surrounds a man who presumably is their leader; he wears a soft hat and a cloak slung around his shoulders, and appears to give an order, gesturing with his unsheathed sword. He turns to a black man on a white horse, perhaps to have him give a signal on the kettledrum (partly covered by a red drapery) mounted at his side. Another command given by an elegantly accoutered officer standing at the left may refer to some goats and sheep, representing the provisions in the form of livestock that the armies of the period had to take along with them. A modest still life of a cannon-barrel, partly covered by a carpet, and a small saddle fills the center foreground. More soldiers can be seen over a rise, and above them is a partly ruined town of vaguely Italian character.

Informative about life in a military encampment as the picture may be, as a work of art it falls decidedly short of the achievements in this genre of the best Dutch painters such as Philips and Pieter Wouwerman, Dirck Stoop, and Hendrik Verschuring. The composition is crowded and poorly organized, the action confusing, and the execution uneven and rather coarse. Certain details, such as the white horse reclining at the left, may have been derived from works of other masters. The attribution of this painting to "Rosa da Tivoli," hitherto unquestioned, points in the right direction but is by no means certain.

Attributed to Roos, *A Military Encampment.*

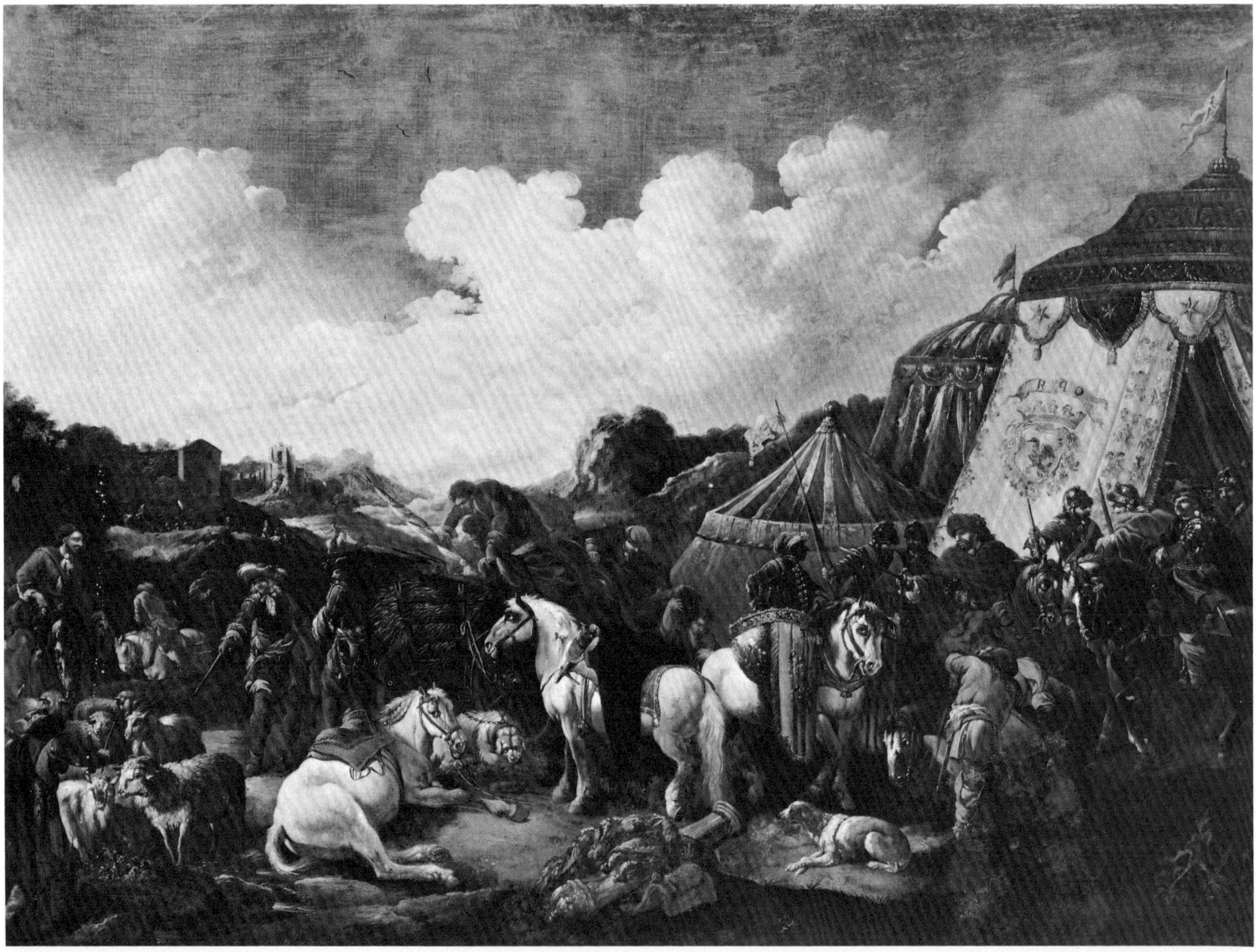

Oil on canvas, 126 × 161.7 cm ($49\frac{5}{8}$ × $63\frac{5}{8}$ in.)

Inscription: on a ribbon painted on or attached to main tent: *R 90* above a heraldic shield bearing an eagle surmounted by a crown.

Conservation: The painting is executed on a coarse-weave canvas that has been glue-lined. The tacking edges on the left and right sides are a continuation of the original paint (the original tacking margins have been cut). Tack holes along the top and bottom, 2.5 centimeters into the picture plane, suggest that these edges were also folded over at one time. There is a reddish, bole-colored ground. The painting has a layer of very discolored varnish. In a large cleaning test patch at the upper left, the sky can be seen to be abraded, with ground color showing through. Ultraviolet examination reveals inpaint along the top and bottom edges (about 3 centimeters in width), and over areas of loss in the foreground (between the dog and the fallen column, near the belly of the reclining horse). The painting has flake losses overall. X-rays show a typical lead-white buildup. Infrared examination reveals no pentimenti and does not pick up any underdrawing. There are no records of conservation treatment.

Provenance: James E. Scripps, Detroit. Acquired in 1889.

Exhibitions: Detroit 1889: 62, no. 78.

References: Detroit 1944: 113, no. 704.

Gift of James E. Scripps (1889.42)

Peter Paul Rubens

1577 SIEGEN – ANTWERP 1640

THE SON of an Antwerp lawyer, the greatest Flemish painter of the 17th century was born on German soil, where his father, who had Calvinist leanings, had taken up residence. At his father's death, when Rubens was ten years old, the family moved back to Antwerp. Rubens' talent must have manifested itself early; at age 14, or perhaps even earlier, he began to train seriously for his future career. Of the three masters with whom he studied, the last one, Otto van Veen, had the greatest influence on him, most likely because Van Veen was not only a skilled craftsman but also a well-educated—indeed, even learned—man. Rubens himself was known to his contemporaries as a scholar as well as an artist, his chief interest being classical, especially Roman, antiquity, which he studied through ancient texts as well as artistic relics like coins, gems, cameos, implements of war and domestic use, and the sculptures in marble and bronze that could be seen at that time. He pursued these studies intensively in Italy, where he went in 1600, but he also used his years there (in addition to one year in Spain, where he was sent by his major Italian patron, the Duke of Mantua) to acquaint himself with the works of the leading Italian artists of the Renaissance and of his own time. While in Italy, he received important commissions for churches in Rome, Mantua, Genoa, and Fermo, and he portrayed many members of the Genoese nobility, who continued to give him commissions even after he had returned to Flanders in 1608. In 1609 he married Isabella Brant, daughter of an Antwerp magistrate; they had three children, two sons surviving to manhood. Four years after Isabella's death (1626), he married Hélène Fourment, whose father dealt in tapestries; there were five children from this marriage.

While he accepted commissions from private patrons, and continued to furnish paintings for churches in Antwerp, Brussels, and many other towns—including 39 paintings for the ceiling of the Jesuit church of Antwerp—Rubens' most spectacular creations were executed for the leading royal courts of Europe: the cycle of the life of Maria de' Medici, painted between 1622 and 1625 for the Luxembourg Palace in Paris (a projected cycle of the life of Henry IV was never completed); the ceiling of the Banqueting House at Whitehall,

London, painted for King Charles I and finished in 1634; and a large number of paintings designed, and in part executed, by him for King Philip IV of Spain between 1635 and 1640, the year of Rubens' death. Of the several large cycles designed as tapestry cartoons, the most important was the *Triumph of the Eucharist*, of around 1626/28, for the convent of the Descalzas Reales, done at the request of Isabella Clara Eugenia, daughter of King Philip II and ruler of the Spanish Netherlands. Rubens also furnished the designs for the many arches and stages erected by the city of Antwerp for the solemn reception in 1634 of Cardinal-Infante Ferdinand, the new Spanish governor.

Despite his extensive scholarly and artistic activities (which also included the design of title pages for books by Antwerp publishers), Rubens found time to engage in important diplomatic missions, which can still be studied in some detail thanks to the preservation of a fairly large amount of his correspondence. He is, in fact, credited with having laid the groundwork for a peace treaty between England and Spain in 1630. By then, he had already been ennobled by the King of Spain, and he was later knighted by the King of England. At the end of his life, he was the owner of a magnificent house in Antwerp, filled with his own paintings and those of other artists—above all, of Titian—and the seigneur of a substantial rural property not far from Mechlin, where he apparently spent his last five summers, when he suffered increasingly from gout. His collections, except for his drawings, were sold soon after his death; when it became clear that no member of his family would follow his profession, the drawings, too, were dispersed at auction.

Philip Rubens, the Artist's Brother

Philip Rubens was the fifth child of Jan Rubens and Maria Pypelinckx; Peter Paul, the sixth. The seventh child, another boy, died in childhood. Two of the older children also died young, while the two first-born lived at least to adulthood, but their lives, too, ended prematurely—as did Philip's. In fact, it was only Peter Paul who reached a more advanced age: he was 63 when he died.

It is necessary to realize the eminence, in his own field, of Philip Rubens, and the close bonds between the two brothers, to see the portrait of Philip in the Art Institute in proper perspective. The records do not allow us to say anything about the promise, or lack of it, of the other brothers and sisters of the artist. However, Philip, in his own way, appears to have been as gifted as Peter Paul, though his fields were literature and jurisprudence. He was the favorite pupil of the most prominent humanist scholar of the age, Justus Lipsius, who expected him to be his successor. Philip was in Italy twice, first, from 1601 to 1604, as the tutor of Guillaume Richardot, the son of Jan Richardot, president of the privy council of the Netherlands. It was in Rome during this period (1603) that he received the degree of Doctor of Law (*doctor utriusque juris*). After a short stay in Flanders, spending much time in close contact with Lipsius, he returned to Rome to take the position of secretary and librarian to Cardinal Ascanio Colonna. Around 1606, he shared a dwelling with his brother, and we have evidence that together they studied the literature and art of ancient Rome. Philip's renown as a scholar was already so great that he was offered a chair at the University of Pisa, which however, he declined; he returned to the Netherlands in 1607. In 1609 (January 14) he received an important appointment as one of the four secretaries of the city of Antwerp, after having received the "letter of Brabantization" required by law for a man born abroad, even as the son of Flemish parents (he had been born in Cologne where his parents were living in exile). On March 26, 1609, he married Marie de Moy, the daughter of another of the secretaries of the city; they had two children, Clara and Philip, the son born two weeks after Philip himself had died, on August 28, 1611, after a short illness. His brilliant career had come to an early end.

In 1608 Philip published a volume of philological studies illustrated with engravings by Cornelis Galle from drawings by Peter Paul, whose

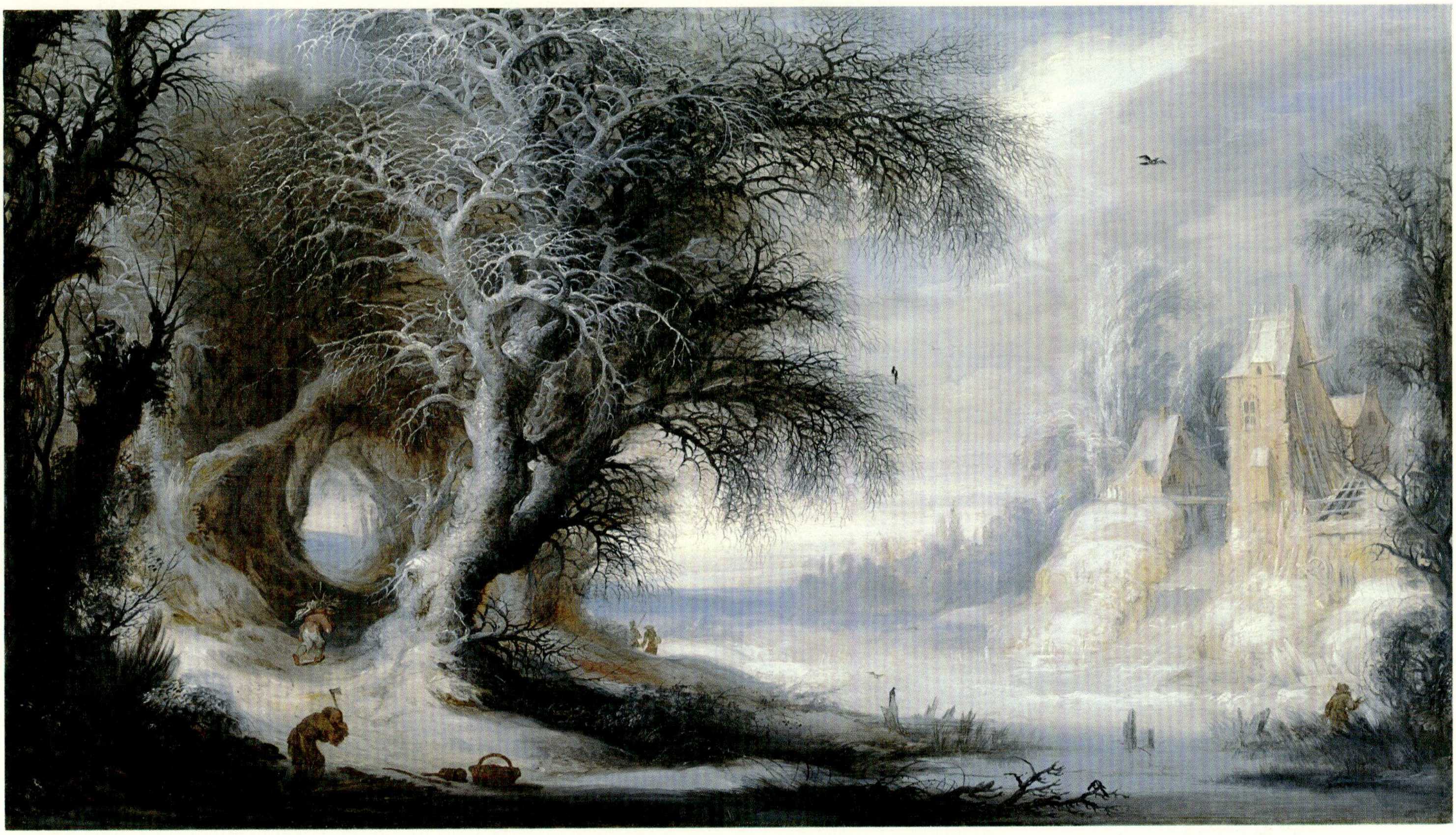

PLATE V. Leytens, *Winter Landscape*.

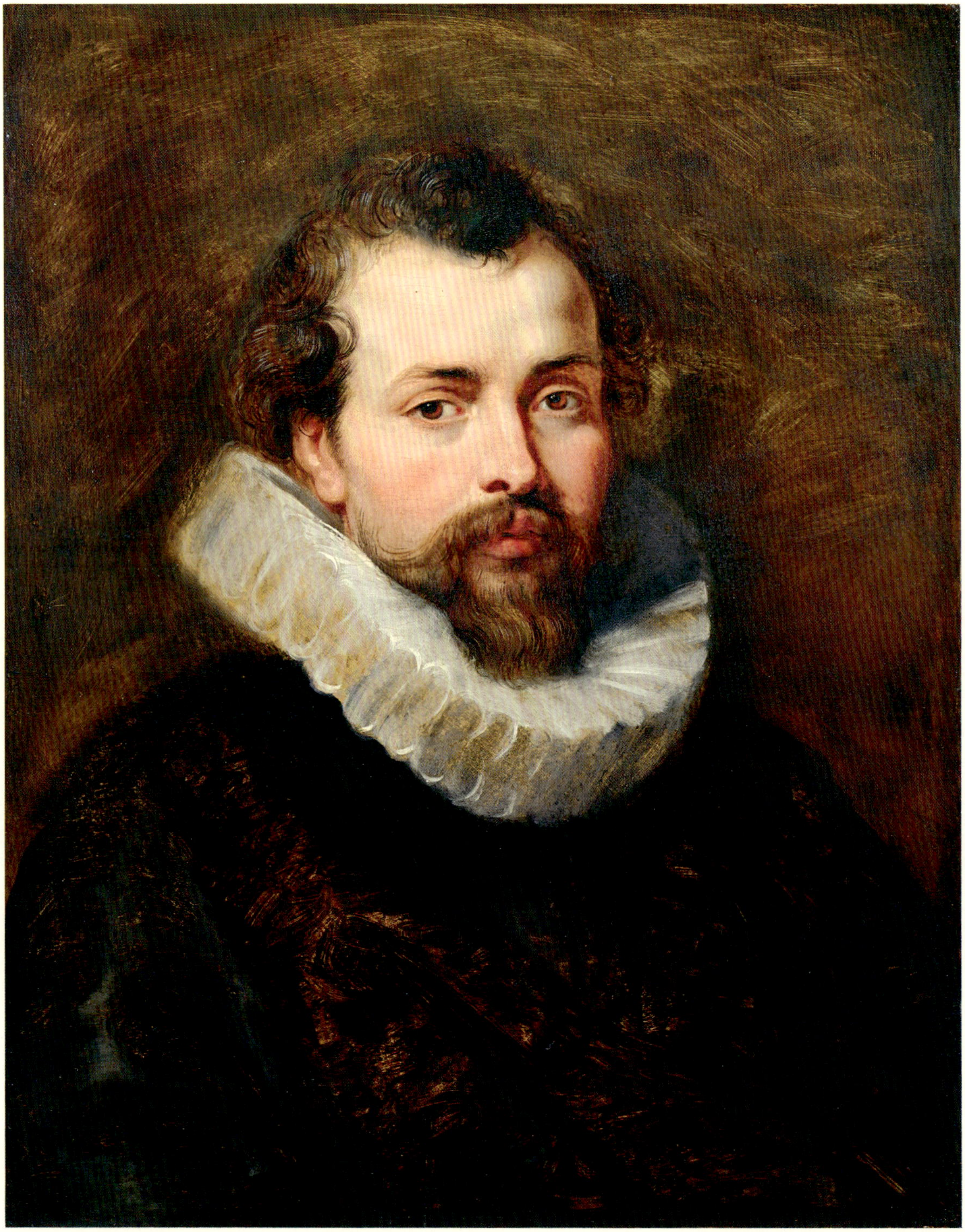

PLATE VI. Rubens, *Philip Rubens, the Artist's Brother.*

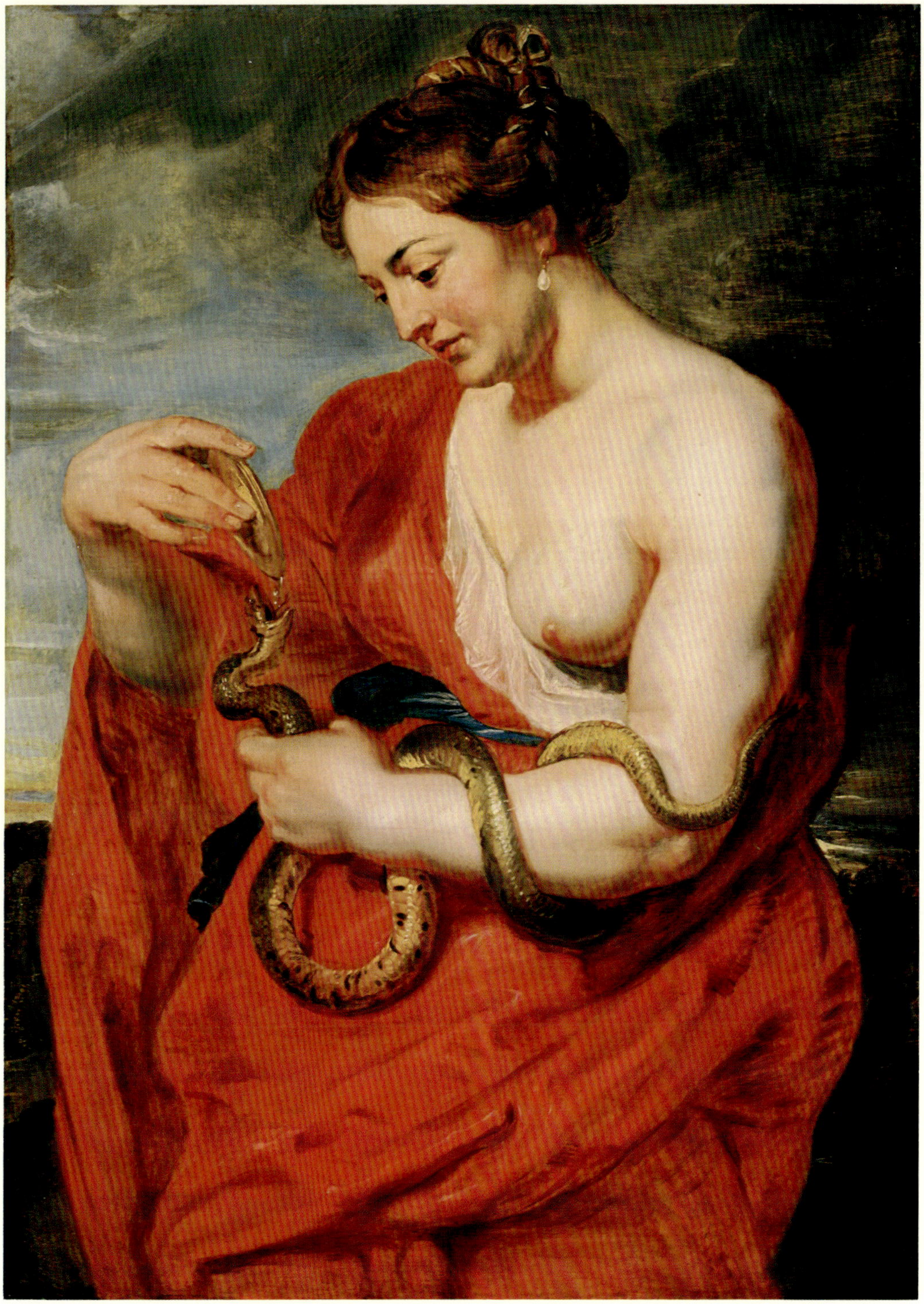

PLATE VII. Rubens, *Hygieia*, *Goddess of Health*.

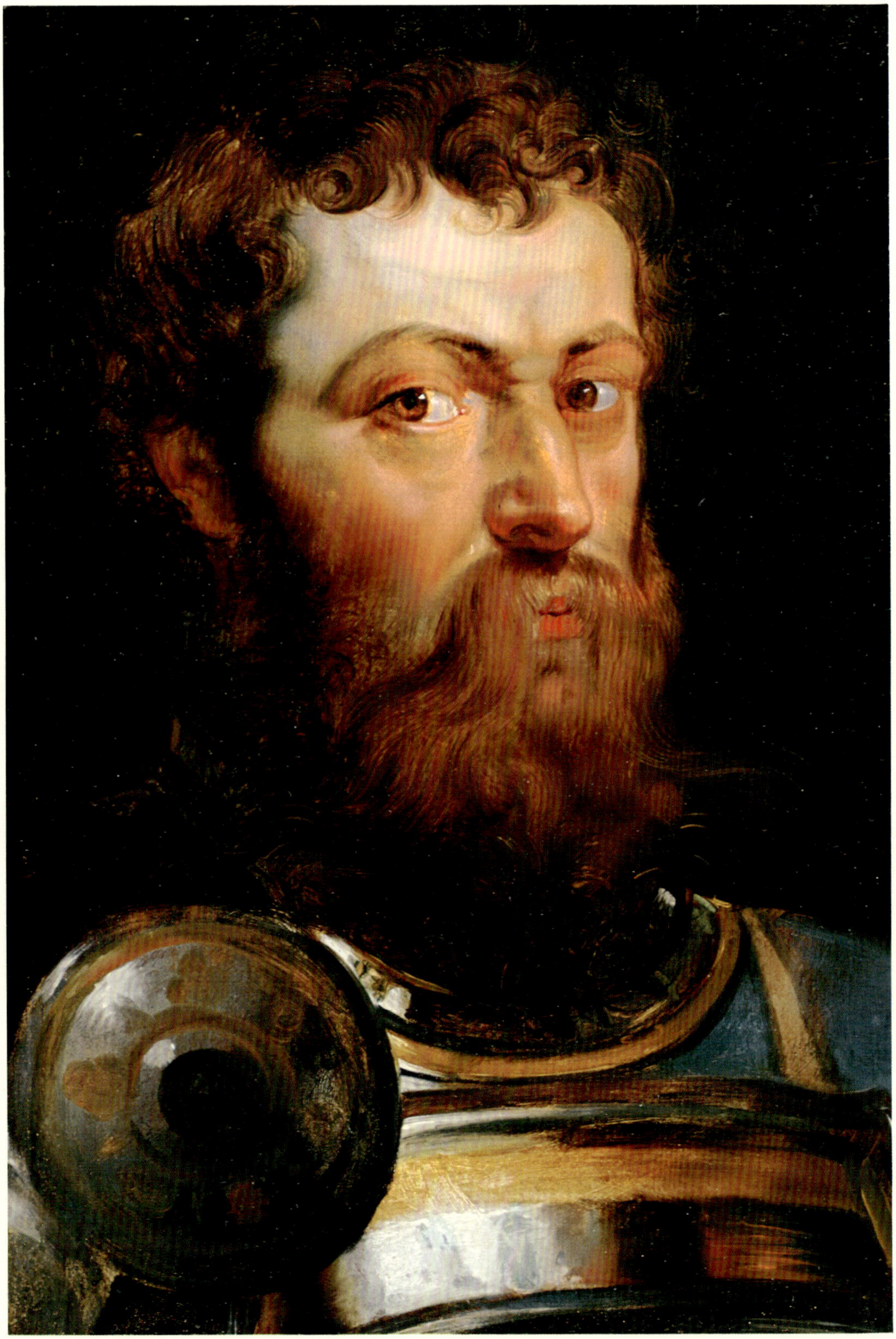

PLATE VIII. Rubens, *Head of a Warrior*.

aid in his studies he acknowledged in affectionate terms. Equally indicative of a very close bond between the brothers are letters that have been preserved, and even a poem (in Latin, of course) Philip wrote on the occasion of Peter Paul's marriage to Isabella Brant in October 1609. After Philip's death, Peter Paul, together with his father-in-law, Jan Brant, was made legal guardian of Philip's two small children. Through the efforts of both Brant and Rubens, a collection of scholarly, epistolary, and poetic writings by Philip was published in 1615, together with somewhat rhetorical, but nevertheless significant, Latin poems by prominent Antwerp humanists in praise of Philip, and for the consolation of Peter Paul.

We are in the dark about the date as well as the original function of this painting. It is known that Rubens inserted a portrait of his brother on Philip's epitaph in the abbey of Saint Michael in Antwerp (where their mother, too, was buried), and it has generally been surmised that the Detroit panel is in fact this picture. There is good reason, however, to question this assumption. In his *Voyage pittoresque de la Flandre et du Brabant* (Paris, 1769: 171), J. B. Descamps described the epitaph and stated unequivocally that the portrait on it was oval ("A côté est l'Epitaphe de Philippe Rubens; tout est en marbre, excepté le Portrait en ovale placé sur le haut, qui est d'une grande beauté & peint par Rubens, son frère"). The Detroit picture is rectangular, and there is no evidence that it was ever framed as an oval. To retain the theory that this is the portrait from the epitaph, one would have to conjecture that the oval frame did not touch the panel, since otherwise there would surely be marks on the surface of the painting. Of Philip's tomb, unfortunately, only the tablet with the inscription has been preserved and is now placed in the garden of the Rubenshuis in Antwerp.

Even if the Detroit portrait is the one placed on the epitaph, there would still remain the question whether Rubens used a pre-existing portrait or painted one after his brother's death. Philip was 37 years old when he died; he looks much younger in the Detroit picture, but this does not necessarily mean that it had been painted from life years before. Philip's smooth skin and youthful expression in the portrait might be due to the painter's desire to idealize the features of his deceased brother. In that case, we would still have to postulate the existence of an earlier portrayal (possibly a drawing), unless we want to assume that Rubens painted the picture entirely from memory.

One argument to support a date for the picture before Philip's death may be derived from a comparison of the portrait with the only other portrayal of Philip by Rubens known to us, in the celebrated painting *Justus Lipsius and his Disciples* (Palazzo Pitti, Florence). There is general and justified agreement that the Pitti panel was painted as a commemorative for both Lipsius and Philip; these two men are "framed" as it were, by the two surviving friends, Jan Woverius at the right and Peter Paul himself at the left. Philip's portrayal in the Pitti picture is unquestionably based on the Detroit portrait; he is seen from the same angle and in the same light, and there is a great correspondence in the details. And yet the expressions on Philip's face are very different. While the Detroit panel shows him with lips slightly parted as if ready to speak, the group portrait in Florence gives him a serious, withdrawn expression appropriate to a portrayal painted after death.

The date of the Pitti panel itself is by no means certain, though the old idea that it was painted in Italy has long been abandoned. It is now generally dated shortly after Philip's death, 1611 or 1612. Yet it could very well be even a few years later, although certainly not later than 1615, the year when the commemorative volume of Philip's writings was published. Peter Paul may have been anywhere between 34 and 38 years of age, and he looks it. Philip, however, who was three years older than his brother, actually looks considerably younger in the Pitti panel. Such a discrepancy is less puzzling if we assume that Philip's face was based on a portrait painted from life several years before.

Philip's head as it appears in the Detroit portrait is also rendered (though naturally in reverse) in a commemorative engraving by Cornelis Galle, which was used to illustrate the above-mentioned collection of Philip's writings published in 1615. The engraver was paid 33 guilders on March 13, 1615, for his work. It is likely that Galle used a drawing, executed either by Rubens or by himself from Rubens' picture, since instead of wearing a contemporary outfit, Philip is portrayed in the print in the manner of a Roman portrait bust, with a classical drapery around his shoulders, which are cut off below in a curve characteristic of such sculptures. The bust is shown on a funerary altar that takes the form of a short, cylindrical base, decorated on either side with cherubs' heads connected by garlands of fruit; on the garlands sit two doves signifying grief and bereavement (Held 1977: 38; 232-233). In front of the base are two torches, turned upside down—common symbols of death—linked together by the coils of a large serpent on the back of which crawls a lizard. Both animals have Dionysian associations, and in some late antique (Neo-Platonic) sources they are symbolically connected with the sun (itself often identified with Dionysus). Thus, they may refer here to the renewal of life through a final resurrection (for this symbolism, see Lehmann-Hartleben and Olsen 1942: 30, n. 60; Judson and Van de Velde [1978: 152], who referred to this study, only made reference to note 61, where it is said that serpent and lizard "are found frequently together on Roman tombs in the Rhineland"; hence, they interpret the animals more narrowly as "signifying death"). The memorial tablet at the front of the base reads: *PIIS MANIBVS PHILIPPI RVBENI(I) SACR.* (Bouchery and Van den Wijngaert 1941: 70, 136; fig. 49). The combined base and bust are placed inside a shallow niche, the top of which is decorated with a stylized conch shell, a combination of motifs that has a long tradition and symbolizes, as William Heckscher has shown, triumph over death by virtue of memorable achievements (Heckscher 1958: 117-121).

Color plate VI, page 78.

c. 1610/11

Oil on oak panel, 68.5 × 53.5 cm (27 × 21 1/16 in.)

Conservation: The original panel appears to have been thinned, adhered to a four-membered oak backing with 1-centimeter-wide borders, and cradled. The added borders hide the original edges of the panel. A grayish imprimatura, applied diagonally over the white-chalk ground, can be seen to have the wide, striated brush strokes typical of Rubens. The paint layer is in excellent condition. There is one minor inpainted loss in the right part of the forehead, and some scattered losses in the background and collar. Blisters were treated and the painting surface cleaned by Edward O. Korany in 1964.

Provenance: Peeters d'Aertselaer, Cleydael, 1817. H. J. Stier d'Aertselaer sale, Antwerp, July 29, 1822. Grand Duke Henry of Mecklenburg. Mecklenburg sale, Paris, December 11, 1854, lot 16. Carl von Hollitscher, Berlin. Camillo Castiglioni, Vienna. Castiglioni sale, F. Müller and Co., Amsterdam, November 17-20, 1925, lot 74. Acquired in 1926.

Exhibitions: Berlin 1909: no. 121. Brussels 1910: no. 396. Detroit 1936: no. 19. New York 1939: no. 321. New York 1942: no. 2. Los Angeles 1946: no. 8. Detroit 1978: cover; no. 1.

References: Smith 1829-42, II (1830): 227, no. 805. Rooses 1886-92, IV (1890): 247, no. 1040. Freiherr von Hadeln 1909: 296. Burroughs 1926: cover, 86-87. Detroit 1930: no. 193. Richardson 1936: 62-63. Scheyer 1937: 46, fig. 19; 49. Detroit 1944: 114, no. 193. Goris and Held 1947: 28, no. 14; pl. 2. Larsen 1952: 215, no. 22. *BDIA* 1964: 53, 55. Gerson 1968: 54 ("whereabouts unknown"). Judson and Van de Velde 1978, I: 152; II: fig. 99.

Gift of William E. Scripps in memory of his son, James E. Scripps II (26.385)

Hygieia, Goddess of Health

Hygieia, in Greek mythology the personification and goddess of health, was closely connected with the worship of Asclepius (Aesculapius), the god of healing. She was generally considered his daughter (in one version she was his wife; *Natalis Comitis Mythologiae*, Venice, 1581: 246, 21). The serpent, symbol of rejuvenation, was sacred to Asclepius, and in Rome, the god was even worshiped in the guise of a serpent. The image of a serpent drinking from a patera offered by Hygieia (representing *Salus*, or health) is known from ancient marbles and coins (for the latter, see Du Choul 1581: 118-119, and Montfaucon 1721, I, pt. 2, chap. 3: 182). The figure of Hygieia is found in Northern art before Rubens in a frame designed by Jost Amman (Butsch 1881, II: title page). The representation of Hygieia actually holding and feeding the serpent appears to have been new with Rubens, but he may have had a valid reason for depicting the goddess that way.

The composition of the Detroit panel is known from several other versions. A small panel (60 by 42 centimeters) was in the sale of Count d'Hane de Steenhuyse of Ghent (Paris, 1840); it was enthusiastically praised in the sale catalogue. The description was reprinted by Rooses (1886-92), but he never saw the picture and I have not found any later mention of the work. The fact that it was on panel makes the citation interesting, since copies are generally executed on canvas (see below); moreover, the Hane de Steenhuyse painting, despite its small size, fetched 3,050 francs, at that time a considerable amount of money. Obviously, nothing definitive can be said about a painting that disappeared nearly 140 years ago, yet I suspect that it was a reduced copy of one of the two larger versions known today. The elaborate catalogue description of 1840 virtually excludes the possibility that the picture was an oil sketch; however, for a finished painting, it was rather small, particularly when we see that two very good versions known today are nearly twice as large. One detail, finally, mentioned in the description, strikes a wrong note: in the Hane de Steenhuyse painting, the goddess held a gold krater (*un cratère d'or*) rather than a simple patera as she does in all the known versions. It is the patera that is justified by all the ancient models, and I very much doubt that Rubens would have replaced the correct object with the improper, albeit more spectacular, form of a krater.

There is another version of high quality; formerly the property of Prince Lobkowitz at Castle Raudnitz, it is now in the Národni Galerie, Prague (no. 0-9300; oil on panel, 130 × 74 cm; Šíp and Blažíček 1963: no. 47). Richardson (1946), without having seen the picture, called it "an old copy" of the Detroit panel, from which it differs slightly. The pearl hanging from the ear of Hygieia in the Detroit work is absent in the painting in Prague; in fact, one sees much less of the ear in that picture, while it is almost entirely visible in the Detroit picture. The paint film in the Prague version is more thickly applied, while it is more translucent and treated in a more abundant glazing technique in Detroit's painting. There are also pentimenti in the Prague panel that are absent from the Detroit one. I am inclined to see the Prague work as the first version, even possibly painted some years before the Detroit one, but the latter is nevertheless of such high quality that it may well be an equally authentic work of the master, even though such self-repetitions are exceedingly rare in Rubens' oeuvre. (The Prague version, while still at Castle Raudnitz, was included in the Rubens volume of the *Klassiker der Kunst* [Oldenbourg 1921: 71], identified, however, as a portrayal of Cleopatra!)

The motif of a serpent wound around the arm appears also in *The Birth of the Dauphin*, one of the canvases from the cycle of the life of Maria de' Medici in the Louvre. There, a winged male figure receives the new-born in his arms while a serpent, curling over his wrist, appears to turn its head toward the infant. As early as the beginning of the 18th century, the exact meaning of the winged figure was in doubt. This is what Moreau de Mautour, in his *Description de la Galerie du Palais du Luxembourg* (Paris, 1704), said: "The nude young man . . . is either the Good Genius as conceived by the Ancients . . . or else the God of Health, because of the serpent which designates Aesculapius" (see Thuillier and Foucart 1972: 80, no. 11).

Among the copies of the *Hygieia* is a canvas, 95 by 81.5 centimeters (Stephane Deurbergue sale, Hôtel Drouot, Paris, February 18, 1974); the absence of the pearl suspended from the ear identifies this painting as a copy of the Prague version rather than the Detroit one. A sketch in black and red chalk (32 × 25 cm), claimed to be the "original drawing" for the composition, was offered in the Charles Haviland sale, Hôtel Drouot, Paris, December 14-15, 1922 (lot 27), and again in the George Haviland sale, G. Petit, Paris, June 2-3, 1932 (lot 98). It was illustrated in both catalogues. This, too, can only be considered as a copy, as it entirely lacks Rubens' sureness and economy of technique.

Rooses (1886-92) also listed a version on canvas (80 × 68 cm) in the sale of the Werbrouck Collection, Antwerp, in 1859, when it was acquired by a dealer, Beeckmans, for 580 francs. Nothing is known about the later history of that work.

A painting described as "een vrouwe met een slange in de handt, van myn Heer Rubens" ("a woman with a serpent in her hand, by Mr. Rubens") was listed in the inventory of the estate of Jeremias Wildens, the son of the painter Jan Wildens, in 1653 (Denucé 1932: 156). Without any further evidence, it is impossible to say whether this picture is the Detroit or the Prague version (assuming that the choice is only between these two works).

Color plate VII, page 79.

c. 1614/15

Oil on oak panel, 106.2 × 74.3 cm ($41\frac{13}{16}$ × $29\frac{1}{4}$ in.)

Conservation: The three-membered panel was originally joined with dowels at 19 and 44.5 centimeters from the left edge. It has been planed to a 4-millimeter thickness and cradled. The top and bottom show part of the original bevel; the sides are hidden by cradle members. There is a vertical crack 35 centimeters in length starting from the bottom, 38 centimeters from the left edge. It is supported from the reverse with a batten. The ground (white chalk) and paint layers reach the edges of the panel, which does not appear to have been reduced in size. There is a gray imprimatura applied in the striated manner distinctive of Rubens' preparations. The paint layer is in good condition, although the background is quite abraded. An area of the background, starting at the level of Hygieia's left elbow and ending at the height of her earring, has been extensively overpainted to cover large losses in this section. Other areas of retouching include the hair, where there is one loss and reinforcement of the darkest lines; the left edge; and the red robe, along the crack and reinforcing the darkest glazes. Infrared examination shows only one minor pentimento: Hygieia's right forefinger was once extended by approximately 1.5 centimeters. Blisters were laid down in 1955 by William Suhr.

Provenance: Jeremias Wildens, Antwerp, 1653 (?). Count Charles de Proli, Antwerp. De Proli sale, Brussels 1785 (580 florins). P. de Smet van Alphen sale, Amsterdam, 1810 (800 florins). H. Francken sale, Lokeren, 1830 (1,500 francs); bought by De Vis, agent for Charles J. Nieuwenhuyse, Brussels. Nieuwenhuyse sale, Paris, 1840. Joseph Allard, Brussels. Senator Prosper Crabbe, Brussels. Crabbe sale, Galerie Sedelmeyer, Paris, June 12, 1890, lot 47. Galerie Charpentier, Paris, 1936. Martin B. Ascher, London. Schaeffer Galleries, Inc. (dealer), New York. Henry Reichhold, Birmingham, Michigan. Acquired in 1944.

Exhibitions: New York 1939: no. 325. Cincinnati 1948: no. 31. New York 1956: no. 11. Detroit 1978: no 2.

References: Smith 1829-42, II (1830): 219-220, no. 779. Rooses 1886-92, III (1890): 110, no. 630. *Bulletin-Rubens* 1897: 90. *Revue de l'Art* 1936: 48. Richardson 1946: 9-11. Valentiner 1946: 159, no. 46. Goris and Held 1947: 37, no. 73. Lewison 1951: 21. Larsen 1952: 216, no. 29. Puyvelde 1964: 132, fig. 26; 211; 249, n. 109. Šíp 1978: 197.

Gift of Mr. and Mrs. Henry Reichhold (44.266)

Head of a Warrior

Whether or not this head of a warrior—the same man who appears in the paintings discussed below (pages 94-102)—is a study for these works or a copy taken from one of them is still an open question. The factors favoring the first alternative appear to me to be stronger than those supporting the second. The sketchy treatment of the armor, as much as is visible, does not, by itself, exclude the possibility that it is a copy. However, there are considerable differences in the details of the single head (the position and size of the eyes, the height and shape of the forehead) compared with both the Althorp and Detroit compositions, which in these respects agree with each other to a considerable degree. Technically, the small panel is thinly painted in the manner of study heads, permitting the viewer to see, especially in the face, the slanted brushstrokes of the grayish priming underneath. The last argument in favor of this view has been provided by x-ray photography. It revealed in the lower half of the picture, and upside-down relative to the head of the warrior, the foreshortened head of a turbaned, bearded, middle-aged man, inclined toward his right shoulder with eyes looking upward with a devout or pleading expression. Although I have not been able to connect this Oriental head with any of Rubens' early pictures, I see no reason to doubt it as his own work; the modulation of the forms by the use of lead white, as well as the strong emotional emphasis in the face point strongly in this direction. Assuming, then, that the study of the Oriental was painted by

Rubens himself, the head painted over it most likely is also his work. A copyist would hardly have taken a panel on which Rubens had begun a sketch to cover it up with a copy, but we know that Rubens himself more than once used a panel with an earlier work on it to sketch or paint something else. Even the practice of turning the panel 180 degrees before painting the second sketch is encountered elsewhere in his work, for instance, in the Chicago Art Institute sketch of *Samson and Delilah*, on which Rubens had first sketched an *Adoration of the Magi* (unfinished), before painting—upside-down in relation to the earlier work—the composition now visible on the surface.

Color plate VIII, page 80.

c. 1614/16

Oil on oak panel, 44.5 × 29.4 cm (17½ × 11 9/16 in.)

Conservation: The panel is unbeveled and uncradled with a slight convex warp. There is a layer of brown paint on the reverse. The paint layer and chalk ground reach the edges of the panel, which does not appear to be reduced in size. The thinly applied paint layer is in excellent condition. There are minor losses along the bottom edge and two other small losses in the background. The x-ray photograph reveals a second portrait underneath, positioned upside-down in relation to the later portrait. It is the head of an old man wearing a turban, his eyes upturned. The pentimento visible in the knight's armor coincides with the turban of the underlying figure. Under infrared illumination, the wide, diagonal brushstrokes of the ground application are evident. The painting was cleaned and inpainted in 1978 by Barbara Heller (CSL). There are no records of previous conservation treatment.

Provenance: Sir Alexander Korda, London. Julius H. Weitzner (dealer), London. Acquired in 1979.

References: Müller Hofstede 1967: 64, fig. 35; 70; 93, n. 152.

Gift of Julius H. Weitzner (79.15)

Saint Ives of Tréguier

The historical Saint Ives or Ivo (1253-1303) studied law in Paris and Orléans and after 1280 was active as an ecclesiastical judge in Rennes and Tréguier. From 1296 on, he was parish priest at Lahonec (Louannec), where he died. (As a resident of Brittany, collector Hippolyte Gonvello may have been interested in Rubens' picture precisely because the saint's entire adult life and activity were confined to this area.) Saint Ives was known for his honesty, his care of the poor, and especially for his interest in the education of orphans. He is the hero of an amusing bit of doggerel: "Sanctus Ivo erat Brito, Advocatus et non latro, Res miranda populo" ("Saint Ives was a Breton, a lawyer, and not a robber, a matter of wonder for all people"). Though they may not always have taken him as their model, lawyers in later centuries turned to him as their patron saint (*The Catholic Encyclopedia* VIII, 1910: 256, and *Enciclopedia Cattolica* VII, 1951: col. 536).

The role of Saint Ives as the legal protector of the poor was illustrated by other Flemish artists of the late 16th and 17th centuries (Knipping 1939-40, I: 223). There are pictures of the subject by Hendrik de Clercq (1590; Musées Royaux des Beaux-Arts, Brussels; no. 102) and Gerard Seghers, but above all by Jacob Jordaens (Puyvelde 1953: 195, lists no less than ten examples of this subject by Jordaens).

The Detroit canvas appears to be, however, the only work by Rubens dealing with the subject. The saint is shown, dressed in the magnificent red robe of a Doctor of Law, as he receives a petition from a poor widow with two small children. Bowing before the saint, she looks toward him pleadingly but also with hope; he, in turn, rests his left hand on a law book to stress the means to which he will resort in her case. At his feet lie a crozier and a miter, symbols of the high ecclesiastical office that he spurned.

Stylistically, the Detroit canvas belongs to the period between 1615 and 1620, when Rubens provided his figures with spacious architectural settings and solid, sculptural bodies. For the head of the young widow, he used a study he had made for the head of the Virgin in the *Descent from the Cross* in Antwerp Cathedral, painted in 1611-12 (Held 1964: 49); the subtler treatment of her features in the Detroit painting, together with

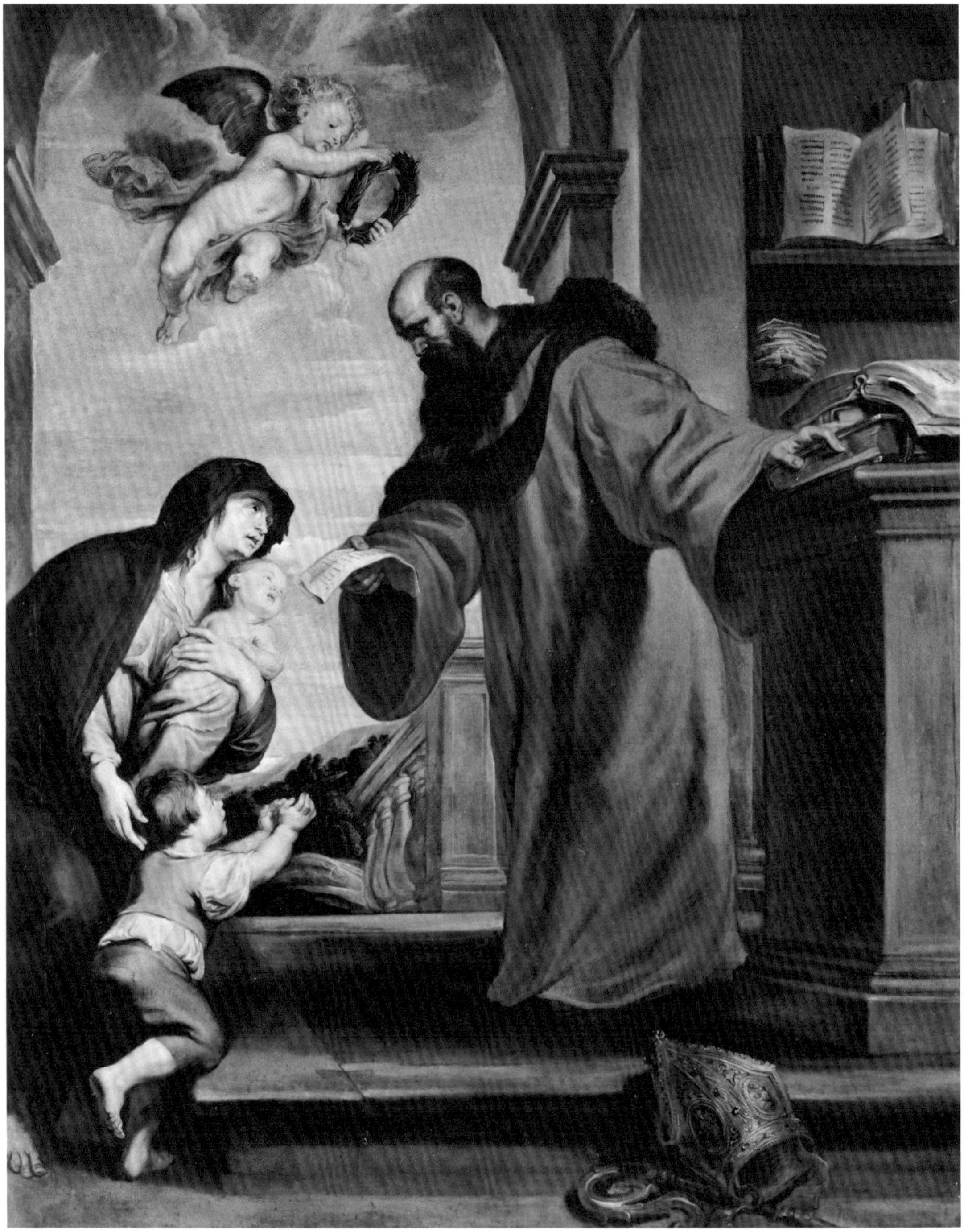

Rubens, *Saint Ives of Tréguier*.

other coloristic and formal differences, suggests a slightly later date, shortly after the middle of the second decade.

c. 1615/16
Oil on canvas, 287 × 221 cm (113 × 87 in.)
Conservation: The original canvas has been glue-lined. In many places the tacking margins are still intact, indicating that the painting has not been cut down. Two horizontal tears, approximately 25 centimeters from the top, starting at the edges of the canvas, were repaired during the lining. The paint layer is in very good condition. The only notably worn or abraded area is the sky. There is one large inpainted loss in the stomach and right thigh of the infant. Smaller losses are located in Saint Ives' beard and hair, the older child's cheek, and the shoulder of the cherub. Under ultraviolet illumination, the right and left edges of the painting, as well as an area around the lower left tip of Saint Ives' red cloak, show retouching. There are three notable pentimenti: the position of Saint Ives' left hand on the book was shifted; the lower right part of his cloak originally extended 6 centimeters to the right, coming closer to the lectern; and the widow's right hand was moved slightly to the left. The painting was last cleaned and inpainted in 1962 by William Suhr, at which time it was noted that "the painting had been restored more than once in the past." The only evidence as to where these restorations took place are remnants of a French newspaper used to repair the frayed tacking margin.

Provenance: The Jesuit church of Saint Michael, Louvain; the church having been secularized in 1773, the picture was offered for sale in Brussels, May 12, 1777 (lot 1), but did not find a buyer; it was offered again on September 12, 1785, and bought by M. de Loose (dealer?), Brussels, for 430 francs. J. J. Bertels (dealer), Brussels. Exhibited London (King Street), 1787, no. 1. Offered for sale, Christie's, London, May 31, 1787, lot 75. Sale, Christie's, London, April 21, 1788, lot 222. Sale, Christie's, London, May 23, 1788, lot 85. Sale, Paris, February 3, 1789 (bought for 6,000 francs). M. Didot (dealer?), Paris. Sale, Paris, April 6, 1825 (withdrawn, after bid had reached 12,000 francs). Marquis Hippolyte de Gonvello, Château de Kerlévénan, Sarzeau (Morbihan, Brittany). Sold by Marquis Renaud de Gonvello (great-grandson of Hippolyte) sometime prior to 1960. Rosenberg and Stiebel (dealers), New York. Acquired in 1964.

Exhibitions: Detroit 1978: no. 3.

References: Held 1964: cover, 47-52. *Art News* 1964: 28-29. Detroit 1971: 98.

Founders Society Purchase, Eleanor Clay Ford Fund and the Estate of Feodosy Kogut (64.459)

The Meeting of David and Abigail

The story of the meeting of David and Abigail is related in I Samuel 25: 18-35. Abigail's husband, Nabal of Maon, had insolently refused to pay for the protection David had provided to Nabal's shepherds while they were on Carmel. Aware of David's anger and his impending attack, Abigail gathered large quantities of food (bread, wine, corn, raisins, and fig-cakes) and went to meet him. When she saw him approaching at the head of 400 armed men, she dismounted from her donkey, begged his forgiveness, and humbly offered him the gifts to be distributed among his men. Impressed by the woman's "good understanding" and "beautiful countenance," David blessed the Lord as well as Abigail's eloquence, thanking her for keeping his hand from shedding blood. Nabal, however, upon learning of the danger she had averted, suffered a stroke and died ten days later, thus opening the way for a happy ending: David sent messengers to Abigail, proposing marriage; she came to him, riding on a donkey (as she had done before) "with five damsels of hers that went after her."

In the Detroit painting the martial force of David and his soldiers is contrasted with the humble and completely defenseless group of young women and servants led by Abigail, who pleadingly kneels on the ground while pointing to the gifts she is offering. David, having dismounted from his white horse, now held by a page, bends down and is about to raise Abigail up, as her two beautiful maids watch the scene with obvious delight. They, in turn, seem to be the focus of attention for several of David's men, who thus are giving expression to the amorous attraction that has not yet visibly affected the two principals.

Although variously said to have been painted with the help of students and as recently as 1977 characterized as "largely a workshop product" (Vlieghe), the Detroit painting has all the hallmarks of an authentic work executed by the master himself. There is also some disagreement about its date; in the Detroit catalogues of 1930 and 1944, and in Valentiner's list of Rubens' paintings in

America (1946), it was dated around 1618, a date first proposed by Rooses (1886-92, I: 148); a later date, 1625/30, was suggested by the present author (Goris and Held 1947: 32), who added that "the landscape, indeed, points forward to the 1630s." The date of 1625/30 was taken over by D'Hulst and Monballieu in the catalogue of the Antwerp exhibition of 1977. In 1964, however, Burchard was quoted as placing the Detroit picture in the 1630s, a view shared by Jaffé (1972).

The problem of the date is complicated by the existence of another version of the theme (oil on canvas, 98.4 × 228.6 cm) now in the J. Paul Getty Museum in Malibu (Malibu 1975: 110; see also Jaffé 1972: 863 ff.). A fairly elaborate modello for the Getty work is in the collection of Mrs. Rudolf J. Heinemann, New York (Held 1980: no. 315, pl. 313). The Heinemann sketch is said to have come from the Wieszbicki Collection in Warsaw. According to the 1930 Detroit catalogue, "an original sketch, or the replica of an original, containing a few more figures" was then in a private collection in Lübeck, and that sketch is said to have formed the basis for the engraving by Adriaen Lommelin. In the Detroit catalogue of 1944 the same sketch—there referred to as "formerly in Lübeck"—is called without qualification an "original," while the Heinemann sketch, listed as "on the New York market," is mentioned without any further comment. The present whereabouts of the Lübeck sketch are unknown to me.

The differences between the Heinemann modello and the Getty canvas are relatively minor (the latter lacks the figure of an old woman that is seen in the sketch, but x-ray evidence shows that she, too, was originally included in the larger version; it also has one additional figure of a servant at the left). On the other hand, the Detroit canvas is markedly different from the Heinemann and Getty versions in that the action concentrates much more on the two central figures; the right half, particularly, has a reduced number of soldiers and a less elaborate arrangement of horses, and Abigail is depicted as more matronly, with a dark veil draped over her head rather than a gauzy white one as in the two other works.

There are also stylistic differences between the Detroit canvas and the Heinemann and Getty versions. The latter are not only more loosely composed but also more lightly painted; in comparison with the solid modeling of all the forms in the Detroit picture, even the larger Getty version appears to have been more sketchily done. The woods are denser in the Detroit canvas, and the foliage richer than in the other two works. How should these differences be evaluated? Which came first, the Detroit picture or the other two? Assuming, as I do, that both versions were essentially planned by Rubens himself, we must ponder the problem of whether the Heinemann and Getty compositions are enlarged versions of the Detroit one, or whether the latter is a condensed and reduced version of the two others.

It is of some note that the only more or less contemporary engraving of the subject, by Lommelin, is of the extended version (Voorhelm Schneevoogt 1873: 7, no. 49; Van den Wijngaert 1940: 70, no. 400; the engraving, based on the Heinemann sketch, is reproduced by Max Rooses [1886-92, I: pl. 34]). This could mean that the larger versions were considered to be the more recent ones, but as we know little about the reasons why some compositions were engraved and others not, it would be risky indeed to draw firm conclusions from such a fact.

There is one observation that could be used as an argument in favor of the priority of the Heinemann and Getty versions: in both of them a piece of the military cloak draped over David's shoulders extends downward, appearing again below his left arm. This same piece of drapery was originally also painted in the Detroit canvas but can now be noticed only as a pentimento, having been painted over by Rubens himself. One might argue that Rubens included it at first, following the lead of his "earlier" versions, but then decided to do without; it certainly is easier to account for this detail in this chronological sequence than in a reversed one. And yet there are, I feel, more weighty arguments supporting the reverse order. The whole tendency of Rubens' development in the later years of his activity was towards a looser, more spacious treatment of his designs. A transformation of a broadly extended action into one more tightly compressed runs counter to the general trend of his art in these years. Moreover, the Heinemann and Getty versions look in some respects like a deliberate improvement or rational clarification of the narrative as depicted in the Detroit canvas. For example, one horseman at the right of the Detroit picture is without a visible mount; in fact, there seems to be no space for one. This has been clarified in the other versions. Also, in the Detroit picture David is without a helmet, which is surely appropriate to the moment when he assuages the fears of the woman kneeling before him; still, as a warrior he must have had one. This was duly acknowledged in the Heinemann and Getty versions where Rubens introduced a second page who holds David's helmet. Even the relationship of David to Abigail in the Heinemann and Getty versions seems to be an improvement over the one in the Detroit picture: being slightly farther apart and thus inclining more toward one another, they convey more convincingly the impression—most meaningful in the light of later developments—that they are mutually attracted and drawn to each other. In the Detroit canvas David seems to loom too closely above the somewhat complacent woman.

The conclusion, hence, favors the priority of the Detroit picture; yet that still leaves the task of assigning actual dates to all three paintings. There should be little doubt that the Heinemann and Getty versions belong to the 1630s, although most likely to the very beginning of the decade. Thus, the Detroit canvas would have to be placed before 1630, in fact, before August 1628, when Rubens left for Madrid and—except for a few days in May 1629—did not return to his studio until the end of March 1630. At the present state of our knowledge, the relatively broad date "1625/28" for the Detroit canvas seems to be the best we can propose.

The various copies mentioned in the literature are all, as far as can be determined, based on the extended (Heinemann and Getty) version rather than the Detroit painting.

In his article in *Art in America* (1922) Valentiner also reproduced (fig. 2) a drawing of two young women in the Albertina, Vienna, suggesting that it was a study for the Detroit picture. That drawing, however, was made in connection with the painting, *Queen Tomyris with the Head of Cyrus*, now in the Museum of Fine Arts, Boston (Vienna 1977: 68, no. 29).

Frontispiece.

c. 1625/28

Oil on canvas, 178.5 × 249 cm (70¼ × 98 in.)

Conservation: The canvas has a wax-resin lining. Traces of the original tacking margin remain on the bottom and two sides, indicating that the original width and the lower dimension of the painting have been maintained. X-rays reveal that a canvas strip along the top, seamed at 26 centimeters from the upper edge, is a later addition. This added section has a grainy, bole-colored ground with a more finely woven canvas than the rest of the painting, which has a brownish gray ground. It is not certain when this strip was added. However, x-ray photographs reveal cusping of the threads in the main canvas just below the seam, which indicates that it was stretched separately from the added strip. The degree of cusping suggests that the main canvas was cut down along the top prior to the addition of the strip. The paint layer of the main canvas is in excellent condition. The added top sixth of the painting is dark and somewhat purplish in hue, due to the bole-colored ground. The most notable losses occur in the central tree trunk in the left middleground, just below the gray horse's mane, and just in front of David's left foot. The remaining losses are minor and scattered, mostly in the foreground. One pentimento can be noted: David's red cape originally fell over his right arm almost to his knee. In 1955 William Suhr removed an older glue-lining and relined the painting with wax-resin. It was surface-cleaned and retouched. The painting was cleaned and inpainted by Barbara Heller (CSL) in 1977.

Provenance: Duke of Richelieu. By gift to Roger de Piles. Jacques Meijers sale, Willis, Rotterdam, September 9, 1722 (690 guilders). Duke of Grammont sale, Remy, Paris, January 16, 1775. Paul, Lord Methuen, Corsham House. Methuen sale, London, May 16, 1840. M. E. Secrétan sale, Paris, July 1-4, 1889, lot 158 (112,000 francs). James E. Scripps, Detroit. Acquired in 1889.

Exhibitions: Detroit 1889: 29-32, no. 29. Detroit 1936: no. 6. Antwerp 1977: 182-183, no. 77. Detroit 1978: no. 6.

References: De Piles 1715 (the reference to the Detroit picture is found in a biography—unsigned—of De Piles added to the 1715 edition; it reads: "M. le Duc de Richelieu . . . lui fit présent d'un fameux tableau de Rubens, que représente David & Abigail: & qui a été depuis à M. le

Duc de Grammont"). Smith 1829-42, II (1830): 170, no. 592. Rooses 1886-92, I (1886): 147, no. 120. Bryant 1915: 228-231. Valentiner 1922: 203-207; reprinted in part in Valentiner 1922a: 10-11. Detroit 1930: no. 194. Scheyer 1937: 42-44, fig. 17. Valentiner 1946: 160, no. 72. Goris and Held 1947: 32, no. 39, pl. 46. Jaffé 1953: 34, 64. Goldstein 1967: 266-267. Goldstein 1972: 863-865. Vlieghe 1977: 642-643. Held 1980, I: 436, under no. 315.

Gift of James E. Scripps (1889.63)

Briseis Given Back to Achilles

In the first line of the *Iliad*, Homer states that the main theme of his work is the wrath of Achilles. The Greek expedition to subdue Troy and to avenge the abduction of Helen was threatened with defeat when Achilles angrily withdrew from combat and retired to his tent; the Greek leaders knew that without their staunchest warrior, they would never conquer Troy.

When the town of Lyrnessus was taken by the Greeks, Briseis, a beautiful woman of that city whose husband had been killed in combat, had fallen to the share of Achilles and had become his favorite slave. Agamemnon, the leader of the expedition (and husband of Helen) took Briseis away from Achilles, who nearly took Agamemnon's life before he was restrained by Pallas Athena. Achilles refused henceforth to take part in the war, and only changed his mind when his best friend, Patroclus, was killed by Hector, the most valiant of the Trojans. He was further assuaged when Briseis was returned to him, accompanied by a gift of seven women, seven tripods, twenty cauldrons, and twelve horses; furthermore, Agamemnon swore that he had never touched Briseis.

Accompanied by old Nestor and by Ulysses, Briseis stands in the center of the Detroit panel; with arms outstretched, Achilles rushes toward her from the right. In back of him we get a glimpse of Achilles' tent where Patroclus, dead on a bier, is bewailed by two women. A number of precious vessels are being placed before Achilles by two servants; four women and three horses (one led by a groom) complete the composition at the left. The action is framed by decorative architectural motifs, chief among them herms of Hermes (carrying the caduceus, symbol of peace) at the left and Peace (with the emblem of concord, two joined hands in a wreath) at the right. Overhead, four putti are busy draping garlands; two horns of plenty filled with fruits lie below, on either side of a palm branch and a caduceus tied together in the center.

The source for this painting was mainly the long passage of the *Iliad* relating the event (XIX, 243-281). Yet Rubens made use of other texts as well: the fact that Achilles appears with shorter hair than in the preceding picture (the Detroit panel being part of a cycle that will be discussed presently) may indicate that he remembered a passage in the *Images* of the Younger Philostratus (III.7) according to which Achilles cut his hair after Patroclus had been killed. In Homer's account Achilles cut his hair only at the funeral pyre of his friend.

The Detroit panel is part of a series of eight sketches made for a group of tapestries narrating the story of Achilles. The other seven are all in the Museum Boymans-Van Beuningen, Rotterdam (for the history of the cycle, see Haverkamp Begemann 1975: 15-19; and Held 1980, I: 169-173). A larger version, painted mostly by assistants to serve as the final modello for the tapestry, is in the Prado (Madrid 1975, I: 309-310, no. 2566; Haverkamp Begemann 1975: 128-129, no. 6b).

The finest set of tapestries based on Rubens' cycle of Achilles, possibly the first edition (*editio princeps*), was in the estate of King Louis-Philippe of France and was sold on January 28, 1852 (lot 17); four pieces of this set, among them the tapestry of the *Return of Briseis*, were bought shortly before 1954 by the house of Bragança for the Paço Ducal at Vila Viçosa, Portugal (Haverkamp Begemann 1975: 81); the Briseis tapestry measures 400 by 570 centimeters and is illustrated as figure 52 in Haverkamp Begemann's publication. Another version, its whereabouts unknown, is reproduced as figure 53. Both tapestries depict the scene, as is usual in tapestries, in reverse, so that the chief personages (Achilles, Ulysses, and Briseis) gesticulate more properly with their right hands, and the groom also holds the horse with his right. Rubens obviously counted on this reversal when he executed the Detroit sketch.

An etching of this composition was done by Franz Ertinger in 1679 (Voorhelm Schneevoogt 1873: 128, no. 15.6; Van den Wijngaert 1940: 44, no. 178, erroneously identified as "Achilles and Polyxena"). An engraving was made by Bernard Baron in 1724 (Voorhelm Schneevoogt 1873: 218, no. 16). Extant copies include a canvas in the Syracuse University Art Collection, School of Art (44.4 × 66.6 cm; gift of Mrs. C. Michael Paul, 1961). This painting came from the Adrian Hope sale, Christie's, London, June 30, 1894 (lot 97), and was sold as an illustration of the tragedy of Alcestis by Euripides; it was later in the collection of Jacob H. Schiff, New York, and while there was reproduced, as Rubens' original, in Oldenbourg's edition of the Rubens volume of the *Klassiker der Kunst* series (1921: 227). This work was sold in the Jacob H. Schiff sale, American Art Association—Anderson Galleries, New York, December 7-9, 1933 (lot 75); it was purchased by Scott and Fowles (dealers). Sold again—at Parke Bernet, New York, on April 15, 1953 (lot 63)—it was acquired by Mrs. C. Michael Paul (for bibliography on this copy see Haverkamp Begemann 1975: 126).

A further copy is at Raveningham Hall, Norfolk, in the collection of Sir Edmund Bacon, Bt., K. G. (paper on canvas, 47 × 69 cm). Finally, there is a drawing—present whereabouts unknown—in sanguine and black chalk (21.5 × 33 cm) by Antoine Watteau, formerly in the collection of Dr. A. Scharf, London (Parker and Mathey 1957: no. 319). For other copies, most of them no longer traceable, see Haverkamp Begemann 1975: 126-127.

Color plate IX, page 97.

c. 1630/31

Oil on oak panel, 44.3 × 66.7 cm ($17\frac{7}{16}$ × $26\frac{1}{4}$ in.)

Conservation: The two-membered panel (joined at 21.2 centimeters from the bottom edge) has been planed to a thickness of 4 millimeters and cradled. No bevels remain. Six-millimeter-wide moldings have been glued to all four edges. There are four small cracks in the right upper and lower corners, as well as an irregular horizontal crack through Achilles' right ankle and the feet of the tripod. The ground (white chalk) and paint layer reach the edges of the panel. The paint layer is in excellent condition. X-ray photographs show no significant losses. There is slight abrasion in the upper left sky and very minor loss along the join and cracks. Infrared examination shows the underpainting of this sketch to be even more free and spontaneous than the final product. The painting was cleaned and inpainted in 1953 by William Suhr. Also at that time, the vertical moldings were slit to allow the panel to "breathe," and the cracks were glued and filled.

Provenance: Daniel Fourment, Antwerp 1643 (?). Joan Baptista Anthoine, Antwerp, until 1691. Dr. Richard Mead, London. Mead sale, London, March 20-21, 1754 (lot 53). R. Fulke Greville, London. Fulke Greville sale, Christie's, London, November 18, 1794 (lot 49). Sir Joshua Reynolds, London. Reynolds sale, London, March 13-17, 1795 (lot 96). Private collection, Rome (?). George John Vernon, acquired 1829. The Vernon family, Sudbury Hall, near Derby. Vernon sale, Sotheby, London, June 14, 1922 (lot 63). Henry Reinhardt & Son, Inc., Galleries (dealer), New York. Sold 1926/27 to Mr. and Mrs. Edgar B. Whitcomb, Detroit. Acquired in 1953.

Exhibitions: London 1835: no. 95 (as *The Death of Ulysses*). Detroit 1926: no. 33. Detroit 1927: no. 54. Detroit 1936: no. 45. New York 1939: no. 330. Detroit 1941: 19, no. 50. New York 1942: no. 23. Los Angeles 1946: no. 33. Cambridge/New York 1956: no. 37, pl. 25. Detroit 1978: no. 4.

References: Smith 1829-42, II (1830): 252, no. 854. Hasselt 1840: 290, no. 646. Rooses 1886-92, III (1890): 43. Heil 1928: 50-51. Puyvelde 1940: 36, no. 7. Valentiner 1946: 164, no. 113. Goris and Held 1947: 36, no. 70; pl. 86. London 1950: 14. Haverkamp Begemann 1953: 77-78. Whitcomb 1954: 60-63. Held 1956: 123. Held 1958: 147. *BDIA* 1964: 54, 58. Gerson and Ter Kuile 1960: 93. Haverkamp Begemann 1975: 126-128. Held 1980: no. 124, pl. 128.

Bequest of Mr. and Mrs. Edgar B. Whitcomb (53.356)

Archduke Ferdinand, Cardinal-Infante of Spain, at the Battle of Nördlingen

The third son of Philip II of Spain and brother of the reigning monarch, Philip IV, the Cardinal-Infante Ferdinand arrived in the Netherlands in 1634 to take the place of his aunt, Isabella Clara Eugenia, as governor of the country, Isabella having died in 1633. He had traveled by ship to Genoa and then, at the head of an army, marched north, joining forces in southern Germany with his cousin, Ferdinand of Hungary, commander of an Austrian army. The joint armies of the two Catholic princes engaged a Protestant army under Duke Bernhard of Saxe-Weimar and Marshal Horn at Nördlingen and on September 5-6, 1634, gained a much-heralded victory. Rubens' modello obviously alludes to this event, depicting a battle of armored horsemen in the distance and a flying imperial eagle and a divine genius hurling a thunderbolt above. The poses of horse and rider are more formal than realistic and certainly are intended to allude to Titian's famous portrayal of Emperor Charles V at the Battle of Mühlberg (Museo del Prado, Madrid). Moreover, it is part of the decorum of princely portraits that the subject's dignity is not sullied by active engagement in combat.

The Detroit panel was probably painted after the prince made his triumphal entry into Antwerp on April 17, 1635. It formed the basis for a large state portrait, now in the Prado, Madrid (no. 1687; oil on canvas, 335 × 258 cm; Madrid 1975, I: 276-277). The large canvas remained in Rubens' house and is probably identical with the picture numbered 101 in the inventory of his estate: "Een portret van den Prins Cardinael Infant, op doek" (Denucé 1932: 61). Acquired from Rubens' widow by the Count-Duke of Olivares for 1, 200 florins, it was taken to Spain by the Marquis of Leganés; when in 1642 Olivares fell from power before taking possession of the picture, the marquis gave it to King Philip IV. From 1666 on it appeared in the inventories of the Alcázar in Madrid.

The phalanx of embattled equestrians in the background of the Detroit modello had been sketched before by Rubens in a beautiful small panel in the collection of the Princes of Liechtenstein, Vaduz (Held 1980, I: 364-365, no. 270; pl. 263). Whatever project it was that Rubens had had in mind when he prepared that sketch (probably a tapestry), nothing apparently came of it; thus, he was free to use the same motif again for his portrait of the Cardinal-Infante.

From the x-ray photograph it can be seen that Rubens first placed the prince about 5 centimeters to the left; the earlier version of the head can be clearly made out. In this version, now completely covered (at least to the naked eye) by an opaque cloud formation, the prince looked straight out of the picture; it is almost to be regretted that this lively first rendering had to make way for a much blander conception of the young prince's countenance.

The painting was engraved by Paul Pontius; an example of the engraving is also in the Art Institute (47.187).

c. 1635

Oil on oak-veneered masonite panel, 122.2 × 93 cm ($48\frac{1}{8} \times 36\frac{5}{8}$ in.)

Conservation: Before its transfer to oak-veneered masonite, the panel consisted of five members (joined at 17.3, 36.9, 57, and 74.5 centimeters from the left edge). It also had a crack at 64 centimeters from the lower left edge. The wood was removed and the original gesso and paint layer transferred and cradled. There is a white-chalk ground with the striated gray imprimatura typical of Rubens. The paint layer is in good condition, even though in many areas the paint was thinly applied and the imprimatura is visible. Some abrasion or tiny flakings (possibly developing during the transfer) are apparent, especially in the foreground browns. Areas of inpainted loss include the horse—his right foreknee, right eye, and the outline of his head; an area on the genius' shoulder, and on the lower edge of its garment; and the joins and cracks mentioned above (particularly the join running through the archduke's left eye). That the painting was a working sketch can be seen from the many major pentimenti visible in the x-ray photographs and even to the unaided eye. These include changes in the position of the horse's head and forelegs, in the archduke's head (which was first painted 5 centimeters to the left of its present position), armor, and left leg (moved 8 centimeters to the left). In 1948 the painting was transferred, due to the "cracks" and "disintegrating" state of the old panel, by William Suhr. In 1953 a small paint chip was restored by Suhr. The work was treated again in 1956 by him for cleavage between the ground and paint layer, and it was varnished and waxed by him in 1957.

Provenance: The Marquis of Bristol. Sir Audley Neeld, Grittleton House, Wiltshire. L. W. Neeld sale, Christie's, London, July 13, 1945, lot 84. Koetser Gallery (dealer), New York. Acquired in 1947.

Exhibitions: Los Angeles 1946: no. 38. New York 1951: no. 30. Cambridge/New York 1956: 41, no. 47. Cleveland 1963: no. 22. New York 1968-69: no. 48. Detroit 1978: no. 7.

References: Smith 1829-42, II (1830): 309, no. 1139. Rooses 1886-92, IV (1890): 157, under no. 930. Valentiner

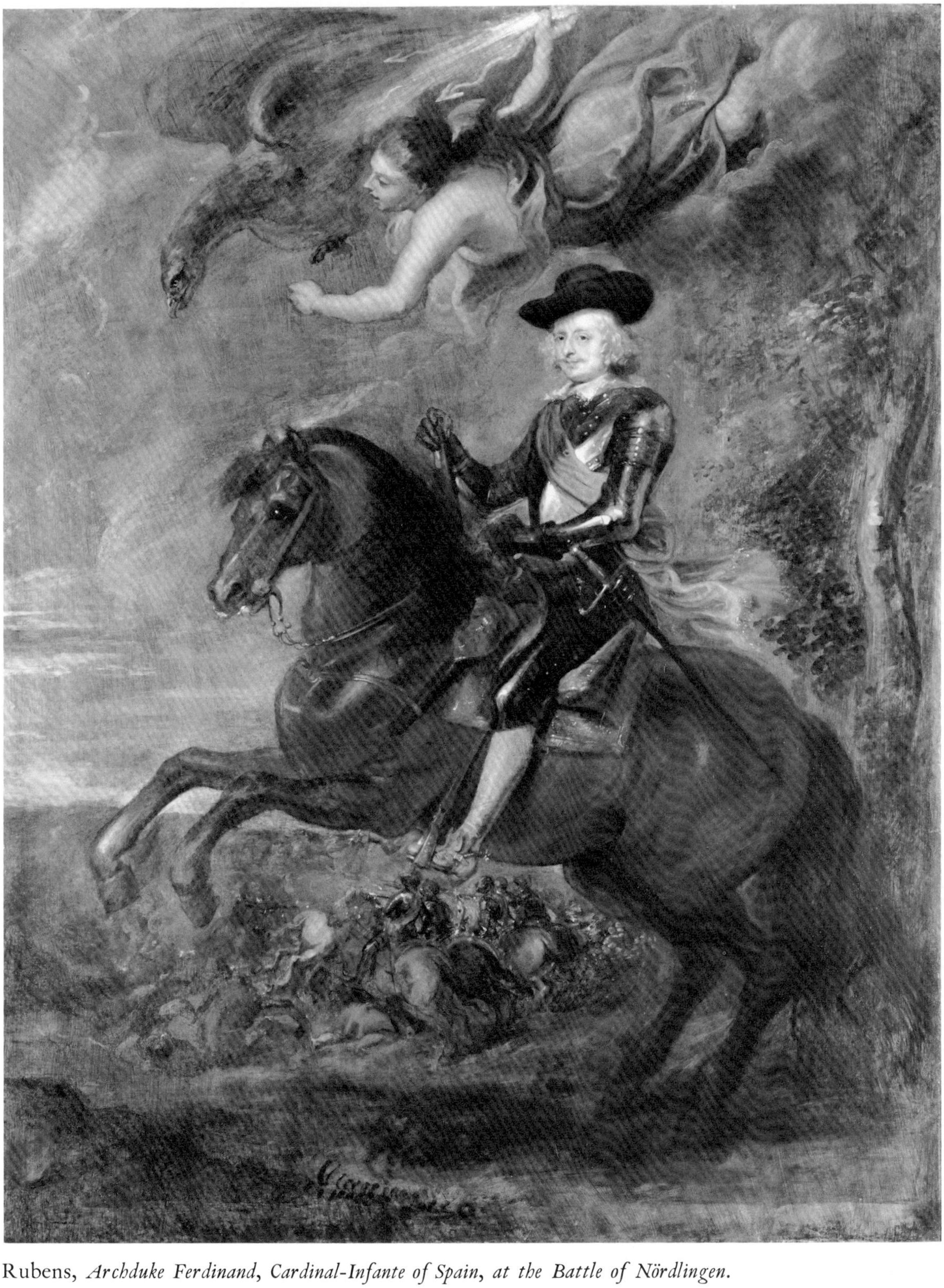

Rubens, *Archduke Ferdinand, Cardinal-Infante of Spain, at the Battle of Nördlingen.*

1946: 168, no. 136. Goris and Held 1947: 26, no. 4. Richardson 1947a: cover, 2-4. Richardson 1949: 135-138. Held 1951a: n. p. Held 1956: 123. Gerson and Ter Kuile 1960: 189, no. 140. *BDIA* 1964: 54, 57. Jaffé 1977: 115, n. 32. Held 1980: 395, no. 293; pl. 295.

Founders Society Purchase, Ralph Harman Booth Fund (47.58)

Studio of Rubens

Portrait of a Warrior Accompanied by Two Pages

Before approaching the problem of whether or not Rubens can be credited with the actual execution of this picture, I should like to emphasize that the work unquestionably represents an invention by the master. The differences of opinion that exist do not affect this aspect; no one has questioned (or is likely to) Rubens' responsibility for the overall design. Equally certain, I believe, is the placing of this invention in the artist's post-Italian period, with about 1615 agreed upon as the earliest date.

Although known to a great many people since it appeared in the late 1950s, until now the painting has received only one serious discussion, in the study by Müller Hofstede (1967). In his view, the knight dominating the composition is an "idealized portrait" (*Idealbildnis*) of Emperor Charles V, founder of the vast Hispano-Austrian monarchy. So certain was the author that he deemed it unnecessary to give any reason for this identification, presumably trusting what to him must have appeared to be a sufficient physiognomic similarity to other portraits of the emperor, several of which (originals or copies) he reproduced in his article. He offered only one historical observation to explain the creation of the painting, and this presupposes acceptance of the identification with Charles V as an established fact. It is known that either this very painting or possibly one much like it was in the collection of the Antwerp merchant and art patron Cornelis van der Geest (Held 1957: 53-84). The name of the house in which Van der Geest kept his collection was "De Keyser" ("The Emperor"), so named from an under-life-sized statue that stood in a niche above the Gothic portal. Müller Hofstede reasoned that this sculpture may have given Van der Geest the idea to have a portrait of Charles V in his collection.

Actually, the identification of the knight with Emperor Charles V is most unlikely for more than one reason. To begin with, the physiognomic argument is unconvincing. It is true that there are different iconographic traditions concerning the emperor's appearance, but none of them agrees with the robust and outgoing personality portrayed in the Detroit panel and in the small sketch of the head alone that preceded it (79.15; see pages 84-85 above). This subject's hair is curlier, his beard more abundant, his glance more piercing than that of any of the authentic portraits (especially those by Titian and also Lucas Vorsterman's engraving based on a design by Rubens [see Müller Hofstede 1967: fig. 16]). One famous distinguishing feature of Charles V is completely absent here: the prominent lower lip (the so-called "Habsburg" lip) always visible in other portraits of the emperor. Moreover, the knight is dressed in a type of armor never worn by Charles V. In none of his portraits in armor do we find a cuirass, the breastplate of which bulges forward in a smooth, unadorned shape; rather, it is always divided by vertical ribs and descends to a point. The only piece of the knight's armor that could have been derived from portraits of the emperor is the circular disk near his right shoulder, hardly sufficient to identify the wearer as Charles V. Most conclusive, however, is an observation which Müller Hofstede failed to make. As a knight of the Golden Fleece, Charles V was obliged to wear, and indeed always did wear, the chain of that order, with the fleece suspended from it. There is no portrait of the emperor, even when in armor, in which he does not display the insignia of the order. This chain would have been shown particularly in an idealized portrait; its absence in the Detroit painting is alone sufficient to subvert Müller Hofstede's thesis on the subject's identity. As a minor point, it might be added that the cuirass, which is so unlike any ever worn by Charles V, does resemble that of Francesco Maria della Rovere, Duke of Urbino, as depicted in Titian's portrait in the Uffizi (Wethey 1971: no. 89, pl. 67).

Without specifically mentioning the armor, the present author pointed out in the study of Van der Geest's collection (Held 1957) that a connection does exist between that picture by Titian and Rubens' composition, which I then knew only from the reproduction in Willem van Haecht's painting of Van der Geest's collection, a picture now in the Rubenshuis, Antwerp. It is most improbable that Rubens should have depicted Charles V (idealized or not) in a pose and a piece of armor that immediately bring to mind the portrait Titian had painted of the Duke of Urbino.

Nor does it seem very likely that a painting of Charles V should have been painted during the period to which Rubens' image belongs, that is, around 1615. As far as we can tell, the well-known revival of interest in the career of Charles V began in the 1620s and seems to have coincided with the early reign of Philip IV of Spain. Rubens himself took part in the renewed glorification of Charles V as a warrior and founder of a great empire, by painting him as the leader of a victorious army in an unfinished composition (possibly only a sketch for a larger work) in Berlin (Held 1980: no. 288), a painting that probably belongs to the second half of the 1630s.

Müller Hofstede explained the interaction of the three figures in the Detroit composition as the preparation of the warrior, assisted by two pages, for combat (his title for the picture was *Karl V als Feldherr, sich zum Kampf rüstend*). This may indeed be correct in view of the fact that, in the period to which the composition belongs, Rubens tended to exalt warlike virtues, although the hero is usually shown, after having overcome hostile forces, being crowned by the goddess of victory (Oldenbourg 1921: 56-57). One could, of course, read the action in a different way: rather than girding himself for battle, the warrior—apparently victorious—might be permitting his pages to remove his armor; the older one appears to be taking off the helmet while looking with admiration and awe at the hero; and the younger one might just as well be unbuckling the leather strap holding a dagger as fastening it. If this is so, the work would be related to one of the most pervasive themes in Rubens' art, the recognition of the heroism required by war but also of the greater glory gained by laying aside the tools of combat for the sake of peace ("swords into plowshares").

The attribution of the panel to Rubens was accepted by Müller Hofstede without question, although he knew that an almost identical version was at Althorp, in the collection of Earl Spencer. In fact, he referred to the Althorp version as "eine zweite eigenhändige Version" ("a second [equally] authentic version"), but he made no apparent effort to compare the two works. More recently, the Detroit picture was accepted as Rubens' work by Michael Jaffé (in a letter of December 6, 1978, to Frederick J. Cummings, Director, Detroit Institute of Arts; museum files); Jaffé declared the Althorp panel to be inferior in quality. The attribution of the Detroit panel to Rubens is also strongly supported by Cummings.

The Althorp panel (122.5 × 98.2 cm) was mentioned, albeit briefly, in the present author's article on Cornelis van der Geest (Held 1957). It was listed as "School of Rubens" in an inventory of 1802, and again as "School of Rubens" by Thomas Frognall Dibdin in his *Bibliotheca Spenceriana* (1814-15: 275). In the 1951 catalogue of the collections at Althorp it appeared as "School of Pourbus," but was again restored to Rubens ("possibly a very early work") by Garlick (1974-76: 74, no. 572; pl. 7; the Detroit picture is not mentioned in Garlick's volume). Nor was the attribution to Rubens of the Althorp panel questioned by J. Douglas Stewart in his rather critical review of Garlick's book (1978: 239). Stewart, incidentally, strongly rejected the identification of the knight as Emperor Charles V: "the title is entirely fanciful. There is no sign of any 'allegory,' and the handsome bearded warrior bears no resemblance whatever to Charles V—whose face is surely one of the most recognizable in European history." Stewart also points out that the composition must have been known in England by the middle of the 17th century as it was adopted by Robert Walker for several of his portraits of Oliver Cromwell. Stewart's review was in turn attacked by Cecil Gould (1978: 470), but he, too, had no doubt that the Althorp picture was an original by Rubens: "'Possibly a very early Rubens' seems a reasonable observation on this particular picture." Lord Spencer's panel was also exhibited at Agnew's in 1947 (no. 41) as by Rubens.

Examination of the Althorp picture is made difficult by the height at which it is hung on the wall. In November 1978 a laboratory examination of both paintings was made at the Courtauld Institute, London. Photographs of details as well as x-ray photographs were taken; a report signed by S. Rees Jones of the Courtauld was submitted to the Art Institute. The report largely avoided the controversial issue of attribution, being content to record that, from a technical point of view, nothing was observed in either painting that was inconsistent with Rubens' autograph works. It did, however, introduce one point that has taken on undue importance in deciding which of the two versions was painted first (the implication being that the one executed first is more likely than the second to be the original). In the Detroit panel a curl of hair falls across the cheek of the youth holding the shining helmet. The x-ray photograph of the Althorp panel indicates that the painter of that picture had at first included a similar strand of hair but had painted it out. From this, Jones concluded that the painter of the Althorp version had copied the Detroit one (including the curl) and then for unknown reasons made the change.

While the presence of the curl in the Detroit picture is of some interest for its history as a motif in Rubens' work, it cannot be used as an argument for the originality of the work. Rather than having been invented for this composition, the full-faced youth gazing upward, his lips lightly parted and his eyes wide open, is a physiognomic *pathos formula* (in Warburg's sense) of which Rubens seems to have been particularly fond; he used it often and in very different contexts. It may have been the strong sense of physical motion resulting in a view from below, combined with an intensely emotional expression on a handsome face, that appealed to the artist.

The upturned head is first encountered in the *Crowning with Thorns* (also known as the *Mocking of Christ*) that Rubens painted in 1601/02 for the church of Santa Maria in Gerusalemme, Rome (now in the Hôpital de Petit-Paris, Grasse; Cologne 1977: 210). Essentially similar to all later renderings of the head, it differs in that the youth wears a feather beret, added almost certainly under the influence of Caravaggio's paintings in the Capella Contarelli of San Luigi dei Francesi (the lock in front of the ear, in fact, is a characteristic feature of all of Caravaggio's youths).

A few years later, in 1604/05, Rubens introduced the same head into the large canvas of the *Transfiguration*, painted for the Jesuit church at Mantua and now in the Musée des Beaux-Arts, Nancy (Jaffé 1977: pl. 247). This painting demonstrates Rubens' ability to adjust a motif to varied contexts and emotional situations; the head, rendered in reverse and provided with a still more luxuriant mass of curly hair, conveys a very different emotion, since the youth's arms are raised, hands joined, in a traditional pose of lamentation or grief as he looks across the foreground to the right where a raving boy is held by his distraught parents.

The youth's head occurs next in the *Adoration of the Magi*, painted by Rubens in 1609/10 for the *Statenkamer* of the Antwerp town hall. A few years later, this composition was taken to Spain, where it ended up in the royal collections (it is now in the Prado). It was enlarged and repainted by Rubens himself when he visited Madrid in 1628/29. Its original appearance has been preserved, however, in an old copy, now in the collection of Christopher Norris at Polesden Lacey (Norris 1963: 129-136). The head appears here again in reverse, as that of one of the pages accompanying the Magi.

Rubens made use of the same head for the figure of Saint Matthew in his Apostle series in Madrid (Vlieghe 1972: no. 14, pl. 46), and again for an angel in the right section of two organ wings with music-making angels in the collection of the Princes of Liechtenstein, Vaduz (Oldenbourg 1921: 66). It

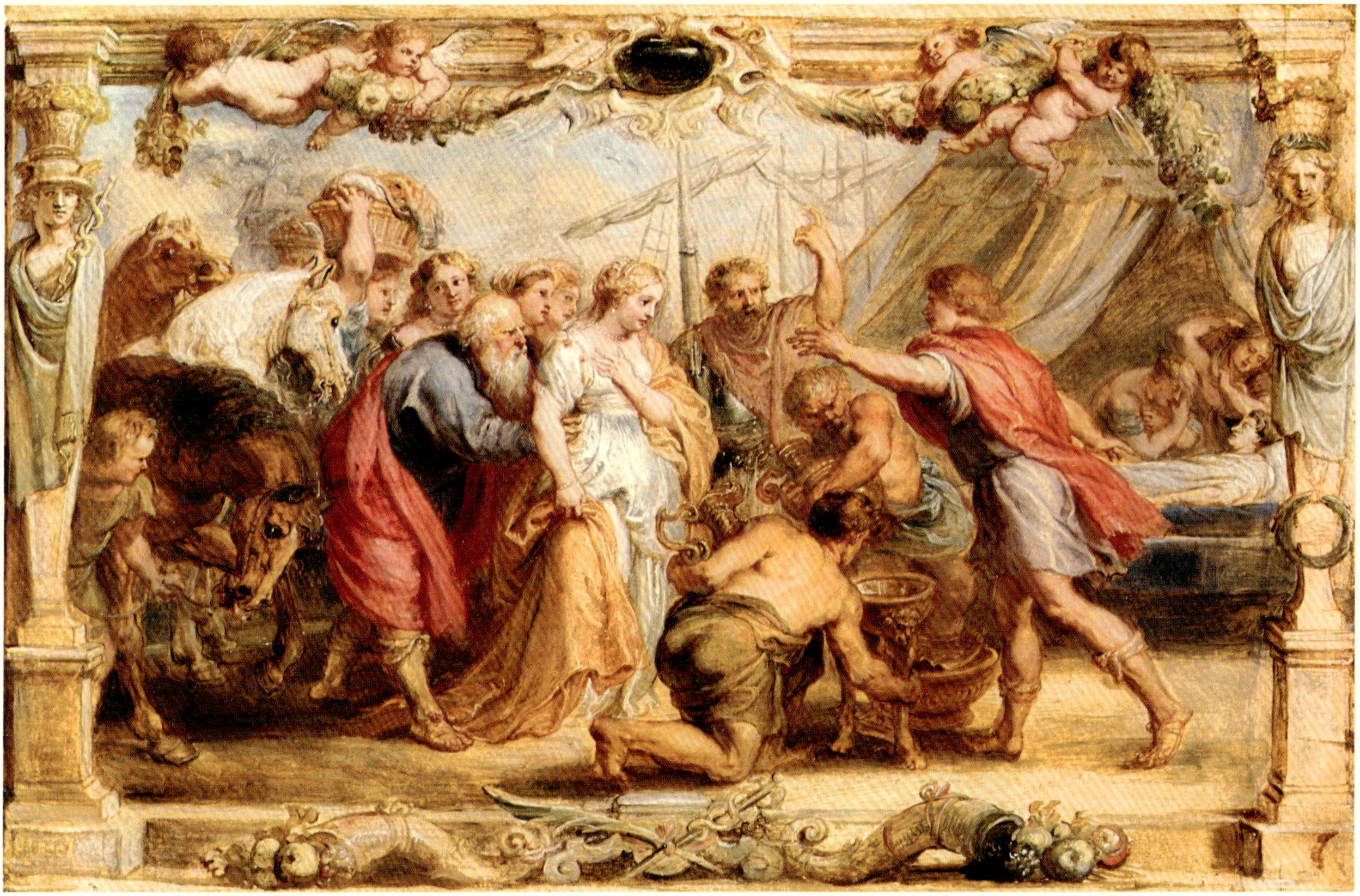

PLATE IX. Rubens, *Briseis Given Back to Achilles*.

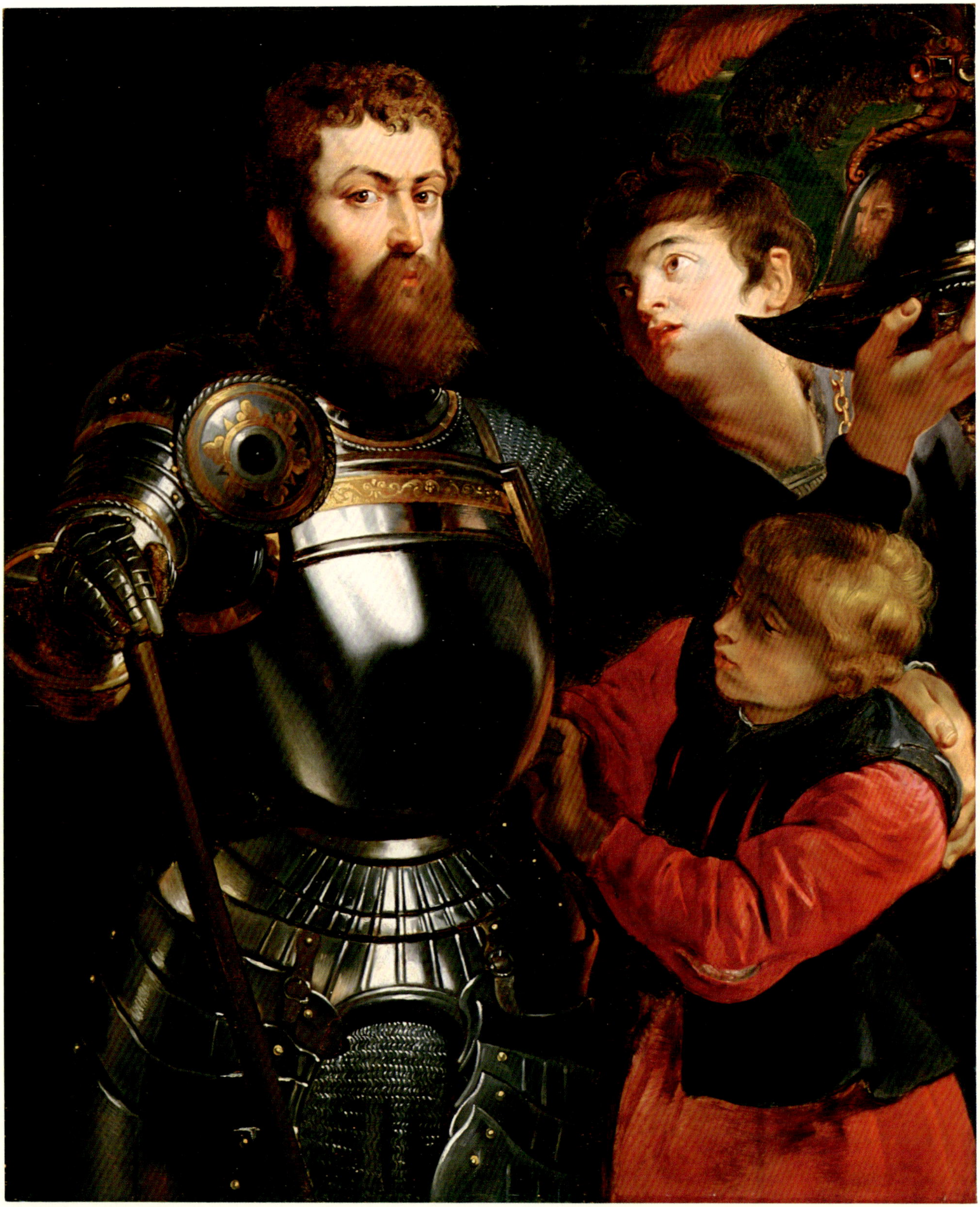

PLATE X. Studio of Rubens, *Portrait of a Warrior Accompanied by Two Pages.*

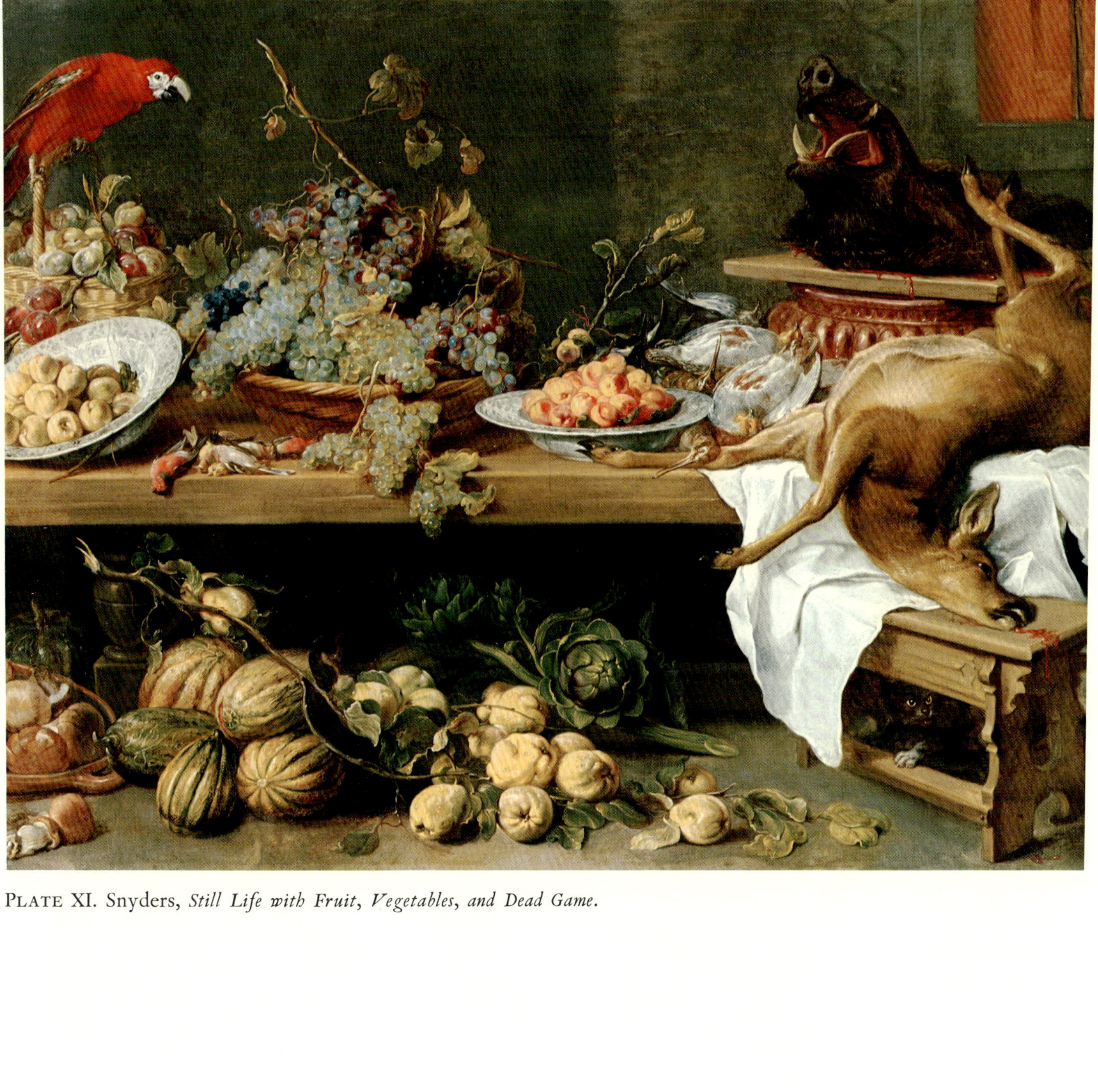

PLATE XI. Snyders, *Still Life with Fruit, Vegetables, and Dead Game.*

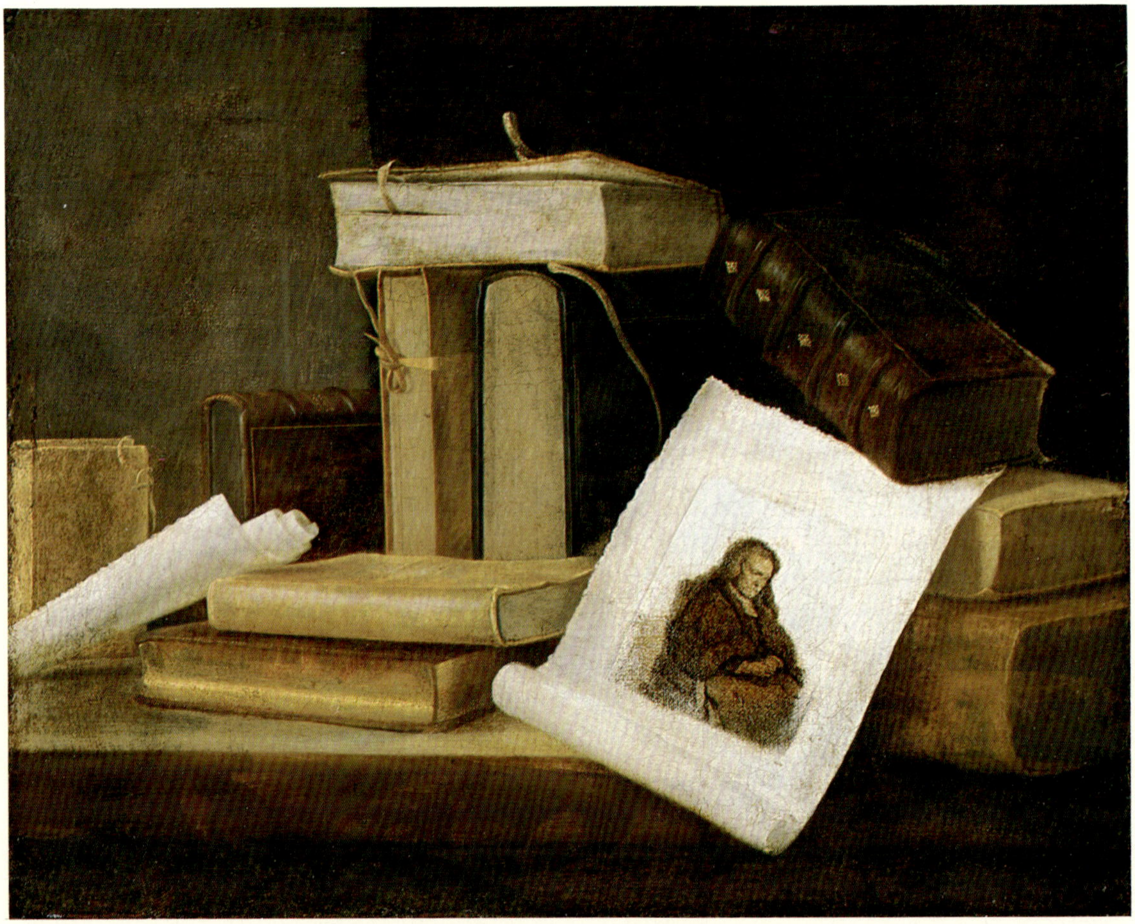

PLATE XII. Stosskopf, *Still Life of Books and a Rembrandt Etching.*

appears also in the *Judgment of Solomon* in the Prado, in the youthful attendant at Solomon's right, who looks wide-eyed at the naked hireling about to divide the surviving child in half (Madrid 1975: 340-341, no. 1543, pl. 215). This picture was published by Glück as an original by Rubens dating to about 1608/10 (Glück 1932: 271-273); this attribution was accepted by J. Müller Hofstede (1968: 249, n. 42), with the difference that he dated the picture to about 1612/14. Díaz Padrón (Madrid 1975), however, demoted it again to "School of Rubens," although it can hardly be doubted that Rubens was responsible for its design and most likely also for its execution.

The frequent appearance of this head with only minor variations in Rubens' early oeuvre (it disappears after about 1615) leads to the conclusion (with which all scholars seem to agree) that there must have been available in Rubens' studio a drawing or an oil study that served as the model for all subsequent renderings of this strikingly expressive face. This study must have been executed by Rubens in the very beginning of his Roman stay, no later than 1601. In fact, an oil sketch on paper mounted on wood (36.8 × 24.6 cm) in the collection of Mr. and Mrs. Robert Manning (Forest Hills, New York) has been identified as this very study (Jaffé 1968: 180; and Jaffé 1977: 19, 60, 62). Müller Hofstede (1968: n. 42) accepted it as Rubens' work but connected it at first with his later paintings; in the catalogue of the Cologne exhibition (1968: no. 34), however, he followed Jaffé in placing it early—around 1601/02. Yet other scholars have been more hesitant to accept the Manning sketch as Rubens' own: it was questioned by David Freedberg (1978: 90, n. 19) and all but rejected by Vlieghe (1978: 471-473). The present author, too, has difficulties seeing Rubens' hand in the work. Even less can I follow Müller Hofstede in his attribution to Rubens of still another rendering of this head, in reverse, but otherwise not any different, which is (or was) in the Grolman Collection, Düsseldorf (also painted on paper, 31 × 27 cm; see Müller Hofstede 1968: 229-231, fig. 161); this sketch is known to me only from the reproduction, which does not inspire confidence. In Müller Hofstede's view, it was painted as a study for the first state of the *Adoration of the Magi* of 1609/10.

For the purpose of this discussion, Jaffé's suggestion that the model for the youth was Rubens' pupil and companion Deodat del Monte (or Van der Mont)—who was about 20 years of age when Rubens used the head for the first time—is immaterial. What should be clear is that in the matter of which of the two paintings under discussion —the Detroit and Althorp versions—came first, the presence or absence of a lock of hair in this head is irrelevant. The curl on the cheek of the page was already present in the first appearance of the head in Rubens' work, the painting in Grasse. Assuming that a study head of this type was available in Rubens' shop, the lock of hair could be used or left out at will; its inclusion could even indicate a lower degree of originality.

Nevertheless, the lock of hair does have a certain significance in establishing the provenance of the Detroit panel, since the version in Van der Geest's collection, as copied by Willem van Haecht in his 1628 "portrait" of Van der Geest's gallery, clearly also had "the lock." Thus, it is probable that the Detroit panel is the one in the house of the Antwerp patron of the arts. A similar version was in the collection of the Duke of Orléans; a drawn copy of that picture, in the Bibliothèque Doucet, Paris, also shows the page with the lock. Of the two extant pictures, only the Detroit panel agrees with the drawing in Paris. There is no record of the fate of Van der Geest's collection; that of the Duke of Orléans was dispersed, mainly in England. The evidence does seem to indicate that the Detroit picture was in both the Van der Geest and Orléans collections, although one can never exclude the possibility that there was still another version, now lost. All that is definitely known about the Detroit panel is that it came from a private collection near Bath, England.

It should be obvious that even a firm location of the Detroit panel in the Van der Geest and Orléans collections would not automatically assure its priority as Rubens' original and its superiority over the Althorp version. In the last analysis, it is the work of art itself that furnishes the decisive evidence about its historical classification. It is only a careful and unprejudiced examination of both paintings with the aim of finding out which of them is "the better"—in other words, more worthy of Rubens' brush—that can lead to a decision as to which is the original. Yet, as the differences of opinion show, even this approach does not guarantee unanimity. This was, in fact, succinctly demonstrated in one of Michael Jaffé's letters (December 6, 1978; museum files), in which he stated that the Detroit picture (then still at Julius Weitzner's in London), "in my view is of distinctly better quality than the Althorp picture." Yet, he also mentioned in the same letter "that there are some who prefer the Althorp version."

Suffice it to say here that after a prolonged and painstaking study of the formal characteristics of both versions, the present author finds the Althorp one in every respect superior, in the care with which decorative elements are handled (in the Detroit version, to mention only one detail, one link of the page's neck-chain is incomplete) and in the understanding of the three-dimensional structure of anatomical parts (one can compare in the two versions the mouth of the page holding the helmet, or the hand of the one fastening the belt holding the dagger). Light and dark patterns are handled with greater subtlety in the Althorp panel, pushed for harsher effects in the Detroit one. In the Althorp version the structure of the warrior's hair remains visible in the x-ray photograph, and a few strands of hair were obviously painted across the expanse of the forehead. In the Detroit panel hair and forehead remain sharply separate, and the locks of hair disappear completely from the radiograph. (Whether or not the Detroit version originally featured the two rivets—functionally essential on the knight's right shoulder—that are visible still in the Althorp panel, I am unable to say. Only one of the rivets in the Detroit picture is old; the other dates from a modern restoration that actually placed it too close to the genuine one.)

The head of the page with the helmet is not the only part of the picture derived from a pre-existing study. By a curious coincidence, the Art Institute acquired, together with the large panel, a study that the present author accepts as Rubens' own, depicting the head of the knight alone (79.15; see pages 84-85 above).

Color plate X, page 98.

c. 1615

Oil on oak panel, 119.7 × 98.7 cm ($47\frac{1}{8} \times 38\frac{7}{8}$ in.)

Conservation: The original oak panel has been thinned to 2 millimeters, adhered to a veneered support, and cradled. The original panel consisted of five members (joined at 13, 28.5, 55.5, and 75.2 centimeters). There is a crack at 87.5 centimeters. The paint layer and chalk ground reach to the edges of the panel, which does not appear to have been trimmed. The paint layer is in good condition. The thinly painted dark colors and shadows are abraded; this is more evident in the hair, belt, and knight's sleeve. Besides the inpainted loss in the center of the breastplate, other minor losses occur along the panel joins. There is a long horizontal scratch on the servant binding the amor. The x-ray photographs reveal reinforcement of the crack at 87.5 centimeters and at the join of the second and third panel members. They also show a slight change in the curl of the page with the helmet. No other pentimenti are discernible. Under infrared illumination, the wide diagonal striations of the ground application are evident in the page's red dress as well as in all three heads. The painting was treated for cleavage, surface-cleaned, and revarnished in 1979 by Barbara Heller (CSL). Previous conservation records supplied by Julius Weitzner include a semi-transfer done by Thorp Brothers and cleaning and inpainting by Gertrude Blumel around 1957 in New York.

Provenance: Cornelis van der Geest, Antwerp (?), Duke of Orléans, Paris (?). Private collection, England. Jan Appleby—D. Koetser (dealer), London, 1957. Julius H. Weitzner (dealer), London. Acquired in 1979.

Exhibitions: Cologne 1968: no. F25, color pl. 19.

References: Müller Hofstede 1967: 67-71; fig. 34. Vlieghe 1981: 143.

Founders Society Purchase, Acquisitions Fund (79.16)

Jan Siberechts

1627 ANTWERP – LONDON 1700/03

ALTHOUGH Flemish by birth, Siberechts owes little to the tradition of Flemish landscape painting of the first half of the 17th century. In his earlier landscapes he followed the lead of Dutch painters of the Italianate school (Jan Asselyn, Jan Both, Karel Dujardin); in the 1660s he developed a personal style of rendering rural scenes, easily recognizable by a cool color scale, almost as if he had used tinted glasses to filter out the warmer shades. He also formulated variations on a theme in which a small body of water in the foreground is traversed by country folk riding on wagons or wading on foot. He stressed the color and texture of rural paraphernalia (shiny brass vessels almost invariably appear in these works) and painted farm animals with precision and a palpable sympathy.

Siberechts left the Netherlands for England in or shortly after 1672 and concentrated increasingly on painting the great English country houses in their lush settings. Many of his paintings, of which approximately 100 are known, are signed and dated, the latest to 1698. He preferred fairly large formats, in which he manipulated a limited number of figural and landscape motifs with considerable skill and occasionally with humor.

Siberechts, *Crossing the Ford.*

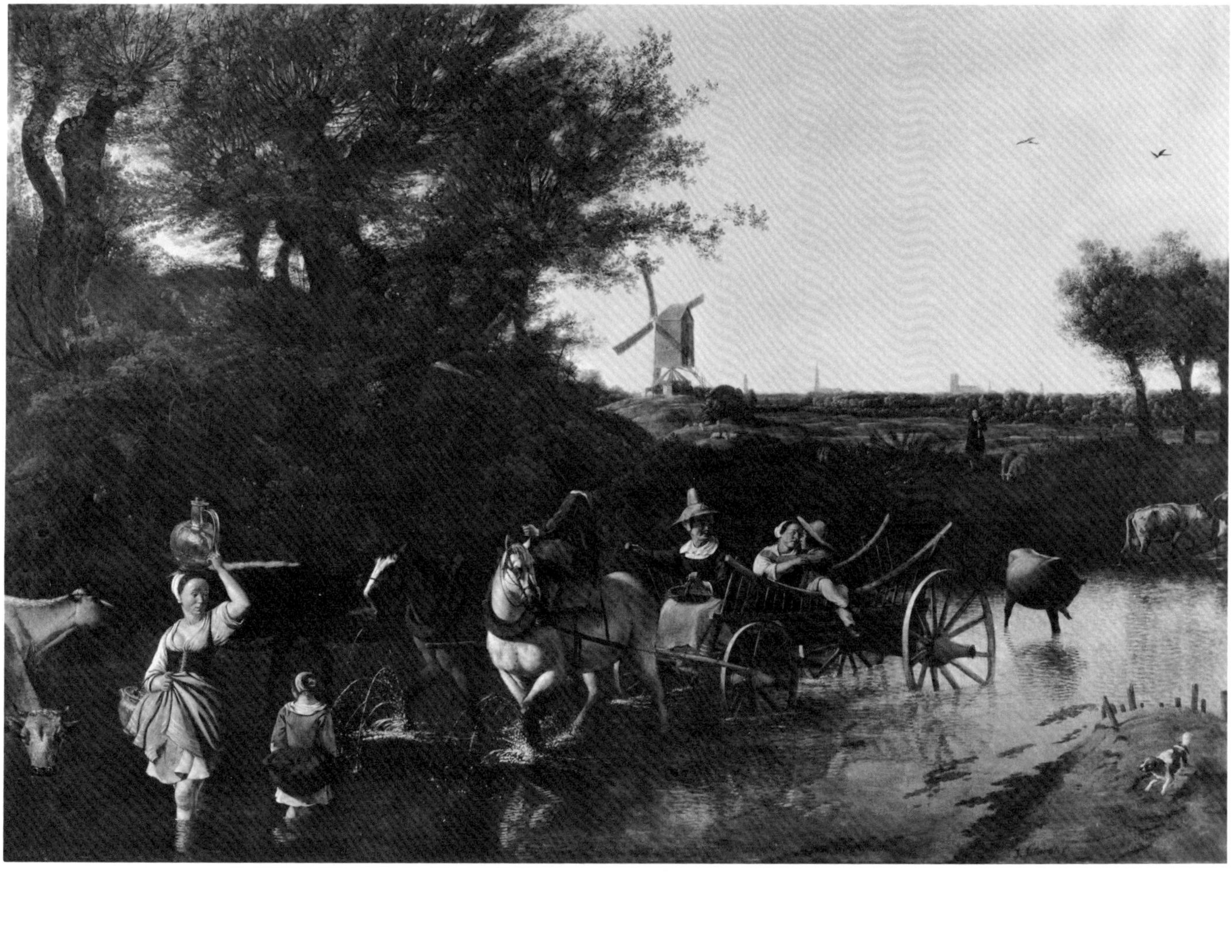

Crossing the Ford

The style and subject matter of this painting represent the last phase of Siberechts' development before his move to England around 1672. That date is supported by the setting, with its prominent windmill and the distant spires which are clearly continental in character. In fact, it is likely that the town glimpsed near the horizon is Antwerp. The tall Gothic spire suggests the Cathedral; the blunt one at its right is probably that of Saint Jacques and the slender one at its left that of the church dedicated to Saint Michael (destroyed in the early 19th century).

A small copy (oil on canvas, 38 × 29 cm) of the Detroit canvas was formerly in the collection of Jules Porgès, Paris, and was sold at Cassirer, Berlin, on December 7, 1921. The painting is also closely connected with another canvas, dated 1665: *The Ford* (Koninklijk Museum voor Schone Kunsten, Antwerp; no. 886), in which the same young woman who is carrying a brass pitcher on her head and a kettle on her arm, and lifting her skirt as she wades through the ford, is seen near the left edge. With slight variations, this figure also appears in a painting, titled *Die Furt* (*The Ford*), in Berlin (Gemäldegalerie; no. 1744), which is dated 1670. The Berlin catalogue (1975) mentions another picture, also containing this young woman, dated 1671, which was at one time owned by K. Loevenich, New York. Particularly characteristic of Siberechts' paintings of this period are the old willow trees with young branches growing in profusion from their twisted and gnarled trunks.

The painter worked with a limited number of figural motifs, for animals as well as for human beings, and the static impression created by many of his canvases is due to the additive method he followed in building up his compositions. The Detroit canvas, nevertheless, contains a slightly more lively touch than many of the others: a pair of lovers in an affectionate embrace, under less than comfortable conditions.

c. 1665/72

Oil on canvas, 153 × 214.5 cm ($60\frac{1}{4}$ × $84\frac{7}{16}$ in.)

Inscription: at lower right: *J. Siberechts F.*

Conservation: The canvas has been wax-lined and its original tacking margins removed. There is a light gray imprimatura beneath the entire painted surface. The paint layer is in fairly good condition although generally abraded. There are large retouchings in the sky, particularly in the upper right corner. Other notable retouchings include the areas of black pigment: the black cow, shadows in the men's robes and hats, and the tree trunks. Other inpainting is minor and scattered. There is one pentimento in the hat of the woman sitting in the front of the cart. She was first painted wearing a small white kerchief similar to that of the woman behind her. In 1963 a hole was filled and retouched by Edward O. Korany. There are no previous treatment records.

Provenance: J. M. Cherry, Bt., Richmond, England. Shaeffer Galleries, Inc., New York. Mr. and Mrs. James S. Whitcomb, Detroit. Acquired in 1960.

Exhibitions: Detroit 1964-65: 14.

References: Payne 1960-61: 54, 56-57.

Gift of Mr. and Mrs. James S. Whitcomb (60.85)

Frans Snyders

1579 ANTWERP 1657

ORIGINALLY apprenticed to Pieter Brueghel the Younger (1592), Snyders may have been more influenced by Pieter's brother, Jan the Elder. It is probably from Jan that he derived his own pervasive interest in still-life painting; and it was Jan who several times, in letters written to his Milanese patrons (1608-09), recommended "mio amico Francesco Snyders" when the latter was in Italy. As early as 1613, Brueghel even went so far as to say that Snyders, "secondo l'openion [sic] mia è unico in quella professione." Snyders had been admitted as a master to the guild of Saint Luke in 1602. His date of departure for Italy is not known, but he returned to Antwerp in July 1609 and two years later married Margareta de Vos, the sister of the painters Cornelis and Paul de Vos (Paul later became one of Snyders' closest followers). The couple had no children.

Much in demand as a painter of large still lifes of animals, Snyders soon achieved economic affluence, acquired a stately house, and established contact with many of the leading Antwerp masters, above all Rubens and Van Dyck. Van Dyck painted his and his wife's portraits (Frick Collection, New York; nos. 09.1.39 and 09.1.42), and Rubens called on his services many times to paint animals and still lifes in his own canvases. Snyders' personal relationship with Rubens remained close to the end; in his will of May 27, 1640, Rubens stipulated that Snyders, together with Jan Wildens and Jacques Moermans, should be charged with the proper disposal of the collections in Rubens' house after his death. Under Rubens' influence, Snyders took up scenes of hunting and animal combat, relying a great deal, however, on models of motion derived from Rubens' designs. Snyders is better remembered, and justifiably so, for his sumptuous and coloristically brilliant still lifes of fruits, vegetables, dead birds, game, and fish than for his pictures of animals in action. He may have painted some of the figures in his paintings himself, but more frequently he was assisted by other painters, among them Van Dyck, Jan Boeckhorst, and Cornelis de Vos.

Still Life with Fruit, Vegetables, and Dead Game

This large canvas depicting various still-life elements on two levels gives an excellent idea of the style of Frans Snyders, but in view of the huge output of works coming from the artist's studio, it would be hazardous to insist on seeing his own hand in every part of the picture. Virtually all the details are familiar from other works of the master—the blue-patterned bowls and wicker baskets filled with fruit, the vegetables on the floor, the dead birds, the deer and the boar's head, both dripping blood, the parrot, and even the cat furtively emerging from under a stool. In fact, as Scott Sullivan (1981) has observed, the central section, containing the basket with grapes and the bowl of peaches on top of the table, and melons, quince, and artichokes below it, corresponds almost literally to the arrangement of the same elements in a still life with two figures (*Frans Rubens with His Nursemaid* is its somewhat fanciful title) in the collection of the Marquis of Bute, Scotland. To this core of the composition, the artist has added various still-life motifs along the left edge of the picture, culminating in the "scarlet macaw" (Sullivan) and the dead birds and game at the right. The somewhat pedestrian arrangement, one object next to another, hardly permits us to claim the painting as one of Snyders' more felicitous compositions. That does not mean that the viewer's eye may not feast on the skillfully rendered shapes, colors, and textures of peaches, plums, grapes, melons, quince, artichokes, and mushrooms, or the plumage, yellow and red, of small birds, the more neutral colors of the larger snipes and partridge, and the bright red of the parrot. The two-tiered arrangement, accomplished with the help of a long table, the front edge of which almost divides the composition in half, is also found in other works coming from Snyders' studio.

To what extent Snyders followed Rubens' practice of putting finishing touches on large canvases executed with the help of assistants, we do not know; as with the greater master, it is not a rewarding effort to try to identify the parts touched by the brush of the head of the studio. This being said, we may conclude that the Detroit canvas, like many others of its kind, probably left the studio with the master's approval, and I see no compelling reason for calling it anything else than a characteristic example of Snyders' still-life art.

Color plate XI, page 99.

c. 1635/37

Oil on canvas, 165 × 200 cm (65 × 78¾ in.)

Conservation: The original canvas, seamed vertically in the center, has been glue-lined and its tacking margins removed. The ground is light gray in color. Approximately 5 centimeters of the top edge of the painting are hidden by the frame. The paint layer is in good condition. Inpainted losses occur in the four corners (particularly in the lower right), along the edges, on the boar's head and nose, and scattered throughout the background. Ultraviolet photographs reveal that the rather thinly applied gray background covers what appears to be a brick wall. The change was undoubtedly made by the artist himself. Besides this change there are two notable pentimenti: a stem and leaf extending down from the branch in the lower left was deleted, as was a melon in the left foreground. There are no records of former conservation treatment.

Provenance: G. C. Baroni (dealer), Florence. Sale, Christie's, London, April 10, 1970, lot 108. Old Master Galleries (dealer), London. Acquired in 1978.

References: Sullivan 1981: 30-37.

Founders Society Purchase, Acquisitions Fund (78.44)

Style of Frans Snyders

Dogs Attacking a Bear

Despite the "signature" and the date inscribed on this painting, its attribution to Snyders himself is unacceptable. The execution of the painting

Style of Snyders, *Dogs Attacking a Bear.*

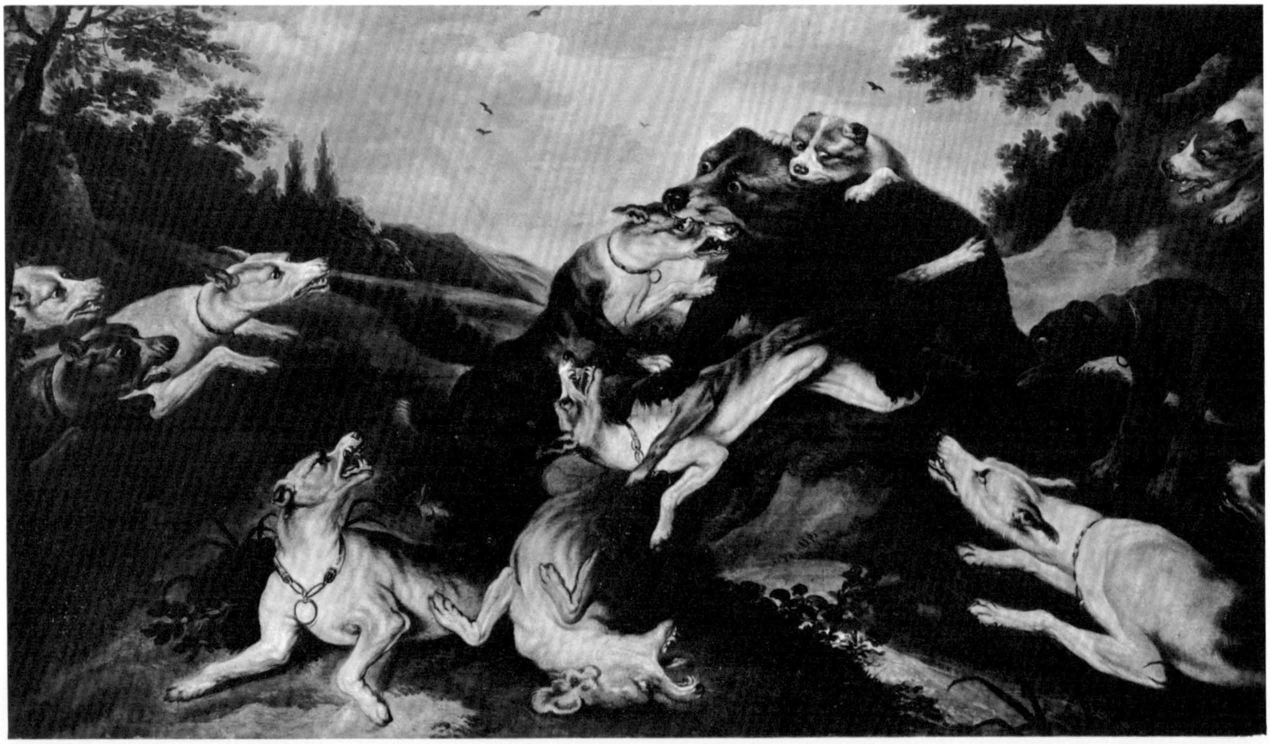

completely lacks the care and skill that characterize Snyders' paintings of animals, as well as the plausibility—however limited—of his depictions of sanguinary encounters between beasts of brute strength (bears, wild boars, or bulls) and packs of fearless hounds. Moreover, the date of 1610 cannot possibly be right, since Snyders turned to these subjects only under the influence of Rubens, who himself began to conceive them no earlier than around 1615. The only question remaining is whether the canvas is a copy of one of Snyders' own compositions or a pastiche by one of his imitators. I am inclined to accept the second alternative. Virtually all the hounds are rendered in poses and attitudes that belong to the general stock in trade of such scenes, but they are introduced without any true sense of dramatic interplay between them and the beast they are attacking. The prototypes of the three principal hounds in the foreground might well have been the similarly placed hounds in the *Hunt of the Wild Boar* in the Staatliche Kunstsammlungen, Dresden (a repetition is in the Alte Pinakothek, Munich), which is now generally considered to be the work of Van Dyck and Snyders although there may have been a drawing or a sketch for the composition by Rubens (Glück 1931: 20). The subject of a combat between a bear and a pack of hounds is also found in a canvas in the Museo Municipal, Vigo, on loan from the Prado (Madrid 1975: no. 1881, pl. 244); it, too, contains two of the hounds seen in Detroit (the one lying on its back and the one to the left looking up at the bear). The Vigo picture is considered to be a copy of a painting by Snyders; in fact, it was formerly thought to be by Paul de Vos, Snyders' brother-in-law. Charles Sterling (museum files) appears to have mentioned the name of Paul de Vos in connection with the Detroit painting, but his suggestion should probably be taken as no more than the reflection of his well-justified doubts about the attribution of the canvas to Snyders.

Oil on canvas, 115 × 199 cm ($45\frac{1}{4} \times 78\frac{5}{16}$ in.)

Inscription: near lower edge at right of center: *F. Snyders F./1610*

Conservation: The canvas has an old, seamed glue-lining. The original tacking margins have been removed on all four sides, and there is a large canvas insert in the lower left corner (22 × 18 cm, roughly in the shape of a half-arch). The ground contains lead white and is covered with a light gray imprimatura. The paint layer appears to be in overall good condition; however, there are inpainted losses in certain key areas of the composition. These include most of the bear's face, the nose of the dog in the lower center, an area in the central sky to the left of the bear's head, sections of the trees in the right background, and the lower and left edges. Examination under the microscope reveals that the bright red details in the eyes of several of the animals, as well as the blood from their wounds, are all later additions. Under ultraviolet illumination, the signature fluoresces like overpaint. The light red signature and date appear, under the microscope, to be in the same layer as the other red additions mentioned above. The painting was treated for bloom in 1959 and 1961 by William Suhr. There are no records of previous treatment.

Provenance: Mrs. J. T. Ijams, New York. Mr. J. Horton Ijams, New York. Duveen Brothers, Inc. (dealer), New York. Acquired in 1939.

References: Detroit 1944: 124, no. 738.

Founders Society Purchase, William H. Murphy Fund (39.665)

Hendrik van Steenwijck the Younger

C. 1580 ANTWERP/FRANKFORT(?) – LEYDEN 1649

TRAINED by his father, Hendrick the Elder, the younger Steenwijck continued the tradition of painting interiors of churches (including their crypts) and other stately buildings, often depicting them at night and introducing artificial sources of light (torches, lamps, fireplaces) for illumination. The figures were often painted after the architectural setting had been completed, and it seems that other artists (among them, Jan Brueghel the Elder, Frans Francken the Younger, Theodoor van Thulden, and Adriaen van Stalbemt) assisted Steenwijck in this task. The latter's main concern, besides rendering all forms with the greatest possible precision, was the exact perspectival construction, with reference to a central vanishing point, of deep spaces and long vistas. The forms remain crystal clear to the furthest recesses of the buildings, and even the most picturesque light effects are never permitted to obscure them.

Few facts are known with any degree of certainty about Steenwijck's life. He may have been born in Frankfort, where his father lived from at least 1588 (and possibly some years before). The younger Steenwijck appears to have returned to Antwerp at an early age; by November 1617, he had settled in London, where he worked for Charles I and collaborated with Daniel Mytens and Van Dyck, but he was again back in the Netherlands, presumably in Leiden, by 1645; his widow is mentioned in that city in 1649. His portrait is preserved in a print by Paul Pontius after a design by Van Dyck, forming part of Van Dyck's *Iconographie* (Mauquoy-Hendrickx 1956: no. 67).

Christ in the House of Mary and Martha

❡ The subject of the Detroit picture exists in two versions by the artist, the finest being the canvas in the Louvre (no. 2581; 64 × 96 cm; signed *Henri V. Steenwick, 1620*), a picture engraved by Jean-Gabriel Caquet in the 18th century and in the 19th by Heina. The third version is in Vienna (according to A. von Wurzbach 1906-11, II: 660). According to the Louvre catalogue (Paris 1922, III: 115-116), the figures in the Paris picture were painted by Cornelis van Poelenburgh, but there is no reason to assume that the figures in the Detroit version were not painted by Steenwijck himself.

The subject of the Detroit picture—a very popular one in the 17th century—is taken from Luke 10:38-42. When Christ was received in Martha's house, her sister Mary "sat at Jesus' feet, and heard his word," but Martha "was cumbered about much serving." When Martha asked Jesus to bid Mary help her, he informed Martha that it was Mary who had "chosen that good part, which shall not be taken away from her." It is the moment in which Christ praises Mary's concern with spiritual things that the artist has chosen to illustrate. At the right, Martha stands carrying food in a fold of her apron (in the distance another woman and a child are busy cooking a meal in a huge open fireplace), while Mary sits before Christ on a low stool, looking down into an open book in her hands.

Important though the human action may be, the artist's chief interest was surely the rendering, in exact perspective, of a large, palatial, and sun-lit dwelling in which a delicate web of lines drawn as if with a ruler lends to all forms a brittle delicacy. An impression of venerable age would have been created for the viewers of Steenwijck's day by his use of Gothic architectural details, the most striking being the passageway between the foreground hall and the kitchen beyond. Gothic filigree ornament is applied to the tall clock at the left, the table, and the wooden partition behind Christ,

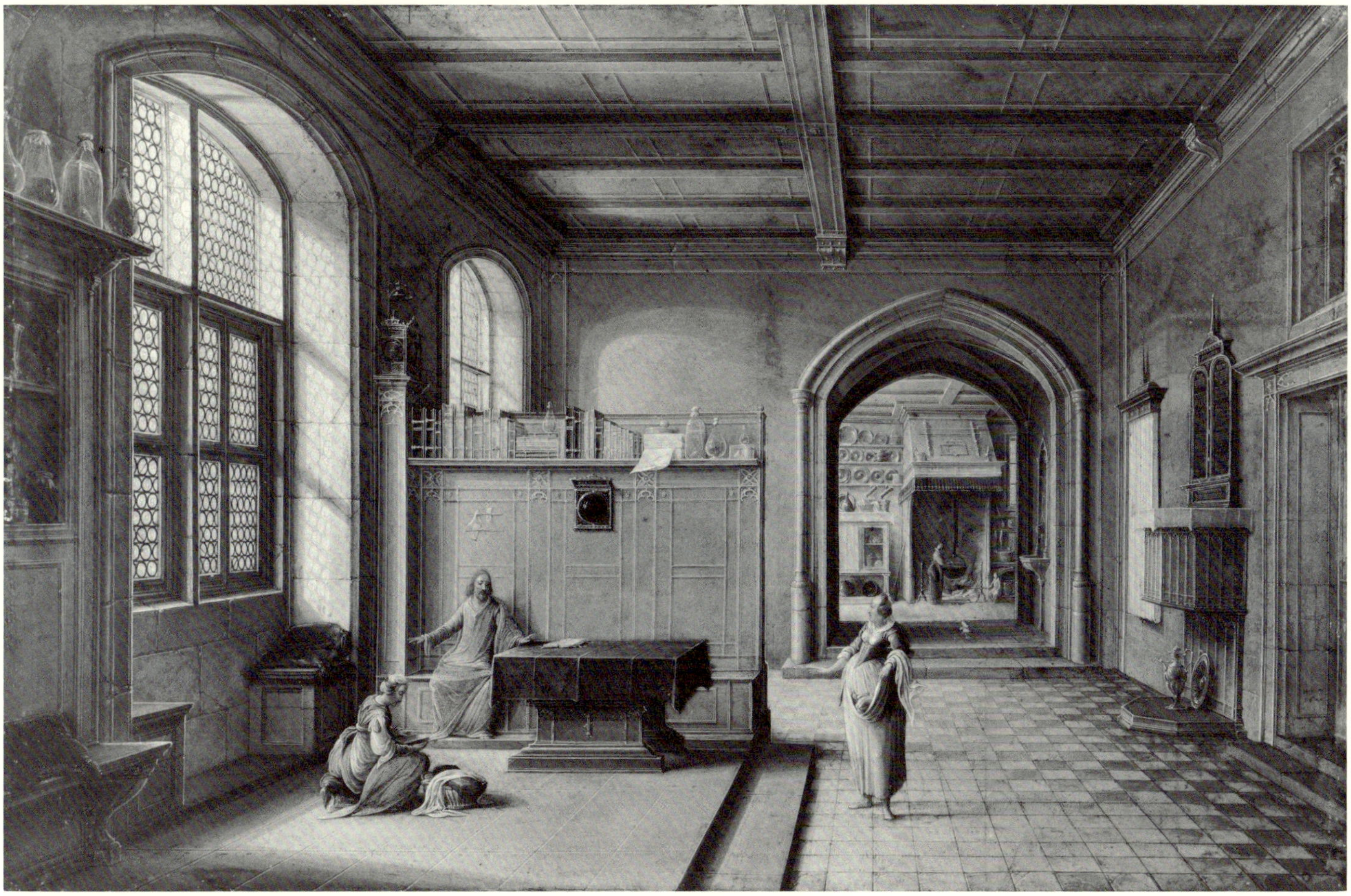

Steenwijck, *Christ in the House of Mary and Martha.*

which supports a small library, all volumes neatly and systematically turned with the hasps toward the front. The "archaic" impression is due, above all, to Steenwijck's clever adaptation of Dürer's engraving of *Saint Jerome in His Study* for the shape of the mullioned windows and glass roundels—and of their function as the primary source of light.

A few details of the furnishings reinforce the religious message: the tablets of the Law—the Ten Commandments, recognizable by shape though not legible—are placed against the right wall, above a credenza (not a pulpit, as Richardson thought [1908]). The washbasin and niche with a kettle suspended in it are ancient symbols of spiritual purification; the convex mirror in the center of the partition is too strikingly placed not to suggest a symbolic significance—perhaps the eye of God that encompasses all.

1620

Oil on copper, 33.2 × 49.7 cm ($13\frac{1}{16}$ × $19\frac{9}{16}$ in.)

Inscription: at lower right (on door jamb): *H. v. S./ 1620*

Conservation: Both the copper support and the paint layer are in excellent condition. Except for one on the wall between the two windows, most of the losses are minor and occur along the edges. Infrared examination shows a major pentimento: the right wall with the Commandment tablets originally had a hood-like structure not unlike that over the hearth in the background room. Also, under infrared, two orthogonal lines (part of the perspective system constructed by the artist) can be seen to traverse the female figure cooking in the background. Blisters were treated in 1955. There are no previous conservation records.

Provenance: Martin Colnaghi. James E. Scripps, Detroit. Acquired in 1889.

Exhibitions: Detroit 1889: 35, no. 36.

References: *BDMA* 1908: 4, 7.

Gift of James E. Scripps (1889.64)

Sebastian Stosskopf

1597 STRASBOURG – IDSTEIN (HESSE-NASSAU) 1657

THE AUTHOR of spare but exquisitely executed still lifes, Stosskopf received his training (from 1615) in the studio of Daniel Soreau, a Flemish artist who, being a Calvinist, had left his homeland and settled in Hanau, near Frankfurt. After Soreau's death in 1619, Stosskopf was briefly in charge of his master's studio, but eventually left Hanau to work in more promising artistic centers, mainly Paris and, for a short period (1629), Venice. In 1640 or 1641 he took up residence in Strasbourg, where in 1646 he married the daughter of a goldsmith. Stosskopf was highly esteemed by his contemporaries but virtually forgotten in succeeding centuries. He was "rediscovered" in the 1930s but the small number of pictures known today represents probably only a fraction of his entire output.

Stosskopf's still lifes are noteworthy not only for his technical skill but also for the attention paid to objects rarely encountered in such contexts—for instance, baskets filled with ordinary drinking glasses—and for the deceptively casual arrangements of these objects within the composition of the whole work. The fragile glasses may allude, as do the more conventional objects in his paintings, such as flowers and books, to the *Vanitas* themes so common in still lifes of this period. Stosskopf also included exact reproductions of readily identifiable prints by contemporary masters, chiefly Callot and Rembrandt, some of them clearly intended as *trompe l'oeil*. One of them, in fact, as was related by Joachim van Sandrart, who was Stosskopf's pupil, was dramatically successful when Emperor Ferdinand III tried to pick up the print before realizing that it was only painted.

Still Life of Books and a Rembrandt Etching

The main elements in this painting are ten books, some bound in leather, others in parchment, which are arranged on top of a table in what may be characterized as an orderly randomness. Two sheets of paper complete the composition, one rolled up so that one cannot tell if there is anything on it; the other one is unrolled and can easily be identified as a very faithful copy of Rembrandt's etching of c. 1630/31 portraying his mother seated on a chair (Münz 1952: no. 85, pl. 98). The presence of this print forces us to date Stosskopf's still life somewhat later than Pierre Rosenberg has suggested (1625/30; museum files). Stosskopf apparently made use of a canvas on which a bucolic scene (a shepherd with sheep and a dog, all on a very small scale) had been painted, almost certainly by another hand, as it has none of the deliberate planning that is the hallmark of his style.

Color plate XII, page 100.

Oil on canvas, 50.4 × 60.7 cm ($19\frac{7}{8} \times 23\frac{7}{8}$ in.)

Conservation: The painting has an old glue-lining, and its original tacking margins have been removed. The still life is coated with a yellowed varnish and is thinly painted. It is somewhat abraded, especially in the figure of the woman in the engraving, in the upper right corner, and along the lower edge. Infrared examination reveals that another composition exists beneath the still life. It includes a flock of sheep, a dog, and a shepherd in the foreground, a cityscape in the middleground (beneath the bottom book in the lefthand pile), and, possibly, mountains in the background. With radiography, only the sheep can be seen, due perhaps to the density of the lead-white ground. There is no record of conservation treatment.

Provenance: Acquired in 1952.

Gift of Dr. W. R. Valentiner (52.199)

Justus Sustermans

1597 ANTWERP – FLORENCE 1681

SUSTERMANS, or Suttermans, as he occasionally called himself, was trained in Antwerp by a painter of portraits and historical subjects, Willem de Vos, a nephew of Marten de Vos. At the age of 19, he left Antwerp, never to return. His first destination was Paris, where he worked for three years with Frans Pourbus the Younger. In 1620 Sustermans settled in Florence where he soon became the favorite portraitist at the courts of three succeeding Grand Dukes of Tuscany—Cosimo II, Ferdinando II, and Cosimo III. Such was his success as a painter of the Italian aristocracy that he received invitations from many other courts; between 1622 and 1624, he worked at the imperial court in Vienna, and in 1653 spent about a year in Innsbruck. In 1627 Pope Urban VIII summoned him to Rome, where he returned in 1645. He also worked at various times in Genoa, Milan, Modena, Parma, Piacenza, Ferrara, and Mantua. In 1627 he was created a Knight of Malta.

Sustermans was in contact with some of the leading artists of his time. Van Dyck visited him in 1624 and included his portrait in the *Iconographie*, and it was apparently through Sustermans that Rubens received the commission for one of his greatest paintings, the *Horrors of War* (1638; Palazzo Pitti, Florence). When that painting was shipped to Italy, Rubens wrote to Sustermans that the latter had Rubens' full permission to retouch it if it had suffered in transit "or from my own negligence"—a remarkable sign of confidence in the judgment and skill of the expatriate master.

Circle of Sustermans

Portrait of a Lady

While this painting of an unknown lady is clearly in the manner of Justus Sustermans, an attribution to the master himself can only be expressed with qualifications. To some extent, this may be due to the canvas' less than satisfactory state of conservation. The extent of damages to the paint film was clearly revealed in a recent (1979) cleaning, which, however, also established that the picture is a work of considerable quality. Physiognomically, the lady portrayed resembles Sustermans' depictions of Vittoria della Rovere; one such example can be seen in his *Holy Family* in the Palazzo Pitti, Florence, where the Virgin has Vittoria's features. The rather Leonardesque hand holding a scroll of paper is also found in Sustermans' portrait of Cardinal Carlo de' Medici (Museo Poldi-Pezzoli, Milan).

c. 1640/50

Oil on canvas, 65.5 × 50.3 cm ($25\frac{13}{16}$ × $19\frac{13}{16}$ in.)

Conservation: The canvas, with its original tacking margins intact, has an old glue-lining. The painting is in fairly poor condition. The varnish is very discolored. X-ray photographs show large losses in the chest, neck, right cheek, forehead, hand, scroll, and scattered throughout the background. There are smaller and more recent unretouched flake losses in the left background and blue garment (lower right). The painting was cleaned in 1979 by Teresa Hensick (CSL). No prior conservation is recorded.

Provenance: Acquired in 1960.

Gift of the Estate of Julie du Charme Marigliano (60.179)

Circle of Sustermans, *Portrait of a Lady*.

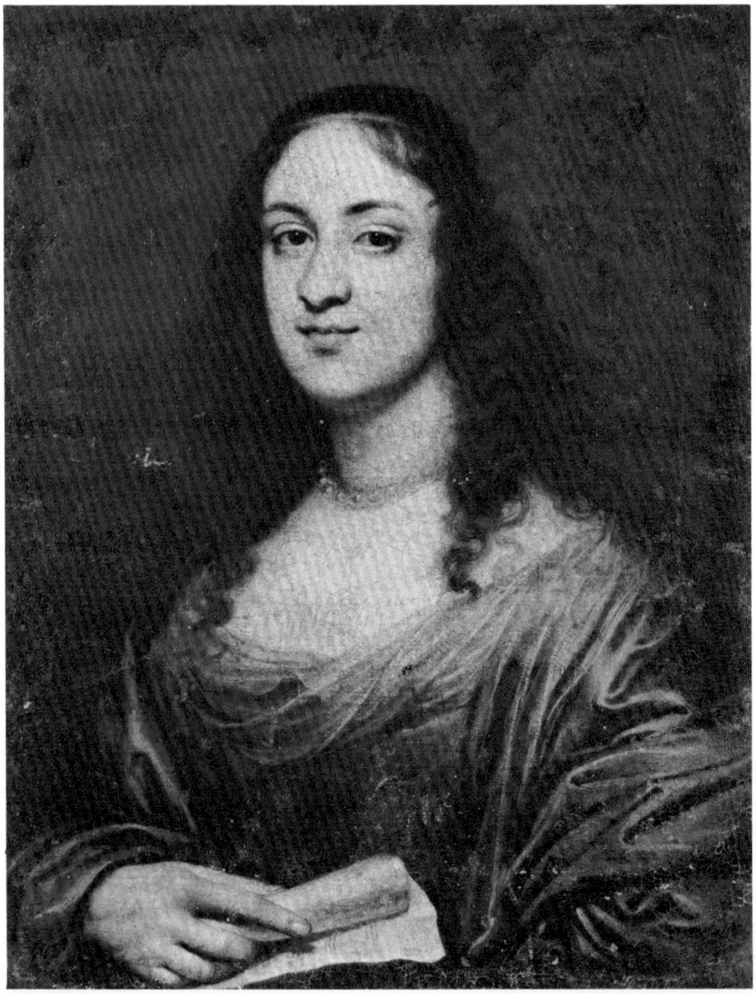

Michael Sweerts

1624 BRUSSELS – GOA 1664

THE earliest documentary evidence about "Cavaliere" Sweerts, as he is generally called (though he was the son of a middle-class Flemish merchant), is found in Rome, where he is mentioned as residing in 1646; he was still there in 1652. In 1656 he was in Brussels, where he founded a short-lived artists' academy, and in 1661 in Amsterdam, where he was esteemed as a painter of portraits. He took part, in 1662, in a pilgrimage to the Holy Land, but parted with his French companions in Persia after a quarrel; he proceeded to Goa to join Portuguese Jesuits active on the island. Nothing is known about the manner of his death.

Only three of Sweerts' paintings are dated (to 1652 and 1656); a chronology of his works and the nature of his artistic development can thus be described only in general outlines. His earliest paintings were Roman scenes in the manner of Pieter van Laer. The strong chiaroscuro of these works later gave way to a rather sophisticated but basically cool colorism that evokes reminiscences of the art of the Le Nain family. Less strong a personality than Jan Vermeer, Sweerts developed in a manner curiously analogous to the slightly younger Dutch painter.

Sweerts' several paintings of artists' studios, where young painters study plaster casts and draw from live models, are important for what they reveal about workshop practices in Rome. His allegories of the five senses represented by five charming half-length figures engaged in delightful, droll actions are among the most original treatments of this theme (portions of two different series exist: *Taste* and *Hearing* in the Staatsgalerie, Stuttgart [nos. 299 and 300], and *Smell* and *Touch* in the Museum Boymans-Van Beuningen, Rotterdam).

In the Studio

¶ In the center of the canvas a young man examines a small sculpture, almost certainly a plaster cast, of a putto(?) whose arms and legs are lacking. Another youth, standing at the left and identified as a painter by the palette and brushes in his left hand, points at a male torso, obviously trying to draw the central figure's attention to this piece. In the background between the two can be discerned an easel with a painting on it. The (plaster) torso is part of a jumble of other casts, mostly portrait heads, all of them taken from ancient sculpture; three are recognizable as women, and one, with a bandage-like wrapping around the head, is of a man with lifelike features and an expression of suffering. There are two other less distinguishable heads, and a cast of a foot. At the right, a servant approaches with another load of such casts, carrying them in his apron. On a stool in the left foreground lies an open music-book and leaning against the stool is a large stringed instrument (*chitarrone*). Some measuring tools used for drawing and drafting are spread out on a flat pillow (or mat) at the lower right. Through a door behind the servant, a second room can be seen in which a seated figure appears to be drawing or reading in a strong light coming from above.

The nature of this second room is such that one may question whether, in fact, we have an artist's studio before us. Shelves filled with books and a large globe line the walls of the back room. Moreover, while one might reasonably expect pictures to hang on walls of painters' studios, the orderly row of five framed paintings—one of them recognizable as a picture of the Virgin with the infant Jesus—on the wall behind the three large foreground figures might also suggest that the locale is the dwelling of an affluent patron who set aside a part of his house, or palace, as a studio for artists in his employ. The best example of a representation of such an artist's work-place is Velázquez' *Las Meniñas* in the Prado.

This does not mean that the various objects in the painting, above all the casts of ancient sculpture, belong to this particular setting. In fact, there is good reason to think that the painting and the combination of objects shown in it are intended to convey a message concerning the training of young artists of the day. A basic requirement, obviously, was the study of the works of antiquity, available everywhere in the form of plaster casts. Yet the conspicuous inclusion of a sheet of music and a musical instrument, as well as of architects' and engravers' tools and the "library" in the second room, may well be meant to stress the importance of a broader "liberal" or academic education for young artists. According to Kultzen (1954) and the 1958 Rotterdam exhibition catalogue, a painting like the Detroit canvas reflects the intellectual ambiance in which Sweerts moved as a member of the *Virtuosi al Pantheon*; it may have been just this academic spirit that prompted him to establish an artists' academy in Brussels (see Passeri 1772: 19-20).

Several of the casts seen in the Detroit picture re-occur in a still larger accumulation of such objects, including a sculpted relief, in Sweerts' painting of an artists' academy now in the Rijksmuseum, Amsterdam (no. 2281). The female cast seen in profile at the left in the Detroit canvas was probably taken from the head of the so-called *Diana of Versailles*, now in the Louvre (no. 589). The head lying in front on its back might have been made from a Hellenistic Aphrodite in the manner of the *Venus de' Medici* in the Uffizi, Florence. According to the catalogue of the exhibition *Gods and Heroes* (New York 1968-69: no. 53), S. Howard and U. Hiesinger submitted the following (tentative) identifications of the different pieces, listing them from left to right:

Meleager head (?); Farnese Hera; a Hellenistic beggar or fishmonger; Hellenistic Aphrodite (?); head of Antonine youth—Geta?; torso, fourth century hero type—Narcissus or Meleager?; fragment of putto, Duquesnoy, seventeenth century; Laughing Satyr or Pan—Pergamon or Alexandria; head of putto; unidentifiable female head; Melpomene mask.

1652

Oil on canvas, 73.5 × 58.8 cm (28 15/16 × 23 1/8 in.)

Inscription: signed and dated on rolled piece of paper draped over table edge: *Michael Sweerts / fecit / Roma / A. D. 1652.*

Conservation: The painting has been lined with primed canvas and its original tacking margins removed. The stretcher dates at least to the early part of the century, as can be seen from a 1911 exhibition label attached where the cross-pieces intersect. The ground is dark brown with, possibly, a reddish brown imprimatura. The paint is in very good condition. There is minor abrasion in the blue coat of the right-hand figure and in the thinly applied dark brown areas. There is inpainting along the lower edge and in the hair of the figure on the left. In 1965 William Suhr removed the painting from its previous lining, cleaned, relined, and inpainted it.

Provenance: Sir George Donaldson, London. Thomas Agnew and Sons (dealer), New York, 1930. Acquired in 1930.

Exhibitions: London 1911: no. 94. The Hague 1928: no. 40. Berlin 1929: no. 91. Baltimore 1946: no. 36a. Muskegon 1949. Hartford 1950-51: 23, no. 61. Rotterdam 1958: 37-38, no. 5. Rome 1958-59: 33-34, no. 5. Hamilton 1964: no. 32. New York 1968-69: no. 53. Cleveland 1973.

References: Martin 1905: 127. Martin 1907: 148, no. 9. Thieme and Becker 1907-50, XXXII (1938): 349. Valentiner 1930: 4-6. Washburn Freund 1931: I, 3. Kultzen 1954: 12ff., no. 6. Waddingham 1958: 68. Schaar 1959: 43. Wilenski 1960, I: 665; II: pl. 768. Waddingham 1961: 50. Bloch 1965: 158, 164-165. Borea 1966: pl. 34. Kindler 1968, V: 464. Bloch 1968: 20; fig. 11.

City of Detroit Purchase (30.297)

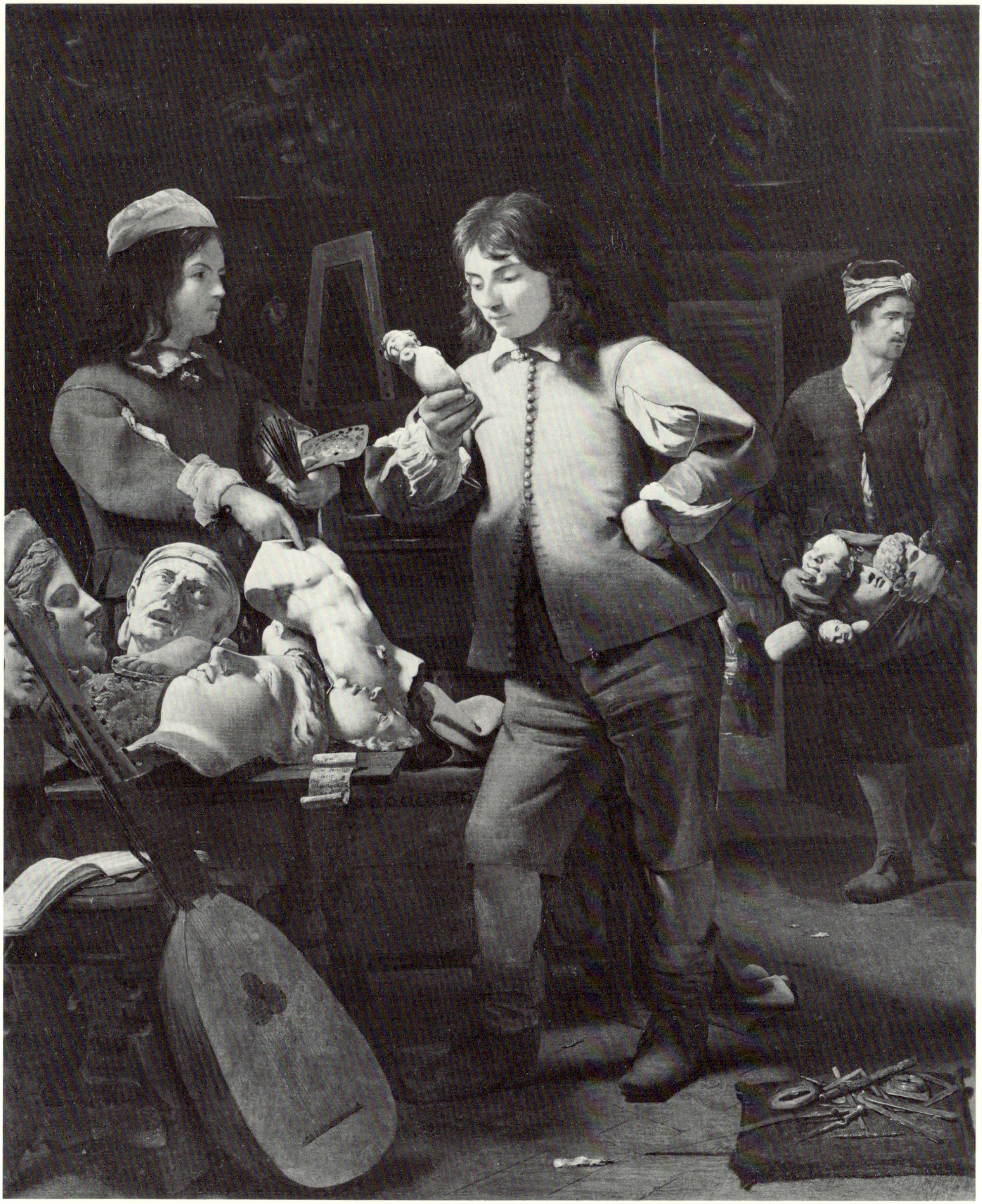

Sweerts, *In the Studio.*

David Teniers the Younger

1610 ANTWERP – BRUSSELS 1690

ALTHOUGH Teniers' father and his three brothers were also painters, only David achieved true—and deserved—prominence. He was received as a master in the Antwerp painters' guild in 1632 and was its dean in 1645. Appointed painter to the court and keeper of the collection of the governor of the Spanish Netherlands, Archduke Leopold William of Austria, Teniers moved to Brussels in 1651. In 1662 he bought an estate in the country ("The Three Towers") and in 1665 founded an art academy in Antwerp; with all these activities he hoped (in vain) to be elevated to noble rank. He was married first (1637) to a daughter of Jan Brueghel the Elder, a ward of Rubens; after her death, he married a second time in 1656.

Teniers' best-known works are scenes from peasant life, mainly moments of leisure at inns or at outdoor festivities often involving country dances. In these works he clearly demonstrated the influence of Adriaen Brouwer but without Brouwer's savage intensity of characterization. Teniers' range also included demonic subjects, such as the *Temptation of Saint Anthony* (Musées Royaux des Beaux-Arts, Brussels), allegories (*The Five Senses*, also in Brussels), satirical themes involving monkeys or cats engaged in "human" activities, group portraits, and "portraits" of picture galleries, especially of the collection in his custody. Still insufficiently appreciated is the fact that Teniers may well have been the most sensitive painter of landscape after Rubens, although he hardly ever painted a landscape for its own sake; they appear largely as backgrounds for his figural compositions. He had a strong influence on later artists, including Watteau, and was often imitated.

Teniers, *Landscape by Moonlight.*

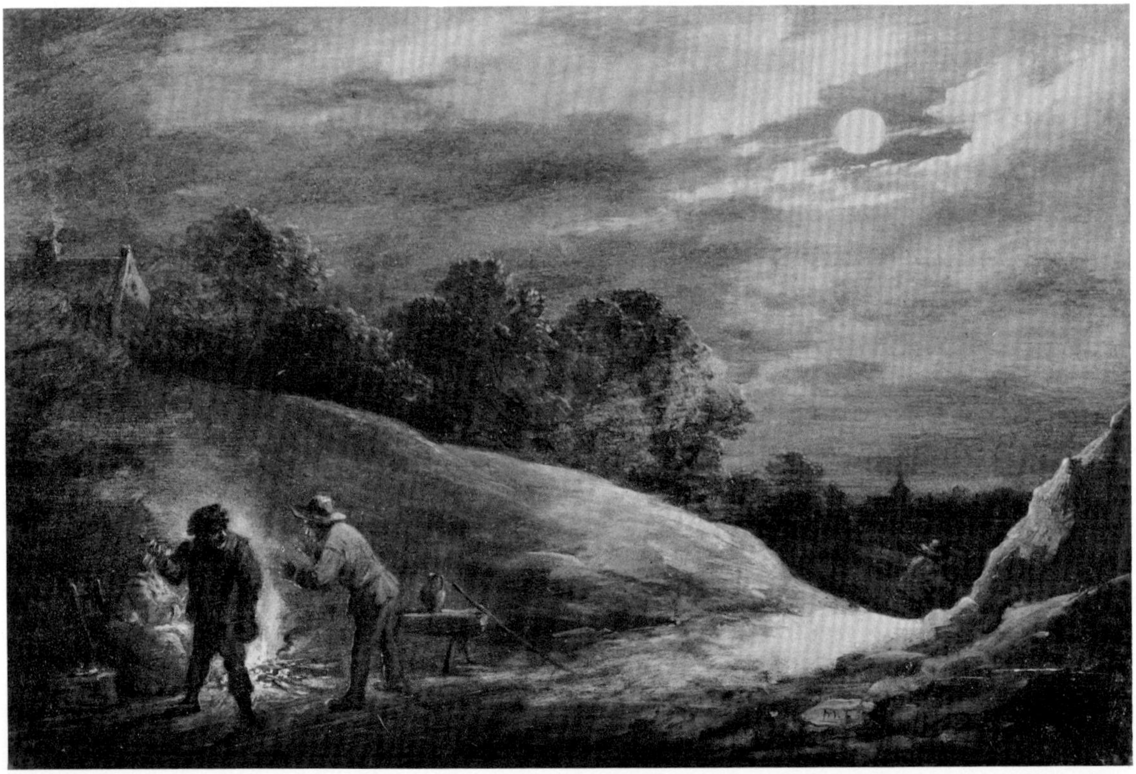

Landscape by Moonlight

By the light of a full moon seen through a break in the cloudy sky, three country folk—one of them a woman seated on a chair—warm themselves by a fire kindled at the side of a road. A gentle hill rises behind the figures around the fire; above it appears a group of trees in full foliage and the gable and roof of a house, smoke coming from its chimney. In the distance at the right are more trees and, just barely visible, the silhouette of a small village church.

This picture is said (museum files) to be identical with one mentioned in Smith's *Catalogue Raisonné* (1829-42) as number 331. The title of that picture reads simply, "A small mountainous landscape," a description hardly fitting the Detroit panel. It is more likely that it is Smith's number 330: "A View of a Village, by moonlight, with peasants warming themselves at a fire." According to Smith, that picture was engraved by Le Bas and etched by Teniers himself.

The striking night scene brings to mind similar pictures by Adriaen Brouwer, who is known to have influenced Teniers greatly. In mood and pictorial technique, it comes close to Brouwer's *Landscape with Dunes in Moonlight* in Berlin (Gemäldegalerie; no. 853G; oil on panel, 25 × 34 cm), but Teniers' technique is smoother and more controlled, and his picture less of a "traumhaftes Stimmungsbild" (Berlin 1975: 67) than a rustic genre scene. Yet the Brouwer panel, being one of his late works (it is dated 1635/37 in the Berlin catalogue), furnishes a *terminus post quem* for Teniers' picture; a date in the years around 1640 would seem to be indicated.

c. 1640
Oil on oak panel, 21.1 × 30.8 cm ($8\frac{5}{16}$ × $12\frac{1}{8}$ in.)
Inscription: at lower right, on stone: *D. F.*
Conservation: The oak panel has a 3-centimeter-wide recessed border on the reverse, which has been thinned from the original 11-millimeter thickness to 6 millimeters. This was done to accommodate a mitered collar that was glued to the panel and is seen from the front as a half-centimeter-wide unpainted border. The panel has one small horizontal crack starting at the right, 3 centimeters from the lower edge. The paint layer and ground (white chalk) reach the edges of the panel. The imprimatura, which appears to be a reddish brown, contains large particles of white lead. These can be seen in the x-rays and under the microscope to be scattered over the entire painting. In 1950 scratches and bloom were removed by William Suhr, and in 1955 the painting was cleaned by him. The painting appears to be in fair condition beneath a discolored varnish. The extent of retouching and overglazing, visible particularly in the sky area, could only be determined if the varnish were removed. X-rays show very few paint losses.
Provenance: Charles Alexander de Calonne sale, Skinner and Dyke, London, March 27, 1795, lot 32. Acquired in 1931.
References: Smith 1829-42, III (1831): no. 330. Scheyer 1937: 56-57. Detroit 1944: 131, no. 763. Page 1952-53: 72.
Gift of Leger and Son (31.341)

The Birth of Jupiter

This little panel is one of 244 copies that Teniers painted of Italian pictures in the collection of Archduke Leopold William of Austria, the governor of the Spanish Netherlands. The painting copied here is a small cassone panel by Andrea Meldolla, called Schiavone, now in the Kunsthistorisches Museum, Vienna (no. 158; oil on panel, 23 × 30 cm; see Fröhlich-Bum 1912: 212, fig. 72). A companion-piece to Schiavone's panel depicts the nurture of Jupiter by the she-goat Amalthea; it too was copied by Teniers (Scharf 1862: 160, no. 62 [128]). The Detroit copy follows Schiavone's picture quite faithfully as regards the figural composition; Teniers had to take some liberties with the background owing to the fact that he chose a panel of different proportions—it is considerably higher than it is wide, while Schiavone's cassone panel is nearly square. As a result, Teniers extended the tree upward, increasing the distance between the kneeling woman and the foliage above her, and adjusting the protective drapery accordingly.

Teniers' copies of the works in Archduke Leopold William's collection were engraved by various artists and published in 1660 (when Leopold William had been succeeded as governor by Don Juan of Spain) in a volume generally known as the "Teniers Gallery"; its full title is *Theatrum Pictorium Davidis Teniers, Antverpiensis pictoris serenissimorum principum Leopoldi Guillelmi Archiducis Austriae, et Joannis Austriaci pro Philippo IV., Rege Hispaniarum Belgii Gubernatorum* (Brussels, 1660). The engraving based on Teniers' copy of Schiavone's *Birth of Jupiter* was executed by Theodor van Kessel.

Schiavone's (and Teniers') rendering of the myth as a scene taking place out-of-doors, but shielded from observation by a large hanging drapery, surely makes reference to the effort of Ops, Jupiter's mother, to protect her child from the violence of her husband, Saturn. To prevent the fulfillment of a prophecy that one of his children would usurp his power, Saturn intended to devour all his offspring. Ops succeeded in keeping not only Jupiter but also Neptune and Pluto alive. The accounts of the nurture of Jupiter vary, but they all agree that he was brought up in secrecy in a rustic environment.

Teniers, *The Birth of Jupiter.*

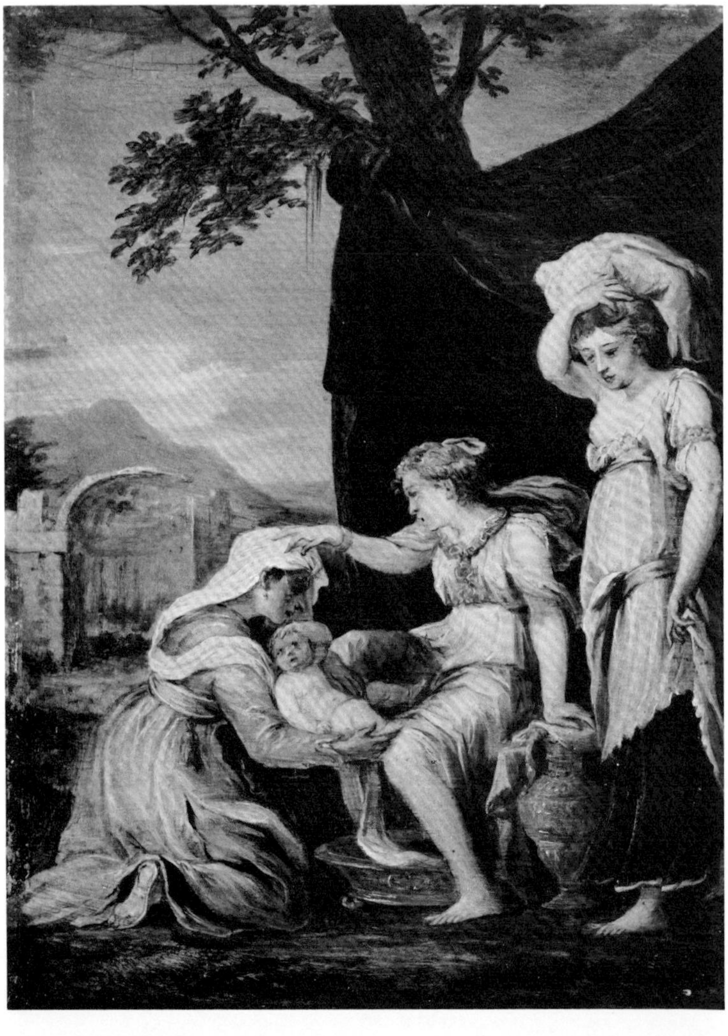

c. 1650/60
Oil on oak panel, 23.1 × 17.1 cm (9⅛ × 6¾ in.)

Inscription: on back of panel (in center in black ink): *A. SCHIAVONE P.*

Conservation: The uncradled oak panel is beveled on the top, bottom, and left sides. On the right, only 2 millimeters of a possible bevel can be seen, indicating that the panel might have been cut down on this edge. The paint film, warm brown imprimatura, and white-chalk ground reach all four edges of the panel, slightly overlapping on the left but not on the right. The paint layer is in fair condition with a tendency to blister horizontally following the grain of the wood. Although x-ray photographs show little paint loss, the faces of the female figures and much of the sky have been overpainted. There are no records of previous conservation.

Provenance: Duke of Marlborough, Blenheim Palace. Sale, Christie's, London, July 26, 1886, lot 140. Emily Charlotte Talbot, Margam Castle, Port Talbot, Glamorgan, South Wales. Acquired in 1960.

Exhibitions: London 1884.

References: Scharf 1862, 1: 160, no. 65 (132).

Gift of Mr. and Mrs. John Schneider (60.217)

Studio of Teniers

Landscape with Castle

In 1662 Teniers bought a property near the village of Perke between Mechlin and Vilvoorde; it had previously belonged to Jan Baptist van Broeckhoven and Hélène Fourment, Rubens' widow, who married Van Broeckhoven in 1644 (Van den Branden 1883: 1004). Hélène Fourment had attended the baptism of Teniers' first son in 1638, and we can assume that the families maintained friendly contact. The small castle that belonged to this property was known as *De Drij Torens* ("The Three Towers"); it appears in several of Teniers' paintings, but the castle in the Detroit picture differs considerably from it, despite the fact that it also has three towers (Dreher 1978: 682-703).

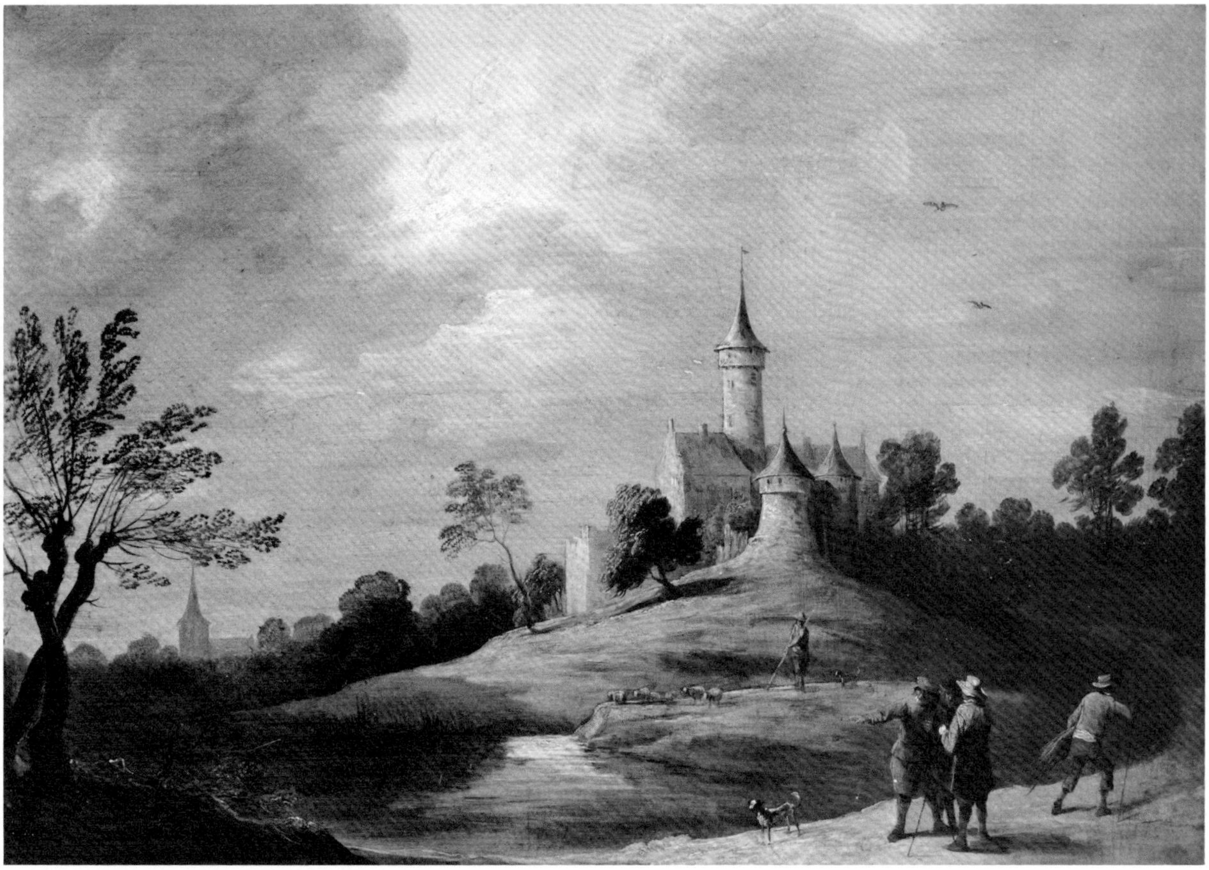

Studio of Teniers, *Landscape with Castle.*

Nor is there sufficient evidence, either in dress or physiognomy, for identifying the pointing man in the left foreground as a self-portrait, as has been suggested.

John Smith, in his *Catalogue Raisonné* (1829-42, III [1831]: 339, no. 296), described a similar painting, but its dimensions were somewhat larger ("18 × 23 in."), and there were four, not three, peasants talking together. The Detroit panel belongs evidently to the type of composition that was often repeated in Teniers' studio with minor variations. Pleasant though it is, the picture was routinely executed and should be classified as a product of the studio rather than a work of the master himself (despite testimony to its authenticity by C. Hofstede de Groot in a certificate of February 25, 1924 [museum files]).

Oil on oak panel, 29.5 × 41 cm ($11\frac{5}{8}$ × $16\frac{1}{8}$ in.)

Conservation: The cradled panel is beveled on all four sides and maintains its original dimensions. Open insect tunneling on the reverse indicates planing. The paint film and ground (white chalk) reach the edges of the panel. The paint layer is in good condition, thinly applied in most of the darker areas with thicker impasto highlights. There is minor inpainted loss in the sky and trees to the right, as well as losses on all four edges. There are no detectable pentimenti or changes in the underdrawing. Blisters were treated and the painting was cleaned and inpainted by William Suhr in 1955. In 1963 further blistering was treated and the painting was surface-cleaned and inpainted by Edward O. Korany.

Provenance: Paul Bottenwieser, Berlin. Acquired in 1925.

References: Detroit 1930: no. 219. Scheyer 1937: 55, fig. 26; 56-57. Detroit 1944: 131, no. 219. Page 1952-53: 71-72.

Gift of Paul Bottenwieser (25.11)

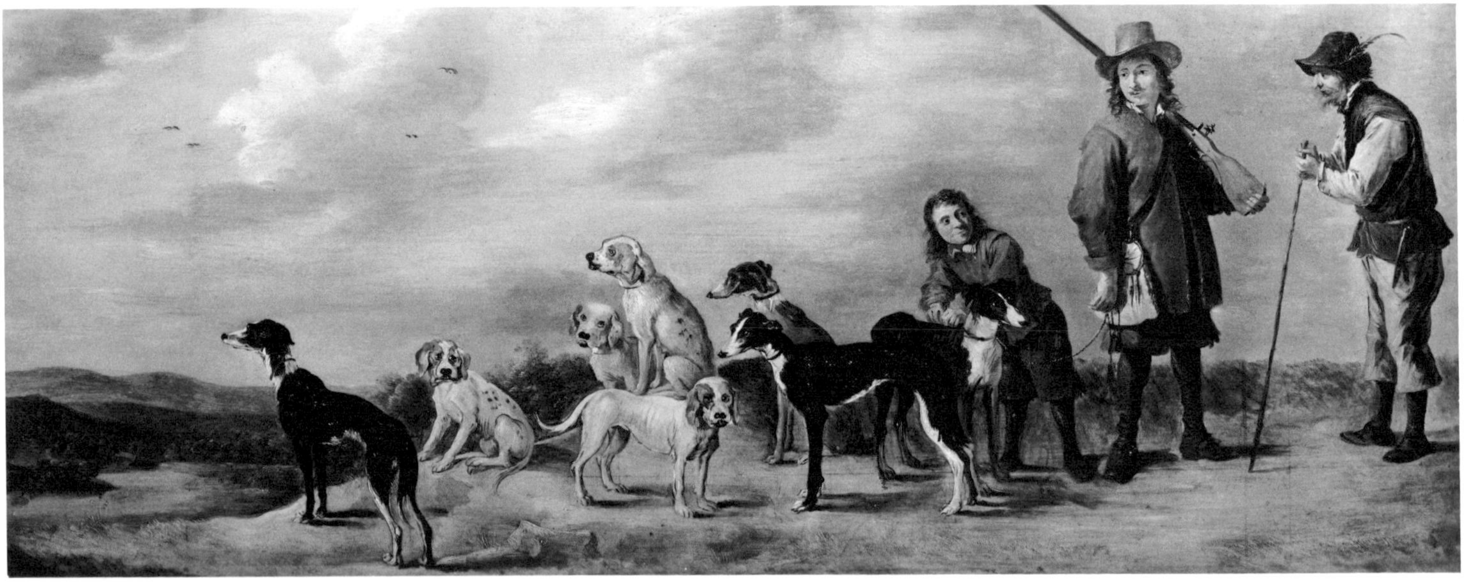

Studio of Teniers, *A Hunter with Eight Hounds.*

Studio of Teniers

A Hunter with Eight Hounds

☙ At the right of this long, narrow panel stands a handsome, well-dressed hunter carrying his rifle across his shoulder. He is accompanied by a boy (his son or a servant?) and an elderly man in modest attire, holding a walking staff with both hands, perhaps his guide or master of his hounds. The hounds are of two breeds—four greyhounds and four beagles—but they show no individuality, nor do they convey any sense of action; their role in the painting is to provide visual confirmation of the hunter's preoccupation and social standing.

This picture seems to be a reduced variant of a painting recorded by John Smith in his *Catalogue Raisonné* (1829-42, III [1831]: 427, no. 632; oil on canvas, "3 ft. 9 in. by 5 ft. 1 in.") as being in the collection of the Earl of Radnor. Smith's description reads in part:

A little retired from the front is a young sportsman, with his pouch and game (a hare); he appears to be in conversation with an elderly peasant, who leans on a stick; nine dogs, consisting of greyhounds, spaniels, beagles, etc., accompany the sportsman. This admirable production is distinguished . . . for the truth and animation displayed in the figures and animals: it is, in truth, a work of the highest excellence.

The Detroit panel, though not without merit, hardly deserves such praise. The hounds, particularly, are painted in a most pedestrian manner. The hunter—surely not a self-portrait of the artist, as has been assumed—and his companions are executed slightly more freely but they, too, lack the sure touch of Teniers himself. The painting is a characteristic example of the many works issuing from the master's busy studio that in the course of time have come to be attributed to Teniers himself, thus obscuring the high quality that characterizes works indubitably by him.

Oil on oak panel, 25.4 × 63.8 cm (10 × 25⅛ in.)

Conservation: The unbeveled panel has been planed and cradled. It is single-membered with a horizontal crack 41 centimeters long starting at the right (12.5 centimeters from the lower edge). The chalk ground and paint layer reach the edges of the panel. The paint layer is in good condition. X-ray photographs show minor losses along the above-mentioned crack and the lower edge. There is retouching in the sky covering minor losses and in the black areas, especially in the dog on the far left. In bright light a grid pattern with at least two horizontal and four vertical lines is visible, but its function is not clear. An inscription, written on the ground layer in the lower center is obvious with infrared illumination and appears as:

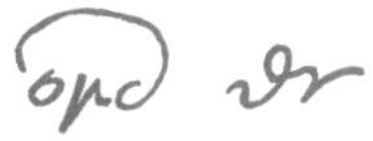

There are no records of conservation treatment.

Provenance: W. R. Valentiner, Detroit. Acquired in 1952.

References: Page 1952-53: 70-71.

Gift of Dr. W. R. Valentiner (52.176)

Style of Teniers

A Tavern Interior

This picture probably reflects a composition by Teniers; the still life at the right is very similar to that in a painting by the master in the Wallace Collection, London (no. 231). Unfortunately, the condition of the Detroit canvas is so poor that it is difficult to decide whether it is a badly damaged work by the master or a later painting, done in his manner—I consider the latter to be more likely.

Oil on canvas, 35 × 42.3 cm ($13\frac{3}{4} \times 16\frac{5}{8}$ in.)

Inscriptions: on footstool: *D T* (the T inside the D); on drawing attached to the wall: *1644*

Conservation: The painting is glue-lined and attached to an elaborately constructed seven-member stretcher. The original tacking margins have been cut off. The paint film is in poor condition on a bole-colored ground. It is very abraded, especially in the browns, which include most of the standing figures and right background. There is a hole in the niche above the candle and there are losses along the left edge. The painting was varnished by William Suhr in 1959 and 1961. It was last treated in 1976, when it was cleaned by Michael Heslip (CSL). The painting was not inpainted.

Provenance: James E. Scripps, Detroit. Acquired in 1889.

Exhibitions: Detroit 1889: 46, no. 50.

References: Detroit 1930: no. 220. Scheyer 1937: 53, fig. 24; 55-56. Detroit 1944: 131, no. 220.

Gift of James E. Scripps (1889.65)

Style of Teniers, *A Tavern Interior*.

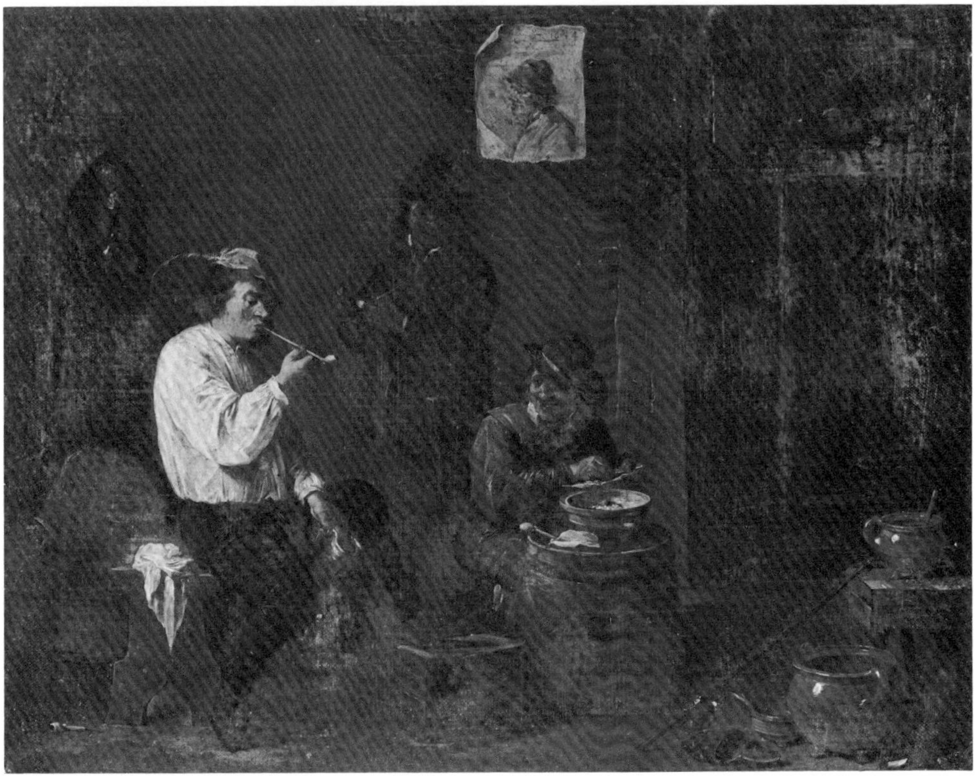

Copy after Teniers

A Country Kitchen

In a plain interior, by light coming from the left, a young Flemish peasant sits on the floor opening mussels while, in the background, two other men flank a woman stirring a pot hanging in the fireplace. In the right half of the picture, a still life of fruits and vegetables, some lying on the floor, some in a wicker basket, dominates the foreground; two dead birds lie on a large barrel, surrounded by pots and kettles of clay. A sturdy post with a broom leaning against it stresses the separation between this part of the picture and the somewhat larger area containing the figures. Attached to the back wall near the fireplace is a piece of paper with a drawing of a man's face and the date 1643 inscribed on it.

An almost identical picture is in the Museo del Prado, Madrid (no. 1798; oil on panel, 35 × 50 cm; Madrid 1975, I: 397; II: pl. 264). Besides being inscribed with the same date, it is also signed *D. Teniers F.*, and there is every reason to assume that it is the master's original version. It can be traced back as far as 1746, when it was listed in the inventory of Queen Isabella in La Granja (no. 1092); its first appearance in a Prado inventory was in 1849 (no. 1502). The Detroit version is unquestionably inferior in quality; it may well be more or less contemporary with the Prado version, although the date 1643 was probably copied along with all the other details from the Prado original and should not be taken literally as the date of the picture. I do not believe that Teniers took any part in its execution.

The title of the painting in Madrid is *The Kitchen*, without any reference to an inn, despite

Copy after Teniers, *A Country Kitchen.*

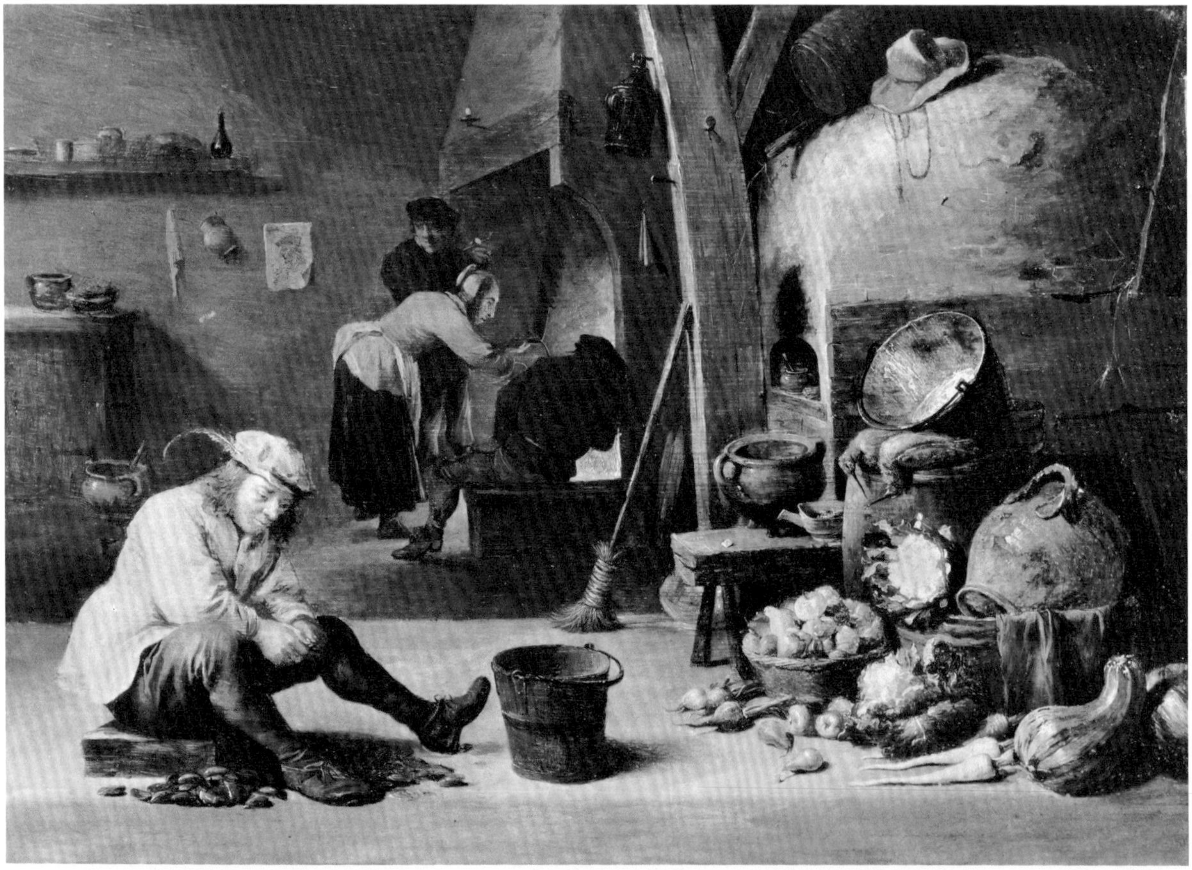

the facts that a piece of chalk lies on a wooden bench and that chalk markings, like those made in inns to count drinks, can be seen on the big timber at the right. These marks are missing in the Detroit panel—one of the few differences between it and the Prado piece—diminishing still further the likelihood of its representing the interior of an inn. *A Country Kitchen*, hence, seems to be a better title for it.

1643 (?)
Oil on oak panel, 36.3 × 52.2 cm (14¼ × 20$\frac{9}{16}$ in.)
Inscription: on drawing tacked on wall: *1643*
Conservation: The uncradled panel is beveled on the right and left sides and slightly beveled on the top. A 2-centimeter-wide wooden strip has been added to the bottom, hiding the original edge. It is reinforced from the back with a canvas strip, indented in the center where the original bevel lies. The panel has a horizontal convex warp. The ground (white chalk), reddish brown imprimatura, and paint layer reach the edges of the panel, except on the added bottom section. A heavy varnish layer and at least two generations of inpaint obscure the condition of the paint layer. The oldest retouching includes the bottom added strip. More recent retouching reinforces many of the abraded dark background colors as well as outlining and re-emphasizing shadows in the figures, still life, and architectural elements. An illegible inscription bearing some resemblance to Teniers' monogram, between the draped blue cloth and the cabbage in the still-life group to the right, is also overpaint. The painting was varnished in 1946, 1959, and 1961 by William Suhr. No prior treatment is recorded.
Provenance: Stanley M. Carper, New York. Acquired in 1938.
References: Detroit 1944: 131, no. 764. Page 1952-53: 72. Madrid 1975, 1: 265, under no. 1798.
Gift of Stanley M. Carper (38.86)

Cornelis de Vos

1584(?) HULST – ANTWERP 1651

LITTLE is known about the beginnings of De Vos' career, beyond the fact that, after his parents had moved to Antwerp, he was apprenticed (1599) to an obscure artist, David Remeeus, with whom he stayed until 1604. He acquired membership as a master in the guild of Saint Luke in 1608—the year Rubens returned from Italy—and was elected dean in 1619-20 and "principal" dean (*opperdeken*) for 1620-21. He had married in 1617 and subsequently had six children.

Although he was commissioned to paint a number of religious subjects, De Vos is principally known as a painter of portraits. Clearly influenced by Rubens as well as by Van Dyck, De Vos developed a style of portraiture that was less powerful and imaginative than Rubens', less sophisticated and intense than Van Dyck's. His is a placid art that, perhaps for that very reason, was exceedingly popular in Antwerp; despite the trappings of curtains, columns, and other devices to ennoble the ambiance of his models, they remain essentially contented members of the upper middle class, well pleased, so it seems, with the thought of having their likenesses recorded for posterity. In 1635 De Vos was one of several painters engaged by the town of Antwerp to paint the decorations, designed by Rubens, for the triumphal entry of the new Spanish governor, the Cardinal-Infante Ferdinand. De Vos is also twice recorded as a dealer in paintings (in 1616 and 1623), and it appears from his will (1648) that he was well-to-do when he died.

Attributed to De Vos

Portrait of a Lady

While the portrait of this sumptuously dressed young woman is somewhat unusual in De Vos'

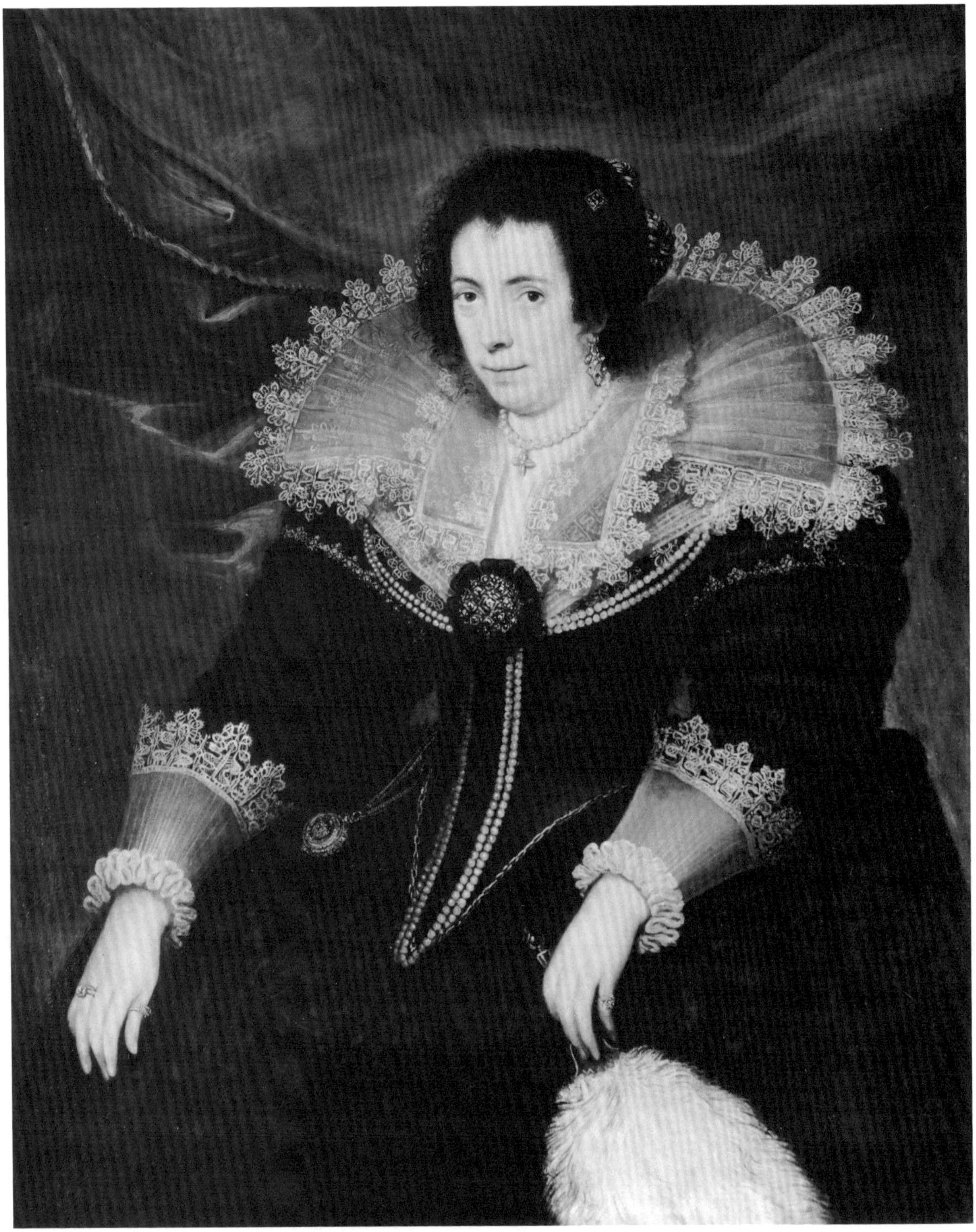

Attributed to De Vos, *Portrait of a Lady*.

oeuvre, its earlier attribution to this master is preferable to one to Frans Pourbus the Younger that was first introduced in the Detroit catalogue of 1944 (although acquired in 1925, the picture was not included in the catalogue of 1930). The fact that it is also listed, without any reservations, in the standard work on De Vos by Greindl (1944) strengthens the attribution. It is particularly the somewhat bland expression and only lightly modulated form of the face, with the dark eyes looking straight at the beholder, that are characteristic of the artist's manner of portraiture. The rather impersonal treatment of other parts of the picture, including the hands and the lace cuffs and ruff, might indicate that the picture was in part executed by assistants.

Greindl's date of around 1630 is almost certainly derived from the costume depicted, which corresponds, without being identical, to fashions worn by ladies in portraits by Van Dyck during his second Antwerp period (1627-32). The fact that the young woman wears a fashion not known before this time furnishes a very strong argument against an attribution to Frans Pourbus the Younger, who died in 1622.

c. 1630

Oil on canvas, 118 × 94 cm (46 7/16 × 37 in.)

Conservation: The painting has two glue-linings, and its original tacking margins have been removed. The paint layer appears to be in fairly good condition beneath an extremely yellowed varnish. The red background, however, has been very liberally reworked. The brightest orange highlights in the red curtain are overpaint and have been spattered with paint in imitation of flyspecks. The outermost lace borders (especially on the left side), as well as highlights in the rings, have also been reinforced. Infrared examination shows pentimenti in the fingertips of both hands. There are no conservation treatment records.

Provenance: Paul Reinhardt, New York. Acquired in 1925.

Exhibitions: Denver 1956.

References: Detroit 1944: 104, no. 683 (as by Frans Pourbus the Younger). Greindl 1944: 81, 138. Puyvelde 1962: 28 ("attributed to Pourbus").

Gift of Henry Reinhardt and Sons, Inc. (25.26)

Sebastian Vrancx

1573 ANTWERP 1647

A PUPIL of Adam van Noort, who was also one of Rubens' teachers, Vrancx traveled for some time in Italy before being admitted in 1600 as a master in the Antwerp painters' guild. He served as a "lower" dean (*onderdeken*) in 1611, and one year later advanced to the principal deanship (*opperdeken*). In the same year he married Maria Pampfi, the daughter of an Antwerp art dealer. He remained one of the most active members of the guild, also acquiring a reputation as a poet and organizer of festivities; the titles of 14 plays written by him for such occasions have been preserved. He also obtained the rank of captain in the civic guard of Antwerp, a position that he held for ten years. The sword worn by Vrancx in his engraved portrait by Van Dyck in the *Iconographie* probably refers to his military career.

The range of themes painted by Vrancx is wide, including genre scenes, church interiors, landscapes, and occasionally even religious subjects. Yet he is principally known for his scenes of military encampments, skirmishes between horsemen, and attacks on villagers or merchants by brigands. He contributed figures to works by other artists, including Joos de Momper and David Vinckeboons, and was also popular as a teacher. He was frequently imitated, and many works unworthy of his talent are still attributed to him.

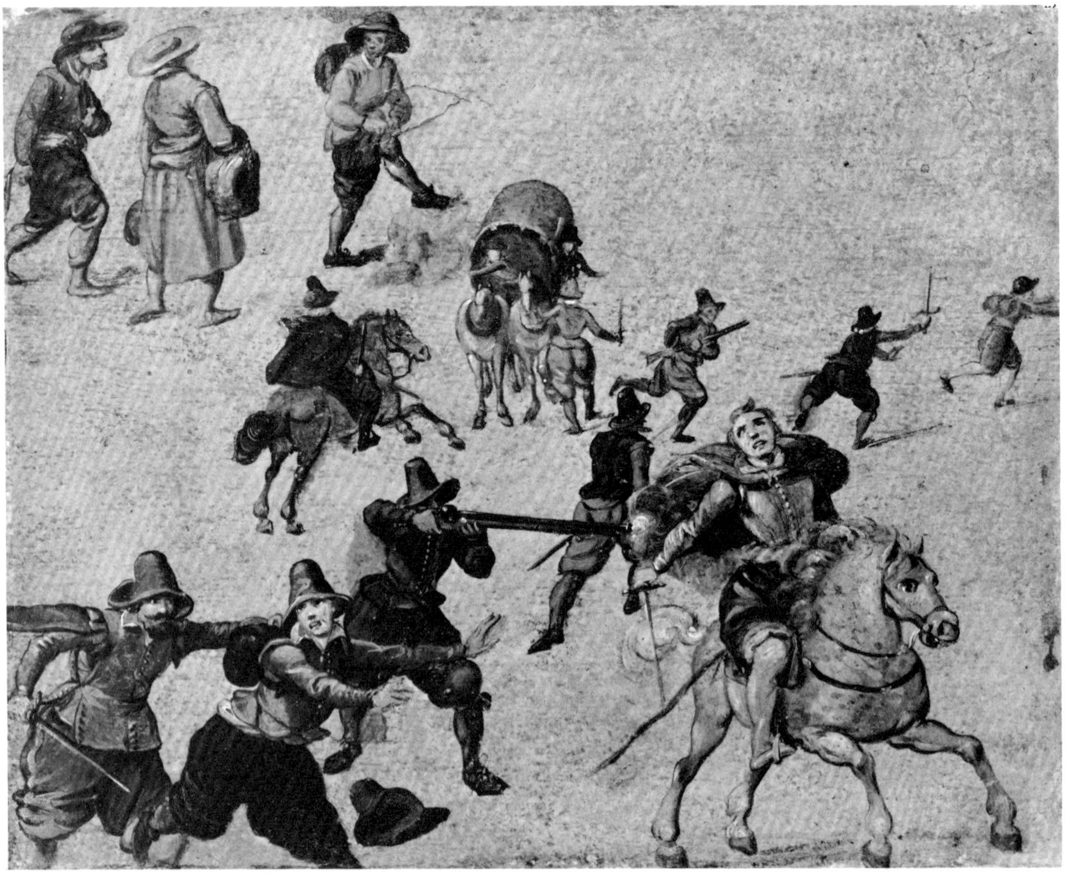

Copy after Vrancx, *Figure Studies of Soldiers and Peasants.*

Copy after Vrancx

Figure Studies of Soldiers and Peasants

The figures depicted on this small panel obviously belong to two different compositions. The majority of them are involved in an attack by military marauders on a party of travelers. The three figures at the upper left, however, are not part of this scene but appear to be peasants moving about peacefully and unafraid. The rendering of the military figures on a diminishing scale, suggesting a distribution in depth, although no indication is given of the actual setting, makes it likely that they were copied from a painting where they indeed occupied corresponding places in an open air setting. The assumption that they (and probably the three peasants, too) were copied gains additional support from the coarse and rather clumsy execution, far below the level of quality one expects of one of Antwerp's most spirited painters.

Oil on paper adhered to panel, 18.7 × 22.6 cm (7⅜ × 8⅞ in.)

Conservation: The paper support is a laminated, pulp (straw) type not used before the 19th century. It is glued to an uncradled, unbeveled (on all four sides) panel. The composition has very likely been trimmed. The paper is torn in the upper right corner, in the figure of the soldier at top center, and cutting through the right ankle of the soldier with the musket and the hand of the man in front of him. There is minor inpainting, mostly in the gray background, and a discolored, greenish coating in blotches over the entire surface. One large paint loss exists in the legs of the second figure from the left at the lower edge. No conservation records exist.

Provenance: Nicholas Roerich, New York (as by Esaias van de Velde). Acquired in 1962.

Gift of Mr. and Mrs. A. D. Wilkinson (62.182)

BIBLIOGRAPHY AND INDEXES

BIBLIOGRAPHY AND EXHIBITIONS

Titles of exhibitions accompanied by a printed catalogue are given in italics; all others are in quotation marks. The abbreviations *BDIA* and *BDMA* signify *Bulletin of the Detroit Institute of Arts* and *Bulletin of the Detroit Museum of Art*, respectively.

Albion 1959. Albion College, Albion (Michigan), "Old Master Paintings," 1959.

Album 1905. *Album der Tentoonstelling Jacob Jordaens*, Antwerp, 1905.

Amsterdam 1935. Kunsthandel P. de Boer, Amsterdam, "Bloemstukken van Oude Meesters," 1935.

Antwerp 1905. Koninklijk Museum voor Schone Kunsten, Antwerp, *Tentoonstelling Jacob Jordaens*, exh. cat., 1905.

Antwerp 1977. Koninklijk Museum voor Schone Kunsten, Antwerp, *P. P. Rubens / Schilderijen—Olieverfschetsen—Tekeningen*, exh. cat., 1977.

Antwerp/Rotterdam 1960. Rubenshuis, Antwerp, and Museum Boymans-Van Beuningen, Rotterdam, *Antoon Van Dyck/Tekeningen en Olieverfschetsen*, exh. cat. by R.-A. d'Hulst and H. Vey, 1960.

Art News 1947. "This Flemish Baroque Gift for Detroit," *Art News* 46/2 (Apr. 1947): 38-39.

Art News 1964. "Entering Public Domain," *Art News* 63/6 (Oct. 1964): 28-29.

Art News Annual 1947. "Art News of the Year," *Art News Annual* 46/9 (Nov. 1947): 140.

Bachrach 1978. A.G.H. Bachrach, review of L. Herrmann, *British Landscape Painting of the Eighteenth Century*, *Art Bulletin* 60/4 (Dec. 1978): 732-734.

Baldass 1930. L. Baldass, "Drei Jahrhunderte flämische Malerei," *Pantheon* 5 (Mar. 1930): 130-136.

Baltimore 1946. Baltimore Museum of Art, *Musical Instruments and Their Portrayal in Art*, exh. cat., 1946.

BDIA 1964. "Other Works of Rubens in the Collection of the Detroit Institute of Arts," *BDIA* 43/3-4 (1964): 53-59.

BDMA 1908. "The Story of Christ, as Related in Paintings in the Museum," *BDMA* 2/1 (Jan. 1908): 1-4, 7.

BDMA 1909. "Mrs. Harriet J. Scripps Presents Fifteen Old Masters," *BDMA* 3/4 (Oct. 1909): 46-50.

Berlin 1906. Gräflich Redernsches Palais, Berlin, *Ausstellung von Werken alter Kunst aus dem Privatbesitz der Mitglieder des Kaiser-Friedrich-Museums-Vereins*, exh. cat., 1906.

Berlin 1909. Königliche Kunst-Akademie, Berlin. *Ausstellung von Bildnissen des fünfzehnten bis achtzehnten Jahrhunderts aus dem Privatbesitz der Mitglieder des Kaiser-Friedrich-Museums-Vereins*, exh. cat., 1909.

Berlin 1929. Galerie Dr. Schäffer, Berlin, *Die Meister des holländischen Interieurs*, exh. cat. by K. Erasmus, 1929.

Berlin 1975. Staatliche Museen, Gemäldegalerie, Berlin, *Katalog der ausgestellten Gemälde des 13.-18. Jahrhunderts*, cat. by E. Schleier, Berlin, 1975.

Berlin-Dahlem 1978. *Peter Paul Rubens/Kritischer Katalog in Besitz der Gemäldegalerie Berlin*, cat. by J. Kelch, Berlin, 1978.

Bloch 1965. V. Bloch, "Michael Sweerts und Italien," *Jahrbuch der Staatlichen Kunstsammlungen in Baden-Württemberg* 2 (1965): 155-174.

Bloch 1968. V. Bloch, *Michael Sweerts*, The Hague, 1968.

Borea 1966. E. Borea, *Caravaggio e i caravaggeschi*, Milan, 1966.

Bott 1961-62. G. Bott, "Stillebenmaler des 17. Jahrhunderts: Isaak Soreau, Peter Binoit," *Kunst in Hessen und am Mittelrhein*, Darmstadt, 1961-62: 27-93.

Bouchery and Van den Wijngaert 1941. H. F. Bouchery and F. van den Wijngaert, *P. P. Rubens en het Plantijnsche Huis*, Antwerp, 1941.

Brussels 1910. Musées Royaux du Cinquantenaire, Brussels, *Exposition d'art ancien / L'Art belge au XVIIe siècle*, exh. cat., 1910.

Brussels 1927. Galerie Fiévez, Brussels, 1927.

Brussels 1937. Musées Royaux des Beaux-Arts de Belgique, Brussels, *Esquisses de Rubens*, exh. cat., 1937.

Brussels 1965. Musées Royaux des Beaux-Arts de Belgique, *Le siècle de Rubens*, exh. cat., 1965.

Bryant 1915. L. M. Bryant, *What Pictures to See in America*, New York, 1915.

Bulletin-Rubens 1897. "Oeuvres de Rubens: Addenda," *Bulletin-Rubens* 5 (1897): 90.

Burchard 1928. L. Burchard, "Jugendwerke von Jacob Jordaens," *Jahrbuch der preuszischen Kunstsammlungen* 49 (1928): 207-218.

Burroughs 1926. C. H. Burroughs, "A Rubens Portrait," *BDIA* 7/8 (May 1926): 85-87.

Butsch 1881. A. F. Butsch, *Die Bücherornamentik der Hoch und Spätrenaissance*, Munich, 1881.

Cambridge/New York 1956. Fogg Art Museum, Cambridge, and Pierpont Morgan Library, New York, *Drawings and Oil Sketches by P. P. Rubens from American Collections*, exh. cat., 1956.

Chattanooga 1952. George Thomas Hunter Gallery of Art, Chattanooga, *Opening Exhibition*, exh. cat., 1952.

Chennevières and Montaiglon 1853-54. P. de Chennevières and A. de Montaiglon, eds., *Abecedario de P. J. Mariette* II (*Archives de l'art français* IV), Paris 1853-54.

Cincinnati 1948. Cincinnati Art Museum, *Nicolas Poussin/Peter Paul Rubens*, exh. cat., 1948.

Cleveland 1963. Cleveland Museum of Art, *Style, Truth and the Portrait*, exh. cat. by R. G. Saisselin, 1963.
Cleveland 1973. Cleveland Museum of Art, *Dutch Art and Life in the Seventeenth Century*, exh. cat., 1973.
Collins Baker and Constable 1930. C. H. Collins Baker and W. G. Constable, *English Painting of the Sixteenth and Seventeenth Centuries*, New York, 1930.
Cologne 1968. Kunsthalle, Cologne, *Weltkunst aus Privatbesitz*, exh. cat., 1968.
Cologne 1977. Wallraf-Richartz Museum, Cologne, *Rubens in Italien (Catalogue Peter Paul Rubens, 1577-1640* I), exh. cat. by J. Müller Hofstede, 1977.
Colorado Springs 1955. Colorado Springs Fine Art Center, "The Changeful Earth," 1955.
Comstock 1954. H. Comstock, "The Connoisseur in America: New Study of a Van Dyck Family Group," *Connoisseur* 134 (Sept. 1954): 71.
Cust 1900. L. Cust, *Anthony Van Dyck*, London, 1900.
De Bie 1661. C. de Bie, *Het gulden Cabinet*, Lier, 1661.
Denucé 1932. J. Denucé, *De antwerpsche "Konstkamers" / Inventarissen van Kunstverzamelingen te Antwerpen in de 16e en 17e Eeuwen*, Amsterdam, 1932.
Denver 1956. Denver Art Museum, *Clothes Make the Man*, exh. cat., 1956.
De Piles 1715. R. de Piles, *Abrégé de la vie des peintres*, Paris, 1715.
Detroit 1889. Detroit Museum of Art, *Catalogue of the Scripps Collection of Old Masters*, exh. cat. by J. E. Scripps, 1889.
Detroit 1926. Detroit Institute of Arts, *The Third Loan Exhibition of Old Masters*, exh. cat., 1926.
Detroit 1927. Detroit Institute of Arts, *The Fifth Loan Exhibition of Old Masters*, exh. cat., 1927.
Detroit 1929. Detroit Institute of Arts, *Eighth Loan Exhibition of Old Masters/Paintings by Anthony van Dyck*, exh. cat. by W. R. Valentiner and L. J. Walther, 1929.
Detroit 1930. Detroit Institute of Arts, *Catalogue of Paintings in the Permanent Collection of the Detroit Institute of Arts of the City of Detroit*, cat. by W. Heil and C. H. Burroughs, Detroit, 1930.
Detroit 1936. Detroit Institute of Arts, *An Exhibition of Sixty Paintings and Some Drawings by Peter Paul Rubens*, exh. cat. by W. R. Valentiner and J. Walther, 1936.
Detroit 1941. Detroit Institute of Arts, *Masterpieces of Art from European and American Collections*, exh. cat. by F. W. Robinson and E. P. Richardson, 1941.
Detroit 1944. *The Detroit Institute of Arts / Catalogue of Paintings*, 1944.
Detroit 1964-65. Detroit Institute of Arts, *The Institute Collects*, exh. cat., 1964-65.
Detroit 1971. *The Detroit Institute of Arts Illustrated Handbook*, Detroit, 1971.
Detroit 1978. Detroit Institute of Arts, *Homage to Rubens*, exh. cat. by M. Grimes, 1978.
Dreher 1978. F. P. Dreher, "The Artist as Seigneur: Chateaux and Their Proprietors in the Work of David Teniers II," *Art Bulletin* 60 (Dec. 1978): 682-703.
Du Choul 1581. G. du Choul, *Discours de la religion des anciens romains*, Lyon, 1581.
Van Dyck 1940. *Anton Van Dyck / Italienisches Skizzenbuch*, G. Adriani, ed., Vienna, 1940.
Ferguson 1954. G. W. Ferguson, *Signs and Symbols in Christian Art*, New York, 1954.
Fischel n. d. [1906]. O. Fischel, *Tizian / Des Meisters Gemälde (Klassiker der Kunst in Gesamtausgaben* III), Stuttgart and Berlin, n. d. [1906].
Fort Wayne 1953. Fort Wayne Art School and Museum, "Picture of the Month," 1953.
Frankfurter n. d. [1934]. A. Frankfurter, *Portrait of a Young Man by Anthony van Dyck*, New York (privately pub.), n. d. [1934].
Freedberg 1978. D. Freedberg, "L'Année Rubens, manifestations et publications en 1977," *Revue de l'art*, new ser., 39 (1978): 90.
Freiherr von Hadeln 1909. D. Freiherr von Hadeln, "Die Porträtausstellung des Kaiser-Friedrich-Museums-Vereins II," *Zeitschrift für bildende Kunst*, new ser., 20 (1909): 296-300.
Friedländer 1936. M. J. Friedländer, *Anthonis Mor und seine Zeitgenossen (Die altniederländische Malerei* XIII), Leiden, 1936.
Friedländer 1975. M. J. Friedländer, *Antonis Mor and His Contemporaries (Early Netherlandish Painting* XIII), Leiden and Brussels, 1975.
Friedmann 1946. H. Friedmann, *The Symbolic Goldfinch, Its History and Significance in European Devotional Art*, New York, 1946.
Frölich-Bum 1912. L. Frölich-Bum, "Andrea Meldolla, gennant Schiavone," *Jahrbuch der kunsthistorischen Sammlungen des allerhöchsten Kaiserhauses* 31 (1912): 137-220.
Garlick 1974-76. K. J. Garlick, *A Catalogue of Pictures at Althorp (Walpole Society* XLV), Glasgow, 1974-76.
Genoa 1955. Palazzo dell'Accademia, Genoa, *100 opere di Van Dyck*, exh. cat., 1955.
Gerson 1968. H. Gerson, *Rembrandt Paintings*, Amsterdam, 1968.
Gerson and Ter Kuile 1960. H. Gerson and E. H. ter Kuile, *Art and Architecture in Belgium / 1600-1800*, Harmondsworth, 1960.
Glück 1930. G. Glück, "Drei Jahrhunderte vlämischer Kunst II," *Belvedere* 15/5 (1930): 167-174.
Glück 1931. G. Glück, *Van Dyck / Des Meisters Gemälde (Klassiker der Kunst in Gesamtausgaben* XIII), Stuttgart and Berlin, 1931.
Glück 1932. G. Glück, "Ein verkanntes Werk von Rubens im Prado zu Madrid," *Zeitschrift für Kunstgeschichte* I (1932): 271-273.
Goldstein 1967. C. Goldstein, review of B. Teyssèdre, *Roger de Piles et les débats sur le coloris au siècle de Louis XIV*, *Art Bulletin* 49/3 (Sept. 1967): 264-268.

Goldstein 1972. C. Goldstein, "Theory and Practice in the French Academy: Louis Licherie's Abigail and David," *Burlington Magazine* 111 (June 1969): 346-351.

Goris and Held 1947. J.-A. Goris and J. S. Held, *Rubens in America*, New York, 1947.

Gould 1978. C. Gould, "Dr. Garlick's Althorp Catalogue," *Burlington Magazine* 120 (July 1978): 470.

Grand Rapids 1959. Grand Rapids Art Gallery, "Community Angels Build," 1959.

Greindl 1944. E. Greindl, *Corneille de Vos / Portraitiste flamand (1584-1651)*, Brussels, 1944.

Greindl 1956. E. Greindl, *Les Peintres flamands de nature morte au XVIIe siècle*, Brussels, 1956.

Greindl 1973. E. Greindl, "Contribution à la connaissance du style de Gysbrecht Leytens," *Pantheon* 31/3 (July-Sept. 1973): 254-263.

The Hague 1928. Gallery Kleykamp, The Hague, 1928.

Hairs 1951. M.-L. Hairs, "Osias Beert, l'ancien, peintre de fleurs," *Revue belge d'archéologie et d'histoire de l'art* 20/3 (1951): 237-251.

Hamilton 1964. Art Gallery of Hamilton (Ontario), *50th Anniversary Exhibition*, exh. cat., 1964.

Hartford 1935. Wadsworth Atheneum, Hartford, 1935.

Hartford 1950-51. Wadsworth Atheneum, Hartford, *Life in 17th-Century Holland*, exh. cat., 1950-51.

Hartford/Andover 1949-50. Wadsworth Atheneum, Hartford, and Addison Gallery of American Art, Andover, *Pictures within Pictures*, exh. cat., 1949-50.

Hasselt 1840. A. van Hasselt, *L'Oeuvre de P. P. Rubens*, Brussels, 1840.

Haverkamp Begemann 1953. E. Haverkamp Begemann, *Olieverfschetsen van Rubens*, Rotterdam, 1953.

Haverkamp Begemann 1975. E. Haverkamp Begemann, *The Achilles Series (Corpus Rubenianum Ludwig Burchard* x), London, 1975.

Heckscher 1958. W. S. Heckscher, *Rembrandt's Anatomy of Dr. Nicolaas Tulp: An Iconological Study*, New York, 1958.

Heil 1928. W. Heil, "The Edgar B. Whitcomb Collection in Detroit," *Art in America* 16/2 (Feb. 1928): 49-58.

Heil 1930. W. Heil, "Sketches by Rubens and Van Dyck," *BDIA* 11/6 (Mar. 1930): 78-81.

Held 1939. J. S. Held, "Malerier og Tegninger af Jacob Jordaens i Kunstmuseet," *Kunstmuseets Aarsskrift* 26 (1939): 1-43.

Held 1940. J. S. Held, "Jordaens' Portraits of His Family," *Art Bulletin* 22/2 (June 1940): 70-82.

Held 1951. J. S. Held, "Sketches by Lucas Franchoys the Younger," *Art Quarterly* 14/1 (Spring 1951): 45-55.

Held 1951a. J. S. Held, "A Rubens Portrait for Sarasota," *Ringling Museum Annual*, 1951: unpaginated.

Held 1956. J. S. Held, "Drawings and Oil Sketches by Rubens from American Collections," *Burlington Magazine* 98 (Apr. 1956): 123-124.

Held 1957. J. S. Held, "*Artis Pictoriae Amator*, An Antwerp Art Patron and His Collection," *Gazette des Beaux-Arts*, ser. 6, 50 (1957): 53-84.

Held 1958. J. S. Held, "Le Roi à la Ciasse," *Art Bulletin* 40/2 (June 1958): 139-149.

Held 1964. J. S. Held, "Rubens' *St. Ives*," *BDIA* 43/3-4 (1964): 47-52.

Held 1969. J. S. Held, "Jordaens at Ottawa," *Burlington Magazine* 111 (May 1969): 265-273.

Held 1977. J. S. Held, *Rubens and the Book*, Williamstown, 1977.

Held 1980. J. S. Held, *The Oil Sketches of Peter Paul Rubens*, 2 vols., Princeton, 1980.

Hertford 1981. *The Hertford Mawson Letters*, ed. by J. Ingamells, London, 1981.

D'Hulst 1953. R.-A. d'Hulst, "Jacob Jordaens, Schets van een Chronologie zijner Werken ontstaan voor 1618," *Gentse Bijdragen tot de Kunstgeschiedenis* 14 (1953): 89-138.

D'Hulst 1953a. R.-A. d'Hulst, "Zeichnungen von Jacob Jordaens aus seiner Frühzeit, bis etwa 1618," *Zeitschrift für Kunstgeschichte* 16/2 (1953): 208-221.

D'Hulst 1956. R.-A. d'Hulst, *De Tekeningen van Jacob Jordaens*, Brussels, 1956.

Jaffé 1953. M. Jaffé, "Rubens' Sketching in Paint," *Art News* 52/3 (May 1953): 34-37.

Jaffé 1967. M. Jaffé, "Van Dyck's Sketches for His Portraits of Duquesnoy and of Van Uffel," *Bulletin / Musées Royaux des Beaux-Arts de Belgique* 16 (1967): 155-162.

Jaffé 1968. M. Jaffé, "Rubens in Italy Part II," *Burlington Magazine* 110 (Apr. 1968): 174-187.

Jaffé 1972. M. Jaffé, "Rubens' *David and Abigail*," *Burlington Magazine* 114 (Dec. 1972): 863-864.

Jaffé 1977. M. Jaffé, *Rubens and Italy*, Oxford, 1977.

Janson 1948. H. W. Janson, review of H. Friedmann, *The Symbolic Goldfinch*, *Gazette des Beaux-Arts*, ser. 6, 34 (Aug. 1948): 137-138.

Janson 1952. H. W. Janson, *Apes and Ape Lore*, London, 1952.

Jongh 1967. E. de Jongh, *Zinne- en Minnebeelden in de Schilderkunst van de zeventiende Eeuw*, n. p., 1967.

Judson and Van de Velde 1978. R. R. Judson and C. van de Velde, *Book Illustrations and Title Pages (Corpus Rubenianum Ludwig Burchard* XXI), London and Philadelphia, 1978.

Kindler 1968. *Kindlers Malerei Lexikon*, Zürich, 1968.

Knipping 1939-40. B. Knipping, *De Iconographie van de Contra Reformatie in de Nederlanden*, Hilversum, 1939-40.

Kultzen 1954. R. Kultzen, "Michael Sweerts (1624-64)," unpub. diss., Hamburg, 1954.

Larsen 1952. E. Larsen, *P. P. Rubens*, Antwerp, 1952.

Lehmann-Hartleben and Olsen 1942. K. Lehmann-Hartleben and E. C. Olsen, *Dionysiac Sarcophagi in Baltimore*, Baltimore, 1942.

Leningrad 1963. *Van Dyck Paintings in the Hermitage*, cat. by M. Varshavskaia, Leningrad, 1963.

Lewison 1951. F. Lewison, "Rubens' Nudes Still Shock the Unwary," *Design* 52/7 (Apr. 1951): 21.

Liechtenstein 1767. *Descrizione completa di tutto ciò che ritrovasi nella galleria di pittura e scultura di Sua Altezza Giuseppe Wenceslao del S.R.I. Principe regnante della casa di Lichtenstein*, cat. by V. Fanti, Vienna, 1767.

Liechtenstein 1780. *Description des tableaux et des pièces de sculpture que renferme la gallerie de son Altesse François Joseph, chef et Prince regnant de la maison de Liechtenstein*, Vienna, 1780.

Liechtenstein 1873. *Katalog der fürstlich Liechtensteinischen Bildergalerie im Gartenpalais der Rossau zu Wien*, Vienna, 1873.

London 1835. British Institution, London, *Pictures by Italian, Spanish, Flemish, Dutch and French Masters*, exh. cat., 1835.

London 1842. British Institution, London, *Works of Sir D. Wilkie, R. A., Together with Pictures by Ancient Masters*, exh. cat., 1842.

London 1866. South Kensington Museum, London, *Special Exhibition of National Portraits*, exh. cat., 1866.

London 1884. Davis's Galleries, London, *A Collection of One Hundred and Twenty Paintings by David Teniers (from Blenheim Palace)*, exh. cat., 1884.

London 1911. Grafton Galleries, London, 1911.

London 1946. Royal Academy of Arts, London, *Catalogue of the Exhibition of the King's Pictures / 1946-47*, exh. cat., 1946.

London 1950. Wildenstein and Company, Inc., London, *A Loan Exhibition of Works by Peter Paul Rubens, KT.*, exh. cat. by L. Burchard, 1950.

London 1970. National Gallery, London, *The Flemish School, circa 1600-circa 1900*, cat. by G. Martin, London, 1970.

London 1979. Brod Gallery, London, *Jan Brueghel the Elder / A Loan Exhibition of Paintings*, exh. cat., 1979.

Los Angeles 1946. Los Angeles County Museum, *Loan Exhibition of Forty-three Paintings by Rubens and Twenty-five Paintings by Van Dyck*, exh. cat., 1946.

Los Angeles 1955. University of California, Los Angeles, "Origins of Landscape," 1955.

Madrid 1975. *Museo del Prado / Catálogo de pinturas I / Escuela flamenca siglo XVII*, cat. by M. Díaz Padrón, Madrid, 1975.

Malibu 1975. *The J. Paul Getty Museum*, Malibu, cat. by B. Fredericksen, London, 1975.

Martin 1905. W. Martin, "The Life of a Dutch Artist in the Seventeenth Century / I—Instruction in Drawing," *Burlington Magazine* 7 (May 1905): 125-131.

Martin 1907. W. Martin, "Michiel Sweerts als Schilder," *Oud Holland* 25 (1907): 133-156.

Mauquoy-Hendrickx 1956. M. Mauquoy-Hendrickx, *L'Iconographie d'Antoine van Dyck*, Brussels, 1956.

McVan 1942. A. J. McVan, "Spanish Dwarfs," *Notes Hispanic* 2 (1942): 96-129.

Milwaukee/Cincinnati 1956. Milwaukee Art Center and Cincinnati Art Museum, *Still Life Painting Since 1470*, exh. cat., 1956.

Montfaucon 1721. *Antiquity Explained and Represented in Sculptures, by the Learned Father Montfaucon*, David Humphreys, trans., London, 1721.

Müller Hofstede 1967. J. Müller Hofstede, "Rubens und Tizian: Das Bild Karls V.," *Münchner Jahrbuch der bildenden Kunst* 18 (1967): 33-96.

Müller Hofstede 1968. J. Müller Hofstede, "Zur Kopfstudie im Werk von Rubens," *Wallraf-Richartz-Jahrbuch* 30 (1968): 223-252.

Münz 1952. L. Münz, *Rembrandt's Etchings*, London, 1952.

Munich 1973. Alte Pinakothek, Munich, *Jan van Kessel der Ältere, 1626-1679 / Die Vier Erdteile*, exh. cat. by U. Krempel, 1973.

Muskegon 1949. Hackley Art Gallery, Muskegon, "Music in Art," 1949.

New York 1939. New York World's Fair, *Masterpieces of Art*, exh. cat., 1939.

New York 1942. Schaeffer and Brandt, Inc., New York, *Peter Paul Rubens*, exh. cat. by L. M. Nash, 1942.

New York 1951. Wildenstein and Company, Inc., New York, *A Loan Exhibition of Rubens*, exh. cat. by L. Burchard, 1951.

New York 1956. Wildenstein and Company, Inc., New York, *The Nude in Painting*, exh. cat., 1956.

New York 1961. Mortimer Brandt Gallery, New York, "Five Hundred Years of Still-Life," 1961.

New York 1967. M. Knoedler and Company, New York, *Masters of the Loaded Brush/Oil Sketches from Rubens to Tiepolo*, exh. cat., 1967.

New York 1968-69. Wildenstein and Company, Inc., New York, *Gods and Heroes / Baroque Images of Antiquity*, exh. cat. by E. Williams, 1968-69.

Norris 1963. C. Norris, "Rubens' Adoration of the Kings of 1609," *Nederlands kunsthistorisch Jaarboek* 14 (1963): 129-136.

Oldenbourg 1921. R. Oldenbourg, *P. P. Rubens / Des Meisters Gemälde (Klassiker der Kunst in Gesamtausgaben V)*, Berlin and Leipzig, 1921.

Ottawa 1968-69. National Gallery of Canada, Ottawa, *Jacob Jordaens 1593-1678*, exh. cat. by M. Jaffé, 1968-69.

Oxford 1916. *Pictures by the Old Masters in the Library of Christ Church, Oxford*, cat. by T. Borenius, London, 1916.

Page 1952-53. A. F. Page, "A Group of Paintings by David Teniers the Younger," *BDIA* 32/3 (1952-53): 70-72.

Pani 1940. A. J. Pani, *La segunda Colección Pani de pinturas/ Catálogo descriptivo y comentado*, cat. by A. J. Pani, Mexico City, 1940.

Paris 1922. Musée du Louvre, Paris, *Catalogue des peintures exposées dans les galeries*, cat. by L. Demonts, Paris, 1922.

Paris 1936. Musée de l'Orangerie, Paris, *Rubens et son temps*, exh. cat. by C. Sterling, 1936.
Paris 1977. Grand Palais, Paris, *Le siècle de Rubens dans les collections publiques françaises*, exh. cat., 1977.
Parker and Mathey 1957. K. T. Parker and J. Mathey, *Antoine Watteau*, Paris, 1957.
Passeri 1772. G. B. Passeri, *Vite de' pittori, scultori ed architetti che hanno lavorato in Roma morti dal 1641 fino al 1673*, Rome, 1772 (J. Hess, ed., Leipzig and Vienna, 1934).
Payne 1960-61. E. H. Payne, "Two Northern Landscapes of the 17th Century," *BDIA* 40/3-4 (1960-61): 54-57.
Philadelphia 1963. Philadelphia Museum of Art, *A World of Flowers*, exh. cat., 1963.
Pigler 1956. A. Pigler, "Portraying the Dead; Painting—Graphic Art," *Acta Historiae Artium Academiae Scientiarum Hungaricae* 4 (1956): 1-75.
Pittsburgh 1954. Carnegie Institute, Pittsburgh, *Pictures of Everyday Life / Genre Painting in Europe / 1500-1900*, exh. cat., 1954.
Princeton 1979. Princeton University Art Museum, *Van Dyck as Religious Artist*, exh. cat. by J. R. Martin and G. Feigenbaum, 1979.
Puyvelde 1940. L. van Puyvelde, *Les esquisses de Rubens*, Basel, 1940.
Puyvelde 1953. L. van Puyvelde, *Jordaens*, Paris and Brussels, 1953.
Puyvelde 1962. L. van Puyvelde, *La peinture flamande au siècle de Bosch et de Breughel*, Paris, 1962.
Puyvelde 1964. L. van Puyvelde, *Rubens*, Brussels, 1964.
Raleigh 1956. North Carolina Museum of Art, Raleigh, *Catalogue of Paintings*, cat. by W. R. Valentiner, Raleigh, 1956.
Revue de l'art 1936. "Les Ventes," *Revue de l'art* 70 (July 1936): 44-54.
Richardson 1936. E. P. Richardson, "The Rubens Exhibit," *BDIA* 15/5 (Feb. 1936): 61-63.
Richardson 1937. E. P. Richardson, "Architectural Painting in the Netherlands," *BDIA* 16/7 (Apr. 1937): 105-113.
Richardson 1938. E. P. Richardson, "From Old Breughel to Van Goyen," *Art Quarterly* 1/3 (Summer 1938): 181-203.
Richardson 1939. E. P. Richardson, "Two Court Fools by Frans Floris," *BDIA* 18/8 (May 1939): 1-4.
Richardson 1940. E. P. Richardson, "A Jacobean Portrait by Gheeraerts," *BDIA* 19/8 (May 1940): 85-86.
Richardson 1946. E. P. Richardson, "Hygeia, the Goddess of Health, by Peter Paul Rubens," *BDIA* 25/1 (1946): 9-11.
Richardson 1947. E. P. Richardson, "The Holy Family with St. Anne by Jacob Jordaens," *BDIA* 26/3 (1947): 56-58.
Richardson 1947a. E. P. Richardson, "Rubens' Portrait of the Cardinal-Infante Ferdinand," *BDIA* 27/1 (1947): 1-4.
Richardson 1949. E. P. Richardson, "A Rediscovered Sketch by Rubens of the Cardinal-Infante Ferdinand," *Miscellanea Leo van Puyvelde*, Brussels, 1949: 135-138.
Richardson 1953. E. P. Richardson, "A Family Group by Van Dyck," *Art Quarterly* 16/3 (Autumn 1953): 229-234.
Richardson 1953-54. E. P. Richardson, "A Family Group by Van Dyck," *BDIA* 33/1 (1953-54): 6-8.
Richmond/Detroit 1964. Virginia Museum of Fine Arts, Richmond, and Detroit Institute of Arts, *The World of Shakespeare 1564-1616*, exh. cat., 1964.
Rome 1958-59. Palazzo Venezia, Rome, *Michael Sweerts e i Bamboccianti*, exh. cat., 1958-59.
Rooses 1886-92. M. Rooses, *L'oeuvre de P. P. Rubens*, Antwerp, 1886-92.
Rooses 1906. M. Rooses, *Jordaens' Leven en Werken*, Amsterdam and Antwerp, 1906.
Rotterdam 1958. Museum Boymans-Van Beuningen, Rotterdam, *Michael Sweerts en Tijdgenoten*, exh. cat., 1958.
Saligny 1967. F. de Saligny, "Lucas Franchoys," *Bulletin/ Musées Royaux des Beaux-Arts de Belgique* 16 (1967): 209-232.
Saltram 1819. *Catalogue of the Pictures, Casts, and Busts Belonging to the Earl of Morley at Saltram*, Plymouth, 1819.
Saltram 1848. *Catalogue of the Pictures, Casts, and Busts Belonging to the Earl of Morley at Saltram*, London, 1848.
Santa Barbara 1958. Santa Barbara Museum of Art, *Fruits and Flowers in Painting*, exh. cat. by W. J. Hesthal, 1958.
Schaar 1959. E. Schaar, "Michael Sweerts e i Bamboccianti: Ausstellung im Palazzetto Venezia in Rom," *Kunstchronik* 12/2 (Feb. 1959): 41-49.
Schaeffer 1909. E. Schaeffer, *Van Dyck / Des Meisters Gemälde (Klassiker der Kunst in Gesamtausgaben* XIII), Stuttgart and Leipzig, 1909.
Scharf 1862. G. Scharf, *Catalogue Raisonné or a List of the Pictures in Blenheim Palace*, London, 1862.
Scheyer 1937. E. Scheyer, *Baroque Painting*, Detroit, 1937.
Scripps 1897. *Catalogue of a Private Collection of Paintings Ancient and Modern*, cat. by J. E. Scripps, Detroit, 1897.
Scripps 1900. *Catalogue of a Private Collection of Ancient and Modern Paintings Formed by James E. Scripps*, cat. by J. E. Scripps, Detroit, 1900.
Šíp 1978. J. Šíp, "Obrazy Petra Paula Rubense V Pražske Národni Galerii," *Umeni* 26 (1978).
Šíp and Blažíček 1963. J. Šíp and O. J. Blažíček, *17th-Century Flemish Painting*, London, 1963.
Smith 1829-42. J. Smith, *A Catalogue Raisonné of the Works of the Most Eminent Dutch, Flemish, and French Painters*, 9 vols., London, 1829-42.
Stewart 1978. J. D. Stewart, "Catalogue of two Famous Collections," *Burlington Magazine* 120 (Apr. 1978): 239-241.
Sullivan 1981. S. A. Sullivan, "Frans Snyders: *Still Life*

with Fruit, Vegetables and Dead Game," *BDIA* 59/1 (Spring 1981): 30-37.
Thieme and Becker 1907/50. U. Thieme and F. Becker, *Allgemeines Lexikon der bildenden Künstler*, 37 vols., Leipzig, 1907/50.
Thuillier and Foucart 1972. J. Thuillier and J. Foucart, *Rubens' Life of Marie de' Medici*, New York, 1972.
Tietze 1936. H. Tietze, *Tizian/Leben und Werk*, 2 vols., Vienna, 1936.
Tietze-Conrat 1957. E. Tietze-Conrat, *Dwarfs and Jesters in Art*, London, 1957.
Vaes 1924. M. Vaes, "Le séjour d'Antoine van Dyck en Italie," *Bulletin de l'Institut historique belge de Rome* 4 (1924): 161-234.
Valentiner 1922. W. R. Valentiner, "Rubens and Van Dyck in the Detroit Museum," *Art in America* 10/5 (Aug. 1922): 203-209.
Valentiner 1922a. W. R. Valentiner, "Rubens and Van Dyck in the Detroit Museum," *BDIA* 4/2 (Nov. 1922): 9-12.
Valentiner 1926. W. R. Valentiner, "Gift of Four Important Paintings: Correggio, Van Dyck, Poussin, and Zurbaran," *BDIA* 8/1 (Oct. 1926): 2-7.
Valentiner 1928. W. R. Valentiner, "Travel Notes," *BDIA* 10/1 (Oct. 1928): 6-12.
Valentiner 1930. W. R. Valentiner, "A Painter's Atelier by Michiel Sweerts," *BDIA* 12/1 (Oct. 1930): 4-6.
Valentiner 1936. W. R. Valentiner, "Still Life Paintings," *BDIA* 15/4 (Jan. 1936): 46-50.
Valentiner 1944. W. R. Valentiner, "The Penitent Saint Peter by Jacob Jordaens," *BDIA* 24/2 (1944): 16-18.
Valentiner 1946. W. R. Valentiner, "Rubens' Paintings in America," *Art Quarterly* 9/2 (Spring 1946): 153-168.
Van den Branden 1883. F. J. van den Branden, *Geschiedenis der antwerpsche Schilderschool*, Antwerp, 1883.
Van den Wijngaert 1940. F. van den Wijngaert, *Inventaris der Rubeniaansche Prentkunst*, Antwerp, 1940.
Van der Velde 1975. C. van der Velde, *Frans Floris (1519/20-1570): Leven en werken*, Brussels, 1975.
Vey 1956. H. Vey, "Anton Van Dycks Ölskizzen," *Bulletin/Musées Royaux des Beaux-Arts de Belgique* 5/3-4 (1956): 167-208.
Vienna 1927. *Die Gemäldegalerie der Akademie der bildenden Künste in Wien*, cat. by R. Eigenberger, 1927.
Vienna 1930. Wiener Secession, Vienna, *Drei Jahrhunderte vlämischer Kunst*, exh. cat., 1930.
Vienna 1977. Graphische Sammlung Albertina, Vienna, *Die Rubens-Zeichnungen der Albertina, zum 400. Geburtstag*, cat. by E. Mitsch, Vienna, 1977.
Vlieghe 1972. H. Vlieghe, *Saints (Corpus Rubenianum Ludwig Burchard* VIII), London and New York, 1972.
Vlieghe 1977. H. Vlieghe, "Erasmus Quellinus and Rubens' Studio Practice," *Burlington Magazine* 119 (Sept. 1977): 636-643.
Vlieghe 1978. H. Vlieghe, review of M. Jaffé, *Rubens and Italy*, *Burlington Magazine* 120 (July 1978): 471-473.
Vlieghe 1981. H. Vlieghe, "Rubens und seine Antwerpener Auftraggeber," *Peter Paul Rubens, Werk und Nachruhm*, Munich, 1981.
Voorhelm Schneevoogt 1873. C. G. Voorhelm Schneevoogt, *Catalogue des estampes gravées d'après Rubens*, Haarlem, 1873.
Waddingham 1958. M. R. Waddingham, "The Sweerts Exhibition in Rotterdam," *Paragone* 107 (Nov. 1958): 67-73.
Waddingham 1961. M. R. Waddingham, "Michael Sweerts in Rome: An Inedited Masterpiece," *Paragone* 139 (July 1961): 49-50.
Washburn Freund 1931. F. E. Washburn Freund, "Vom New Yorker Kunstmarkt," *Weltkunst*, Jan. 25, 1931.
Waterhouse 1953. E. Waterhouse, *Painting in Britain / 1530 to 1790*, London, 1953.
Wessely 1865. J. E. Wessely, "Zusätze und Verbesserungen zum Werke über Wallerant Vaillant," *Archiv für die zeichnenden Künste* 11 (1865).
Wethey 1971. H. E. Wethey, *The Portraits (The Paintings of Titian* II), London, 1971.
Whitcomb 1954. *Catalogue of the Paintings and Sculpture Given by Edgar B. Whitcomb and Anna Scripps Whitcomb to the Detroit Institute of Arts*, cat. by E. P. Richardson, 1954.
Wilenski 1960. R. H. Wilenski, *Flemish Painters, 1430-1830*, 2 vols., New York, 1960.
Windsor/London (Ontario) 1969-70. Willistead Art Gallery, Windsor, and London Public Library and Art Museum (Ontario), "Things: Still Life Painting from the 17th to the 20th Century," 1969-70.
Worcester/Philadelphia 1939. Worcester Art Museum and Philadelphia Museum of Art, *The Worcester-Philadelphia Exhibition of Flemish Paintings*, exh. cat., 1939.
Wurzbach 1906-11. A. von Wurzbach, *Niederländisches Künstler-Lexikon*, 3 vols., Vienna, 1906-11.

INDEX OF ARTISTS

Numbers in *italics* denote illustrations.

INDEX OF SUBJECT MATTER

Religious Subjects

I OLD TESTAMENT

II NEW TESTAMENT

III HOLY FAMILY AND SAINTS

Secular Subjects

I ALLEGORY AND MYTHOLOGY

II ANIMALS

III GENRE

IV INTERIORS

V LANDSCAPES

VI PORTRAITS, KNOWN SUBJECTS

VII PORTRAITS, UNKNOWN SUBJECTS

VIII STILL LIFES

INDEX OF PREVIOUS OWNERS

NUMERICAL INDEX

Flemish and German Paintings
of the 17th Century

was designed by Klaus Gemming, New Haven, Connecticut.
It was set in Monotype Van Dijck by
Stamperia Valdonega, Verona, Italy.
The text and the illustrations were printed
in offset lithography by The Meriden Gravure Company,
Meriden, Connecticut, on Mohawk Superfine Text paper,
made by Mohawk Paper Mills, Cohoes, New York.
The color plates were printed on Lustro Offset Enamel Dull,
made by the S.D. Warren Company,
a division of the Scott Paper Company.
The book was bound by Robert A. Burlen & Son, Inc.,
Hingham, Massachusetts.

The Detroit Institute of Arts

THE COLLECTIONS OF · THE DETROIT INSTITUTE OF ARTS ·

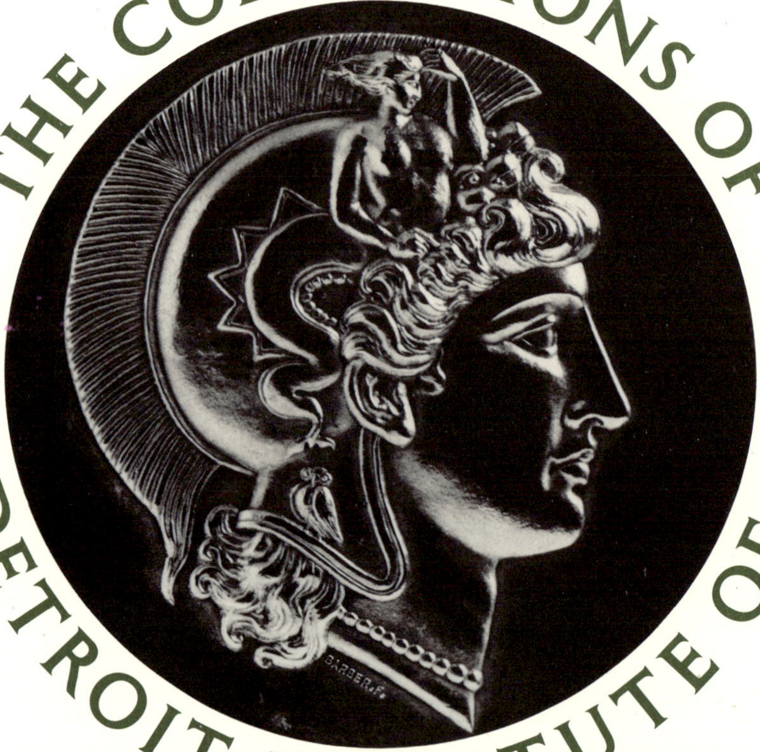